NATURE FIRST

OUTDOOR LIFE THE FRILUFTSLIV WAY

Edited by Bob Henderson & Nils Vikander

NATURAL HERITAGE BOOKS
A MEMBER OF THE DUNDURN GROUP
TORONTO

Published by Natural Heritage Books
A Member of The Dundurn Group
3 Church Street, Suite 500
Toronto, Ontario, M5E 1M2, Canada
www.dundurn.com

Library and Archives Canada Cataloguing in Publication

Nature first : outdoor life the Friluftsliv way / edited by Bob Henderson & Nils Vikander.

Includes bibliographical references and index.
ISBN 978-1-897045-21-3

1. Outdoor life. 2. Human ecology. 3. Outdoor recreation. 4. Outdoor education.
5. Environmental responsibility. I. Henderson, Bob, 1956– II. Vikander, Nils, 1941–

GV191.6.N375 2007   304.2   C2007-903318-0

1   2   3   4   5   11   10   09   08   07

Front cover: Clockwise from top left, #1 Courtesy of Bob Henderson, #2 & #3 Courtesy
of Nils Vikander, #4 Courtesy of Bob Henderson.
Back cover: Above, Courtesy of Bob Henderson. Below, Courtesy of Nils Vikander.
Cover design by Neil Thorne
Text design by Sari Naworynski
Edited by Jane Gibson
Printed and bound in Canada by Marquis

We acknowledge the support of the Canada Council for the Arts and the Ontario Arts
Council for our publishing program. We also acknowledge the financial support of the
Government of Canada through the Book Publishing Industry Development Program
and The Association for the Export of Canadian Books and the Government of Canada
through the Ontario Book Publishers Tax Credit Program and the Ontario Media
Development Corporation.

TABLE OF CONTENTS

Acknowledgements

Bob Henderson

I would like to thank all the contributors to *Nature First*. I have learned from you all and made many a new friend and deepened other relationships.

The crew at Natural Heritage deserve much praise for working through the melee involved in producing an anthology with a wide variety of authors and a less-than-perfectionist Canadian editor. Thanks to Barry, Jane and Shannon.

I must reserve special praise for my first reader, advisor and computer/typist extraordinaire, Greer Gordon, who will be one of the few North Americans who can spell friluftsliv without batting an eye.

Finally, I would like to thank the many artists who have contributed art to this project: Don Burry, Josh Gordon, Emily Robertson, Helena Juhasz, Zabe MacEachren, John Kaandorp, Anna Downes Catterson, Erika Blomqvist, Signy Ramsem and Sigurd Falk. A thank you also goes to John Flood of Penumbra Press, Moonbeam, Ontario, for permission to use artwork by Anna Downes-Catterson.

Nils Vikander

First I bow to nature, my irresistible mentor who draws me out into Her inexhaustible richness, always teaching me, always inspiring me. But I am not often alone in my journeys – my wife, Margarita, shares her well of insight and wisdom with me, pointing to the many wonderful threads in nature's fabric that I sometimes miss; and my students in Norway and Canada, who stretch my capacities and my imagination, sometimes beyond what I thought possible. Reverberating, humming through all these, are my parents and brothers for whom nature was a home to be loved. How could I not, with this marvellous nature-pack on my back, approach our contributing authors with passion, and in turn be yet more infected by their vitality and reverence for our task?

Is a Tree Transplanted to Another Continent the Same Tree?
Some Reflections on Friluftsliv in an International Context

Andrew Brookes and Børge Dahle

How can and how should individuals, families, and communities experience nature in the modern world? Now, just beyond the twentieth century, with nature itself under threat from every quarter, these are perhaps the most important educational questions for this century. Their apparent simplicity tempts two quick responses. One that of course we must "get back to nature." Two, that the end of nature was a foregone conclusion a century ago, and it is time to concentrate our efforts on the social, cultural, and environmental problems of a post modern world – all that now remains of nature are copies of copies, and perhaps that is all there ever was. There is some truth in both responses. Perhaps the most important tasks for outdoor educators is to deal with some of the resultant complexities.

It is hard to be certain what is going on each time a small party sets out to paddle a river, a family heads to a cabin in the mountains, or old friends meet at a favourite fishing spot. A return to nature perhaps, but mixed with some capillary effects of modernity, creeping into all of the nooks and crannies previously untouched by the industrial and electronic revolutions. For those who accept the responsibility of teaching or guiding in the outdoors, and for those interested in the overall shape of education, indoor and outdoor, both getting the mix right and knowing it is right are difficult. Returning to nature is not as simple as it may seem; we should not be too ready to congratulate ourselves. At the same time, we are not ready to accept that nature is finished and it is "post-modern" all the way down. We are in agreement here with Nils Faarlund, "it is too late to be pessimistic." In the industrialized democracies, the ways and means by which nature is encountered and understood by individuals and communities will contribute importantly, one way or another, to the ontological assumptions on which future environmental histories will be made. We see outdoor education as shaping the accumulated experiences of communities. While the power of education (and for that matter of the nation state) may seem diminished in the face of global forces beyond the reach of either, it remains important to find what can be achieved through outdoor education, and to achieve it.

Norway has a special contribution to this discussion. The Norwegian tradition of friluftsliv (literally free air life), or more accurately traditions of friluftsliv, give some cause for optimism about the possibilities for maintaining routine involvement in the outdoors as a kind of stabilizing influence, or point of reference, within, or alongside, a modern industrialized society. The case of Norway also illustrates some of the difficulties and dilemmas, which emerge when friluftsliv is accommodated in a changing world. Friluftsliv may be, as Arne Næss has suggested, Norway's gift to the world, and the principles of deep ecology, rooted in the Norwegian landscape, culture, and history, provide some guidance for educators trying to interpret what friluftsliv might have to offer outside of Norway and Scandinavia. However, friluftsliv cannot be simply uprooted and translated into different cultural, historical and geographical contexts. In considering outdoor education in particular contexts, educators face dilemmas in balancing tradition and change, concrete experience and textual abstraction, local perspectives and broader views. Environmental education, which is not sensitive to the particular environment in which it is developed, is potentially flawed.[1]

These dilemmas arise when considering friluftsliv in an international context. The older Norwegian traditions (which we will call here nature-life) from which friluftsliv has grown are specifically local, and somewhat personal; they might be seen more as part of living family histories than expressions of national identity. The nature-life traditions of particular groups – community, friendship, or family – are associated with specific places, in this respect resembling an indigenous relationship with the land. They resemble oral traditions, kept alive by repetition and subtle improvisation in response to the patterns and variations in nature, encountered along well-known paths. They are part of, not out of, the ordinary. Their meaning derives from the slow accumulation of stories and familiarity around certain places in the forest, particular cabins, a summerhouse, and a berry patch. They represent the unselfconscious inclusion of the nearby hills and forests in "home." In important ways they are rather personal, and perhaps private, akin to the everyday intimacies within a family. They are grown into rather than derived from principles; they are lived and performed rather than recorded.

In order to share in traditional nature-life as an outsider, perhaps one must be invited to join a family or to form a friendship; then come the Sunday walks, the ski trail, the small rituals, the tree under which lunch is taken – these are simply there, part of the relationship. It may be that to fully understand one must wait a lifetime, to experience the full expression of the tradition from grandchild to grandparent. To share these traditions in a different way – through their adaptation for inclusion in formal education, or after adjustments to allow for urbanization and the complications of modern living, or after attempting to transport them across geographical, cultural, and political boundaries – inevitably entails changes. There may be good reasons for considering such adaptations. Nature-life traditions seem to have provided some Norwegians with a sense of local and national identity linked to an environmentally helpful conservatism (while avoiding the militaristic nationalism for which the twentieth century will be remembered).

However, the environmental history of Australia provides numerous cautionary tales, if any are needed, about the dangers of pressing on, with the best of intentions, in transplanting culture and beliefs into different landscapes. What seems right in Norway may not be right for Canada or Australia. We see an international discussion on "friluftsliv" as means to direct attention towards differences in the forms (which outdoor activities take), to location-related differences (geographical, cultural, and historical) and to the significance of these differences.

It is in the nature of abstraction, and friluftsliv is no exception, that when a tradition, or constellation of local traditions, is compressed into a single word – friluftsliv – later to be unpacked in a new context (a school, a glossy magazine, over the border in Sweden, in North America ...) we find a new concrete expression of friluftsliv, which may differ so much from the prototype as to be, in some respects, its opposite. It is appropriate that friluftsliv be adapted to the circumstances in which it is being made concrete. However, such changes have implications for the validity of the connections we might wish to make between friluftsliv and deep ecology, and for the educational qualities we might suppose are associated with friluftsliv. Here the educational dilemmas are not only between tradition and change, concrete experience and textual abstraction, local perspectives and broader views, but also form around these questions: which tradition, what form of experience, which locality and whose view of that locality should shape our practice? The cautionary tales that emerge from Australia are not just about the environmental consequences of transplanting species and practices, but of "transplanted" intentions and beliefs.[2]

Within Norway, friluftsliv is multiple. We refer here not to the uniqueness of each local expression of traditional friluftsliv, or nature-life, but to manifold, somewhat contradictory forms of friluftsliv. Perhaps 30 per cent of the Norwegian population continue with some form of the "everyday" nature-life tradition. This should not be interpreted in a fundamentalist way; members of that 30 per cent may also experience a world of satellite television, motor vehicles and ski resorts. They drink coffee, which contains, as has often been pointed out, the whole history of western imperialism. We could say, however, that the collective consciousness, or constellation of worldviews, in Norway still contains nature as understood through the nature-life tradition. For others, friluftsliv is understood differently. It may be learned through formal instruction. It may consist of discrete single episodes, rather than an on-going repetitions and variations. It may be more consumerist. It may be organized around the themes of adventure, challenge, and exploration – leaving home – rather than familiarity and coming home, as Sigmund Kvaløy-Sætereng puts it, "inside nature."

Friluftsliv has been associated in the last decades of the 20th century with some towering figures in modern exploration, particularly Fridtjof Nansen. It is possible to see Nansen as a hero who exemplifies national characteristics, in the same way that Norwegians, as a skiing nation, might see their Olympic skiing team as truly representative of the nation. No doubt life in Norway provided an excellent preparation for polar exploration; but the fact remains Nansen is famous not for his mundane participation in Norwegian life, but because of his exceptional achievements. Perhaps he was moulded by the everyday, but his fame comes from breaking the mould. What is striking about contemporary forms of friluftsliv in Norway (apart from the 30 per cent already mentioned) is the resonance not with the ordinary Norwegian life, which shaped Nansen, but with his more exceptional exploits. The distinction is important. Quite different, perhaps opposite, understandings of nature are embedded in nature life as mundane, familiar, and local, compared to friluftsliv as exciting, risk-entailing, and exploratory.

There are a number of evident social explanations for this emphasis on the exceptional over the mundane (and perhaps too there are cultural explanations for it going largely unnoticed). Adventure is news; indeed, turn of the century polar exploration (1900) was deeply implicated in laying the foundations for sensationalist journalism (not a pejorative term then).[3] A middle-class, urban friluftsliv revival in Norway reflected a literate, abstract view of nature. The adoption of friluftsliv by educational institutions also helped friluftsliv to become something shaped by literature, while the unwritten rural traditions of friluftsliv have remained largely undocumented.

Friluftsliv in educational institutions, and the friluftsliv associated with backpacking tourism has mainly involved people in their late teens and twenties. Research into how traditional nature-life has been maintained and reproduced suggests this is the group least important to the tradition, or put another way, this is the stage of life where individuals are most likely to abandon the tradition (perhaps temporarily until they start families of their own).4 One way or another, friluftsliv must move to accommodate the realities of urban life, competing interests and so on. But educators must pay attention to the educational implications of changes in friluftsliv driven by consumerism, marketing, convenience or necessity. It is possible that the supposed educational benefits of friluftsliv may be reversed or negated when friluftsliv is treated as a kind of product or brand.

These dilemmas intensify when the study of friluftsliv is taken across national borders (perhaps referred to as outdoor education or adventure education). Differences in culture, history and social arrangements must be considered, and especially the landscape. The particularities of landscape are often neglected in outdoor education discourse. We do not mean to imply that the consumable qualities of the settings for outdoor education have been neglected. On the contrary, scenic value, suitability for skiing, camping, rock climbing and so on have had a high priority in outdoor activity-based education. But what educational aims and practices should apply for populations in urban or highly developed rural landscapes? Must outdoor education involve travel to somewhere more suitable? How might familiarity be developed – should Danes, for example, adopt particular places in Norway? What of landscapes that do not share the particular qualities, which have so, suited the Norwegian landscape to friluftsliv? (The Norwegian landscape seems to represent an archetype of western visions of nature.) We will not attempt to answer these questions here, but make two points. First, we should pay careful heed to how local outdoor education, outdoor recreation, or friluftsliv respond (or fail to respond) to the local landscape, and how these practices sort and select landscapes for attention or neglect. Secondly, we should consider carefully how educational imperatives and the principles of deep ecology might lead us to forms of "friluftsliv" outside of Norway, which, by responding appropriately to the local landscape, take quite different forms from those which have hitherto characterized outdoor education and some contemporary friluftsliv.

Introduction

An Outdoor Life and Literary Ecology:
Connections Between Nature and Culture

by Kathleen Osgood Dana and Students in Literature and Film of the North

At the Center for Northern Studies in Northern Vermont, Sterling College, the divide between nature and culture is slight. When we step out of the classroom, we are right in the northern forest, part of the great circumpolar sweep of hardwoods that circles the globe. And, when we walk down into adjacent Bear Swamp, we enter a boreal world.

In the classroom, we study and think deeply about these natural connections around the globe, whether by studying snowload in Winter Ecology, or spring migrations in Polar Biota, or climate change in Quaternary Studies, or the rifts and connections between humans and their environments in Stories and Storytelling. So, it is not a very large stretch for students in northern literature to grasp the essential concepts of friluftsliv and to connect them to poems they have been studying. Here I (Kati Dana) provide a commentary on "The Great Sea" by Uvavnuk. The commentaries written by the students precede the opening chapters of each of Parts I, II and III.

When Knud Rasmussen, the great explorer (1879–1933) set out to demonstrate the continuity of Inuit culture from Greenland to Chukotka, he recorded a beautiful song by an angagok, a shaman, Uvavnuk. She is transported in utter delight by the natural world.

The great sea stirs me.
The great sea sets me adrift,
it sways me
like the weed on a river-stone.
The sky's height stirs me.
The strong wind blows through my mind.
It carries me with it,
so I shake with joy.

Whether Uvavnuk experiences an ecstatic trance or a transcendental moment of revelation by her immersion in nature is probably a matter of interpretation, but the simplicity and power of her experience is undeniable.

A Canadian Meets Friluftsliv

Bob Henderson

Seven years ago (January 2000), I found myself in Norway with an international group of Outdoor Educators. We had gathered for a symposium entitled Deep Environmental Education Practice (DEEP). Here is an excerpt from the conference abstract:

> Papers at this [gathering] will explore ways in which "outdoor life" may maintain links with nature, weakened by developments in the last century, and maintain traditions of knowledge and respect, which have been placed at risk by globalization and modernization. The papers will explore the imperatives for developing [a] deeper analysis of the environmental and cultural dimensions of outdoor life, with particular emphasis on pedagogical implications.[1]

We as conference delegates were, and are still, concerned with how to preserve that quality of outdoor life that helps us behave and belong as true dwellers of the earth, comfortable with nature as a place to know and be at home. And we were concerned with how to actively take on the task of this preservation of certain land-based traditions. In Scandinavia, particularly Norway, the word friluftsliv represents a tradition of thought attentive to the folkways of "nature life" in the country and outdoor life for the urban excursioner, the weekender and/or expeditioner.

Upon returning to Canada, I had a new perspective on certain North American conventions in outdoor life practices and Outdoor Education, both of which had caused me a certain discomfort. In the past, I had left these feeling poorly articulated. I am of the view that nature in North American outdoor education and recreation is all-too-easily lost in the mania of skill development, personal growth and technological conveniences. Nature becomes a backdrop, perhaps even a sparring partner to test one's skill and resources. The self is the focus, but not the "Self" in nature. Here I use Arne Naess' notion of a capital "S" Self to denote the self aware of a potential for Self-realization – to develop a connection of knowing and being within nature.[2] Strangely, even outdoor education with the language used, the activities conducted, and mostly, the "way" the life activities are conducted, can reinforce a detachment from nature, rather than an engagement with nature. *Nature First* has slowly taken shape since my first visit to Norway. We (Nils Vikander and I) wanted to be true to that first impetus to produce a collection of Scandinavian, Canadian and International writers following that January 2000 symposium. Thus, many authors here were present for the DEEP symposium in Rennabu and Oslo. We then sought out authors who, each in their own way, have fully engaged in friluftsliv traditions in Canada and beyond. Finally, aware of certain outdoor education dynamics in Scandinavia, we sought out authors who would bring variety to the fruluftsliv message that dominated at the DEEP symposium without generating conflicting messages.

Have Outdoor Experiential (Environmental/Adventure) Educators taken "Nature and Place" out of our education?[3] Nature is there, of course, but has it become scenery and therefore more of a backdrop for our programs than the centre of our relational immersion? Are we building ego relationship at the expense of eco-relationships? There is a place for both together. A friluftsliv tradition (there is not one specific friluftsliv understanding of the term) as part of the Norwegian/Scandinavian tradition has much to offer those who seek a healthy balance of the eco and ego goals. A

friluftsliv education can address a shift in the experience and adventure
that is compatible with teaching and learning about place, nature and heritage lore, craft and the general art of living outdoors. Friluftsliv in literal
translation means "nature free life" or "open-air life." Friluftsliv is well-
grounded in Scandinavian educational and philosophical thought. The
idea relates to eco-activism and deep ecology (delving deeper into the root
causes of the environmental cultural crisis). Most simply put, it means outdoor recreation education following a particular Scandinavian tradition.

The dominant, cultural value orientation is an orientation more in
keeping with nature as commodity, and self-esteem as the hallmark of
outcomes based educational programming and life pursuits. The variant
to this, of which friluftsliv is one example, is not entirely new or unique to
Norway. Conference delegates, Øysten Dalhe's "talking terms with nature"
and Sigmund Kvaløy-Sætereng's "inside relationship with nature," clearly
resonate with Canadian Sharon Butala's "friluftsliv-like" writing in "The
Perfection of the Morning: An Apprenticeship in Nature":

> It is one thing to come from the city and be over-
> whelmed by the beauty of nature and to speak of it, and
> another thing entirely to have lived in it so long that it
> has seeped into your bones and your blood and is insep-
> arable from your own being, so that it is part of you and
> requires no mention of hymns of praise.[4]

While there is a big difference between the week-long "apprenticeship"
of the short-term canoe or snowshoe trip compared to full-time habitation in a place, friluftsliv education as a goal for experiential educators and
the outdoor recreation community generally seeks this seeping of nature
into one's bones. Home with nature is home with a quietly celebrated,
respected presence, not an awe-struck spirit of worshipped otherness. The
way of friluftsliv is for nature to seep under one's skin, solidifying in our
being, and not for nature to be worshipped outside ourselves.

The friluftsliv idea shares common sentiments with Henry David
Thoreau's quest for the "tonic of wilderness," Sigurd Olson's attention to
"ancient rhythms," P.G. Downes,' "ways of the north," Aldo Leopold's,

"primitive arts," Grey Owl's, "giving of a single leaf," and Butala's, "seeping of the beauty of nature into your bones."[5] All are writers and speakers who have embraced nature and tried to teach reconciliation with nature. Their words are expressions acknowledging the importance of a "free" nature, with attention to traditional ways of the local culture/place. It is this spirit of reconciliation that is the foundation tying together the work of the writers of the chapters appearing in this book.

In the boreal forest of the Canadian North, the Cree First Nations people have an expression *miyupimaatisiium*, which means "being alive well." Like friluftsliv, the word is a complex one, saturated in values. *Miyupimaatisiium* implies "alive well" or "living well" based on Cree beliefs and practices. While there is no Cree word for health as understood in English, *miyupimaatisiium* can be understood as the Cree understanding of "connections between land, health and identity." The practices of these connections centre on securing food, warmth and physical ability. There is a wealth of wisdom to be explored in an inquiry of the beliefs and practices tied to this Cree place-based orientation to land, health and identity. The outdoor experiential educator would find sound social and ecological learning in such a pursuit.[6]

As a Canadian outdoor educator/recreator who travels in these same boreal forests, certainly I should be looking for local indigenous meanings that inspire wise place-based practices. We might also explore our own traditionally rooted ancestries for those practices still relevant that might inspire. In moving forward in time, we would gain ways to bring nature and place back into our education and life experiences back through an inquiry attentive to traditional land-based life ways. Friluftsliv, as a way of thinking and being in nature taken from the Norwegian/Scandinavian tradition, is one such way to achieve such goals. Friluftsliv inspires an experiential practice grounded in place. It is a reminder of the importance of place-based connections to dwelling well in health and being of sound ecological identity.

Now seven years since that January 2000 gathering of international outdoor educators, many of this same group are well represented here in this book, sharing the imperative to explore cultural dimensions of outdoor life and pedagogical principles. Our relationship with nature is among the most important questions we can ask in the twenty-first century. The writers of this first friluftsliv English-language anthology volume bring these concerns of relationship to nature centrally to their work. Some write directly of friluftsliv ideas, some write of related traditions. All embrace the importance of place and heritage, activity and nature. Scandinavians will learn how their friluftsliv tradition is being actively interpreted outside of their own countries. Canadians, specifically, will learn of traditions worthy of exploration that can help us embrace our nordicity and inspire our life experiences and educational practices to heightened relational qualities within nature. On an international level, friluftsliv is presented as a way to explore age-old traditions toward nature and health and identity. There is an awareness of a departure from many current conventions in common outdoor educational practices.

FEET ON TWO CONTINENTS: SPANNING THE ATLANTIC WITH FRILUFTSLIV?

Nils Olof Vikander

In the early 1970s, when Canada caught the irresistible virus of cross-country skiing, a path was beaten to my door by virtue of my Scandinavian background. The setting then was the Atlantic coast province of New Brunswick, and it was assumed that skiing knowledge and skills had been ingested with my mother's milk. In 2003 I returned to Canada, to Ontario this time, after many years in Norway, and experienced an intense déjà vu, this time in the shape of friluftsliv. During my two years as a visiting scholar I became deeply immersed in the professional/academic outdoor arena as I realized that Nordic traditions of friluftsliv in their conceptual, philosophical and realized dimensions were making intriguing inroads in North American life. Curiosity had drawn colleagues on that continent to examine the panorama of their field and passion elsewhere.

That their attention had been directed to northern Europe was not without its inner logic – that region having strong historical, cultural and geographical ties with Canada. It was reasonably surmised and hoped that fresh inspiration might be gained there for the further development of the outdoor education/recreation field. Of particular importance in this regard is the shared northern heritage. Although the *National Post*[1] acidly

8

has queried " … what exactly is a 'northern identity' and why should anyone care about affirming it?" This "northernness" carries with it deep life
implications. As William Lewis Morton writes, " … Canadian life to this
day is marked by a northern quality, the strong seasonal rhythm … the
wilderness venture … ."[2] Especially intense is life in the northern winter;
after all, everyone has summer, but winter is a privilege for the few. From
this vantage point I came to understand that in New Brunswick in the
1970s I was part of a Nordic winter friluftsliv vanguard in Canada. And
now, many years later, I was back, being carried by another friluftsliv
wave, this one deeper, more inclusive and subject to more reflection. How
had this come about and what was its future? Most extraordinary was the
encounter of the word friluftsliv, not in italics or in quotation marks. Like
smorgasbord and ombudsman it was becoming anchored in the English
language. If anything, this could be a portent of things to come.

Skiing may, indeed, be a Nordic/Russian invention, but what about
friluftsliv? In my recent years in Canada I have felt on my body and in my
mind, a deep unease among outdoor professionals, a kind of existential
anxiety about their place in the maelstrom of post-modern life. Hopes of
having a significant, ameliorating impact on dubious patterns of life
appeared dashed for many. Could reaching out and learning about alternative approaches lead to a rejuvenation of their professional selves and
point the way to a more harmonious human existence where nature once
again could feel like home? Could the absorption of a friluftsliv "model"
fuel such a process?

What, then, is this friluftsliv? Can it be transplanted? Is it worthy of the
attempt? After some decades in North America, many years in Norway
and a childhood in Sweden, I, it might be thought, could provide some
reflections on these questions, particularly from my site in the social sciences and physical education/friluftsliv. Or, a ruminating journey might,
at least, open a path to some insight and wisdom.

In the Beginning was the Word? In parallel fashion, friluftsliv, though the
word has taken deep and historical meaning, can be argued to have preceded Ibsen in 1859. The word does not create the phenomenon, but sym-
bolizes it.

My years in Norway have taught me that there is no consensus on the meaning of the word "friluftsliv." There is a saying in Swedish that "the dear child has many names," but the converse appears to be true for friluftsliv; "the dear name has many children." The debate is so alive and well in Norway that from time to time the volume and intensity of the arguments as to what is appropriately friluftsliv reaches religious fervour. Such engagement does not appear to be generally the case in the other Nordic countries. In itself, this points to the necessity of understanding that many contextual variations on the theme of friluftsliv exist.

During my most recent stay in Canada I slowly arrived at an understanding that friluftsliv was viewed as a Norwegian term. Indeed, the phenomenon itself in all its nuances was regarded as anchored in the Norwegian setting. It is true that Henrik Ibsen pioneered the use of the term in its written form in the mid-19th century. However, the present identification of the term as Norwegian may be more a reflection of vigorous international contacts in past decades by Norwegians in the outdoor field, than a correspondence with historical reality. Friluftsliv as a broadly recognized concept and an applied philosophy has a long history also in other parts of the Nordic region. It was well-established long before the dissolution of the union with Norway in 1905, and I grew up with it as a matter of course during my childhood in Sweden. The era of romanticism in late 19th and early 20th centuries was the crucible within which the concept of friluftsliv and its expression were initially formed, and these powerful reverberations may still be felt today.

Since friluftsliv has always been understood to have a deep anchoring to place, embedding the person in the inexhaustible settings of nature, it becomes apparent that friluftsliv must possess a dynamic quality, varying not only with geographical (and cultural) contexts, but also with the characteristics of the individual. As such, the debate in Norway becomes understandable, indeed predictable, as long as the human/nature relationship remains an issue high in the consciousness of a society. After all, though small in area, Norway possesses great variety in topography, climate, vegetation and local traditions. What, then, does all this mean for people elsewhere?

As a first step, it is essential to cast the net more broadly. It is self-defeating to focus on Norway only, important though it unquestionably is in the development of friluftsliv. The other Nordic countries should also be brought into purview. This has the consequence of greatly increasing the diversity of geographical, cultural and historical settings, thereby creating broader opportunities for finding patterns and variations on the friluftsliv theme that could inspire fruitful adaptations outside the Nordic region.

Secondly, it is of essence to approach friluftsliv with a more critical acumen than is generally the case in the English language literature. This advice is founded on the human predilection to selectively perceive. If there is dissatisfaction at home, then the positive aspects there are downplayed, while the apparently positive dimensions of life in the arena in question elsewhere are pointed to as a contrast. Without doubt, the human species is afflicted with the converse disposition as well. This perspective leads to some musings about the friluftsliv sphere in Scandinavia, with some clarifying juxtapositions vis-à-vis the Canadian/American context.

A Friluftsliv Mosaic

History – The Right of Public Access: It is difficult to deny that this element of the cultural context has had the deepest significance for the development of the friluftsliv ethos in the Nordic countries. As well, in all likelihood it is the element that sets that part of the world most apart from North America in the human/nature interface. Its ancient historical roots may, moreover, be regarded as having been reinforced by the growth in importance of friluftsliv in the 20th century. The centrality of this "Right of Public Access" becomes in many ways a problematic phenomenon to overcome in a quest to adapt friluftsliv to Canadian and American settings, and in other countries of the world as well. The distinction is immediate and striking when entering the outdoors in North America. It has been noted that in the United States the individual is burdened by the oral "No" about 150,000 times in the first 18 years of life. When written sign messages are added, such as "No Trespassing," the total is even more formidable. The constraint that this produces on the human/nature relationship is immense, particularly when the high correlation is taken into account between the "No" word and where most of the population now lives – in the urban conglomerations. In the Nordic region, as a contrast, the path to nature is almost everywhere through a nearby open door. Fortunately, North America possesses a redeeming quality in its very geographical vastness, where large public land areas have been out of reach to the dominant privatization ethos. Nevertheless, for the public it often takes considerable time, money and energy to reach them.

The deep kinship with nature that North American observers frequently have noted in many Scandinavians is surely a consequence of many centuries of tradition of public access to land, river, lake and seashore. From the perspective of Edward O. Wilson's[3] biophilia hypothesis (that of the innate affinity of the human species with all living organisms), the friluftsliv ethos may be viewed as an expression of biophilia, facilitated by the right of public access, and carried forward in a world otherwise increasingly inimical to such human/nature symbiosis. The continued cultivation of the mythological dimension of nature in the Nordic area with trolls, gnomes and elves, which has intrigued many observers and which still infuses friluftsliv for many, may be understood as mirroring this. The roots of friluftsliv, with its plethora of implications, can then be traced back through human evolution, and suggest that the friluftsliv ethos is anchored in a world view imbued with deeply "heathen" elements. From this perspective, could the pre-Christian Viking culture, with its dramatic exploratory drive to unknown lands and seas have sown the decisive seeds from which friluftsliv later sprang forth?

Such mental voyages aside, the question of friluftsliv's relevance and possibility for North American outdoor life must be posed. The path to a successful adaptation of friluftsliv in that part of the world appears to lie in a rejuvenation and incorporation of the deep bond to nature of North American First Nation cultures, a bond formed by truly common, public access. Here, there is a rich well of wisdom, similar to the pre-Christian Nordic cultures, anchored in the millennia of life experience within the particular natural conditions of their continent. Many North American residential summer camps, those seminal contributions to the international spectrum of human development and education in the outdoors, intuitively grasped this more than a century ago, often locating themselves in areas sufficiently remote to avoid the growing encroachment of *homo* "builder" *faber*. Here, then, is a powerful foundation for a vigorous North American friluftsliv with its own distinctive colouring.

Societal Underpinnings: The way society is organized has wide-ranging impacts on the potential for friluftsliv. In the Nordic region a number of such characteristics have facilitated the development of friluftsliv.

Although the private car is as established here as in North America, the Nordic public transportation system far exceeds that of the lands across the sea. It is extensive, attractive, affordable and efficiently coordinated – a vehicle for all to reach the natural areas of their choice.

For overnight friluftsliv, there are several structural advantages that characterize the Nordic area. The right of public access permits camping freely in virtually all natural areas, governed only by modest restrictions on private land (such as time, usually two nights, and at a distance from inhabited dwellings of no closer than 150–200 metres. In the extensive system of public and private campgrounds, most have cabins and trailer parking available and are often open year-round. Of yet greater importance is the hostel system in the Nordic countries, which far exceeds that of North America. Well over 600 inexpensive, attractive hostels are located often in or near natural areas, and are staffed by people well equipped to provide friluftsliv advice. Shorter working hours is a further facilitator, giving Nordic people abundant possibilities to engage in friluftsliv. A 2003 Ipsos-Reid[4] study found that while Americans worked on the average 1,815 hours per year, and Canadians, 1,778 hours, the Swedish figure was only 1,581 hours, with the Norwegian as low as 1,342 hours.

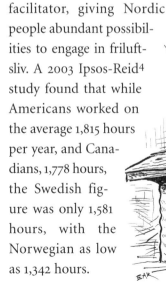

Competition among leisure activities is as intense in the Nordic area as it is in North America, but in relation to enabling engagement in the outdoors, the former has an edge in its large, prominent and long-standing voluntary national organizations, all of which have a focus on friluftsliv. Of course, there are outdoor-focused organizations in Canada and the United States, but they do not match those of the Nordic countries in the comprehensiveness of their impact. National "touring clubs" (literally they are "tourist associations," however, "tourist" in English does not have a friluftsliv flavour) with roots in the romantic era of the late 19th century and with hundreds of thousands of members, provide regional and local chapters with outdoor programs, trips, courses, marked trails, wilderness cabins and mountain stations; the latter facilities are often provided in cooperation with various levels of government. National land and forest management authorities in Scandinavia also have cabin systems for individual and groups planning to overnight. In Sweden, an additional national voluntary organization, *Friluftsfrämjandet* ("The Friluftsliv Advocator" freely translated) has been part of the social fabric for generations; its extensive programs being deeply anchored in local communities where cadres of passionate volunteers provide friluftsliv knowledge and programs to the general public. The existence of The Friluftsliv Advocator in addition to the Swedish Touring Club (*Svenska Turistföreningen* or STF), which has a broader mandate than its Norwegian counterpart, *(Den Norske Turistforeningen*, DNT), may partially explain distinctions between Norwegian and Swedish friluftsliv development.

In Norway, the friluftsliv ethos has in recent decades been affected to a considerable degree by the Deep Ecology movement with philosophers, scholars and activists, such as Naess, Faarlund, and Kvaløy-Saetereng,[5] to name but a few who have been highly visible in the national debate. Across the border, the Swedish Touring Club (though with academic roots at the University of Uppsala), and particularly The Friluftsliv Advocator with its origin from 1892, have shaped more of a "from the ground up" friluftsliv, with a lesser academic colour. Debates on philosophically or politically correct notions of friluftsliv have, in any case, been less common in Sweden.

The strength of the national organizations in the Nordic region has had a particularly dramatic consequence in one area that is critical for understanding the divergent paths outdoor life has taken there in comparison to North America. The commercialization of outdoor activities, characterizing the latter, has not had an impact in the former. The expensive (often marketed as "exclusive") and for profit wilderness trips and outdoor skills development courses, so ubiquitously offered in Canada and the United States, are strikingly juxtaposed in the Nordic countries by widely available, low-cost variations on the theme by the not-for-profit national organizations. It does not require deep insight to understand that the latter has consonance with the nature of a "friluftsliv for all," whereas the former does not.

The structural facilitation of the particularly important "near friluftsliv" (nature settings, close to home, work and school, making friluftsliv possible as a daily activity) is conspicuously illustrated in the Nordic countries in wintertime. Cross-country ski trails, maintained for free public use, are found in virtually all communities with modest population densities. In North America such facilities are rarely without fees. Skating on prepared lake loops in or adjacent to towns and cities is another growing form of Nordic winter friluftsliv, increasingly provided through the public sector.

The Nordic sky, however, is not without its foreboding clouds. In Norway, some sectors of the tourism industry have recently attempted to reverse its earlier failure of achieving acceptance for a form of "tourist tax," intended to shift costs of facilitating friluftsliv from industry and tax payer on to visiting user. And in Sweden, The Åre alpine ski complex, the largest in Europe north of the Alps, has instituted a voluntary payment system for its cross-country ski trails that could be a step in a strategy to eventually charge for trail use, as is done in North America.

In the educational system, as many as six aspects of pedagogy are worthy of particular attention. The Friluftsliv Advocator pioneered friluftsliv pre-schools decades ago, where children are mainly outdoors year round. As well, it has developed initiatives whereby regional staff and local volunteers offer their services to schools to enhance the delivery of outdoor programs and the friluftsliv pedagogical competence of teachers. At present, its initiatives have resulted in 200 schools at different levels, all of which are committed to implementing the Friluftsfrämjandet "I Ur och

Skur" pedagogy ("Come Rain or Shine"). Required preparation for teachers includes a purpose-designed university course. The friluftsliv preschool concept is spreading quickly beyond the seeds of The Friluftsliv Advocator to other Nordic countries. Secondly, recesses after each class or period in school, where pupils are outdoors, provide the foundation of a life routine whereby "near friluftsliv" is woven into the life pattern. Thirdly, outdoor education centres, designed mainly for residential stays by school classes, have a long tradition, as they have had in areas of North America. However, these centres appear to have suffered more from financial cutbacks than in Scandinavia. In Norway, with a population of 4.5 million, there were, in 1998, 58 such centres listed and recommended by the national Camp School Association.[6] This computes to approximately one per population of 77,500 citizens, not taking into account additional centres not listed by the Association. Fourthly, the Norwegian touring club (DNT) has in recent years in an outreach program, educated thousands of teachers in friluftsliv and enabled large numbers of their pupils to take part in DNT activities. Presently, the DNT is modifying their mountain huts to better facilitate school class trips. Fifthly, and of pivotal importance for encouraging winter friluftsliv, is the culturally iconic school winter and Easter vacations. These are highlights of the year and are closely connected to striking out on skis for the high country. And, finally, what may well be viewed as the Nordic area's most significant contribution to international pedagogy, possibly best translated as the "Folk Academy," *Folkhögskola* has for much of its history elevated friluftsliv to a position of prime importance for its students. From its roots in mid-19th century Denmark, the Folk Academy movement spread quickly to the other Nordic countries, and today there are several hundred such schools, each with its freely established identity and programs. These intimate, largely residential academies are often located outside the urban centres, and with their one- or two-year, mainly non-examination-oriented offerings aimed at students wishing an alternative educational experience after high school or adults searching for rejuvenation, they offer outstanding opportunities for making friluftsliv a life pattern. As at all levels of education in the Nordic countries, there are no financial accessibility barriers to the Folk Academies; they charge no tuition fees.

The Nature of Nature: Nature itself in the Nordic region may be viewed as inviting friluftsliv. Due to its northern reaches, the vegetation is often sparse in comparison with that of the more populated, more southerly, areas of North America. Not only is tree growth less dense, but the relative lack of undergrowth leads to ease of access.

Water for recreation is abundant in many parts of North America, and especially in Canada, but even there it is not so evenly distributed. Norway, Sweden and Finland not only have great amounts of inland waters in relation to their overall surface area, but these waters are also very clean and, through the right of public access, eminently available to the population for swimming, canoeing, kayaking, rowing and sailing. Coastline lengths compared to the size of these countries is extraordinary, and the Baltic and Atlantic archipelagos may well be without peer internationally. This unusual geographical phenomenon is also widely found in their many inland lakes; swimming is even great in downtown Stockholm! In the Baltic, low salinity even permits that most exotic of northern friluftsliv, winter-skate touring among the myriad islands far out at sea.

Topographical variation is highly compressed, which in conjunction with the considerable biological variation resulting from the north/south alignment of the region, results in vast opportunities for a differentiated friluftsliv. In North America, the scale is much larger, perhaps with the exception of the American New England states and the Canadian Maritime provinces, which means that greater travel distances are required to reach the forms of nature desired.

Urban planning appears, as well, in the Nordic area to have been characterized by a more determined focus on including green friluftsliv areas within town and city borders than is the case in North America. Indeed, the concept of near-friluftsliv is well established in the Nordic countries, mirroring this planning priority. It is likely that this is a consequence of the more restrictive philosophy of nature privatization.

On the other hand, the establishment of large parks and nature reserves in North America in late 19th century preceded that of the Nordic countries, and could be viewed as a strong statement of public responsibility. However, Sweden was not far behind, beginning with the shaping of its system of national parks in 1909 and the establishment of ten such parks, the first in Europe.7 More importantly in the present context, friluftsliv in these protected areas has been given strong inducement through the complete lack of user fees, a strong contrast to the practice in North America. The right of public access, then, is applied universally to the land and does not discriminate according to economic status.

The Path Ahead

Nature, as the consummate teacher, will always point our way as we enter her domain. If we are only alert and receptive, her hints will show us how to live in her home, and this will always vary according to any place on earth. But, what then of the intervening cultural context?

In North America, it is a paradox that the waves of European immigrants escaping constrictive societies did not shape nations with freedoms extended into nature. It may be unrealistic to expect that the North American unfortunate restricted access to nature will, in the foreseeable future, be relegated to history. However, life is never stagnant, and with political mobilization fuelled by will, societies have been and will continue to be restructured. The point of departure for a journey freeing North-American access to nature could be a concerted action to eliminate user fees from all levels of parks and reserves, thus shifting their financing from individual pockets to the public purse. Simultaneously, the heavy bureaucratic structures governing such areas should be de-escalated. My contrasting experiences with organizing student friluftsliv trips in Canada vis-à-vis Norway/Sweden/Finland vividly illuminates this need. Bringing Canadian students into a provincial park was an expensive, time-consuming, complicated and often frustrating project, reminiscent of a military operation, whereas on the other side of the Atlantic we would simply point our feet in the direction of our hearts' desires, never dealing with anyone but ourselves.

At the more local political levels it should be within closer reach to invigorate school pedagogy with friluftsliv, both in everyday practice and at well-supported outdoor centres. Most, if not all, school subjects could be taught partly outdoors, but of equal significance would be instituting the Nordic "play-friluftsliv," made possible by frequent outdoor recesses during the school day. For this to be facilitated, more green planning and implementation needs to be prioritized by local school and municipal authorities. Winter and Easter school holidays with structured opportunities for friluftsliv on the Nordic model should not be beyond the capacity of North American educational authorities to institute.

In conjunction with such public objectives, immediate attention should be given to expanding the modest and fragmented hostel system in North America. With the solidly anchored International Youth Hostel Federation as an organizational framework, it should be feasible to emulate the fine-meshed hostel networks found in many other countries. With the expense and time required to reach prime areas for friluftsliv in North America, it is crucial that inexpensive accommodation be widely available as a compensating factor. As "base camps" for venturing out into nature, especially during the winter season, such hostels would be of inestimable value. It should be emphasized that hostels around the world today are not only for youth – after hostelling's early history, the movement became fully age-inclusive, and moreover, long ago ceased being identified with stark simplicity and enforced collective living.

Closure

The cultural factor, then, is of decisive importance in the friluftsliv spectrum; it is the critical mediating variable between the individual and nature. Nordic friluftsliv has been markedly shaped by collaboration between public and private sectors. Rather than viewing each other from an adversarial perspective, they have generally complemented each other in working to actualize values deeply embedded in society. Similar bridges between levels of government and voluntary outdoor organizations, echoing the experience of the Nordic countries, is a formidable challenge for North America in the creation of such partnerships for the benefit of all. For it to succeed, the notion of "user pays" must transcend the strictly individual level and be moved to the sphere of the "public good," where a simple and authentic friluftsliv is not only made possible but is actively encouraged for all, according to the mosaic of personal dispositions, societal enabling and the tapestry of nature.

This mental voyage spanning the North Atlantic may serve as a springboard for further explorations of body, mind and soul in our nature home. Like Vikings of the future, we can search our varied heritages, cast our eyes on distant horizons and build creatively upon them for a more natural, fulfilling, and harmonious life.

PART I

Scandinavian

A Commentary on Nils-Aslak Valkeapää's
"I Converse With the Earth"

Contribution by Benjamin Gaglioti

The piece that I chose to represent the idea of friluftsliv for today's world is from *The Sun My Father* by Nils Aslak Valkeapää. The few lines that present the philosophy of living a free air life are in the eighth poem of this famous Sámi book of poems.

I converse with the earth
and hear the creeks answer
their voices the sound of silve
I converse with the earth
beyond time.

These lines fly off the paper and are followed by the reader into a long relationship to the natural world. A dialogue is portrayed between land and humans, which is precisely what is necessary in defining an active life outdoors. Whether this interaction is done by farming for years, subsistence hunting, observing nature, or glancing out the window during a busy day. It is a moment or a lifetime of space silence and wonder that comes through to humans in many forms of environments. Open air that answers our questions and satisfies our hungers. These connections can be made everyday or never, but they are responsible for a life in the open air. A life that is interrupted by episodes outside the boundaries of time and place.

CHAPTER 1

Norwegian Friluftsliv: A Lifelong Communal Process

Børge Dahle

A master's student defending his thesis closed the defence by asking, "Why has 20 years of research in friluftsliv not managed to capture the essence of the phenomenon of friluftsliv?" Perhaps the student is right, or perhaps he has not found the right sources. But the question at least is interesting. What is the essence of the cultural phenomenon – friluftsliv?

I believe that friluftsliv, first and foremost, is about feeling the joy of being out in nature, alone or with others, experiencing pleasure and harmony with the surroundings – being in nature and doing something that is meaningful.

What is the Essence of Norwegian Friluftsliv?

A description of people's practice of friluftsliv can be structured in the following way: The clearly dominant form of Norwegian friluftsliv is that people, starting from their own homes or cabins, go out into nature on walks alone or together with others, family and friends, in order to come back later in the day to their own home or cabin. The motives for these walks are often many and complex – to experience nature, to be sociable, to exert physical activity, and so forth. The walks are often longest on

Saturdays or Sundays, but are often taken during the week. This is "daily walk friluftsliv." The essence of friluftsliv is the simplicity with which people can engage with nature in a meaningful way – without the trappings of expensive gadgets or equipment.

When the typical Norwegian friluftsliv individuals go out, they are often on foot or, in winter, on skis. A small group bicycle, and even fewer use other means of transportation such as boats, canoes or skates. In addition to the nature wanderer satisfying the motives mentioned earlier, a relatively large group, as a part of their walk, may want to engage in other interests such as fishing, hunting, berry picking, mushroom gathering, photography, looking at plants and birds, and other such outdoor activities.

Another important part of the practice of Norwegian friluftsliv is a tour over several days, staying overnight in tents or cabins. These trips are usually taken during the weekends or on vacation time – "vacation friluftsliv." The motives are the same as for the daily-walk friluftsliv.

The Norwegian touring culture has been passed on from generation to generation, and has its own rituals that must be learned. The following are some examples of the Norwegian friluftsliv tradition:

> Day Trip 1:
> Breakfast together on Sunday morning. Everyone knows that the family is soon on its way to the woods. The thermoses are filled with coffee or tea for the adults and, with hot chocolate for the children. The necessary clothing and equipment for the temperature and weather are found. Some extra clothes are put in the backpack. In a short time, without any particular discussion or planning, the family is out walking in the forest, where they are likely to meet neighbours and acquaintances, stop for a chat, looking at and talking about phenomena in nature and the cultural landscape. The social high point

of the trip involves sitting down, taking out the thermoses and having lunch, perhaps lighting a fire and talking in friendly tones about things that have happened, future plans and dreams. Then the trip home starts. It is good to get home, to take a shower and cleanse sweaty bodies and have dinner together, followed by lounging about on the sofas or on the throw rugs.

Friluftsliv needs the family to continue to be a living cultural phenomenon and the family needs friluftsliv to ensure positive ways of sharing times together.

Day Trip 2:
In Tuesday's newspaper there was an article on where "Wednesday's exercise" would meet, the tour for this week. Most of the group are single retirees. For most, "Wednesday's exercise" is perhaps their most important social network. Every Wednesday at 10:30 a.m., throughout the year, 40 to 70 enthusiastic walkers meet. The tour goes to one of the cabins in the forest. The path varies from time to time.

These are people who have practised friluftsliv throughout a long life, and friluftsliv is the foundation upon which they have built a lifetime of quality experiences, and they have continued this practice into this last phase of their lives.

Overnight Tour 1:
A group of women teachers have talked for a long time about taking a common tour in the mountains. They have used many work breaks to plan; they have looked forward to it, but have also considered the challenges. They have to find a time that suits leaving their children and husbands behind for a period of time. They ask themselves, "Am I in good enough condition? Do I need to train a little bit before the trip?"

Now the day is here. The backpack is carefully packed. Some experienced mountain backpackers still have their old "pink" anorak (wind jacket) – this makes the group feel confident. But some have a new multicoloured anorak and are pretty excited about how the tour will be. They get on the train. At last they are on their way to the first Norwegian Tourist Association (DNT) cabin. They walk and talk excitedly. They worry about their husbands and children, stop often, eat and talk, look at the magnificent landscape. Soon they feel free. They manage to forget children, husbands and the worries from a long and tiring school year. They get a four-person room in the cabin, where the conversation continues. They put on the clean sweaters they have knitted and go down to be served dinner, coffee and cake in front of the fireplace. They massage their sore thighs and get ready for the next day.

Friluftsliv gives us breathing room in a busy world. Friluftsliv gives us an experience of freedom.

Overnight Trip 2:
He has read books about hunting and fishing during the entire winter. He has tied some trout flies. He doesn't meet his old school friend very often, but the yearly fishing trip holds them together. They can talk for a long time on the telephone. The conversations have to do with last summer's fishing trip and mostly about the big one that got away. What will next summer's fishing trip be like?

The day is here. This year both men take their sons with them. They drive a long way to get to this year's spot. They buy food on the road. With heavy bags they arrive at the "fishing water" and set up camp. It doesn't take long before all of them are at the water with their fishing poles in hand. It has been 30 years since the men met at elementary school as young boys, but now it is as

if time has stood still. Family, colleagues, economic problems and stocks are forgotten. There is only one thing
important in the world. The situation is here and now –
the boys that need to be taught, the friends from school,
the fishing poles and the trout that will soon take the fly.

Friluftsliv gives us excitement. Friluftsliv gives us dreams. Friluftsliv is a
gift from the parent to the children.

Friluftsliv: Lifelong Learning

What characterizes the cultural phenomenon of friluftsliv? What sepa-
rates its practice from the practice of other more commercial international leisure-time culture in nature activities? The following points
illustrate the significant elements:

- experiencing nature is key,
- practising friluftsliv is not dependent on large costs for travelling
  and equipment,
- the nature and cultural landscape used is easily accessible from
  permanent residences and holiday cabins,
- the passing of tradition is strongly anchored in natural social
  groups such as family and friends,[1]
- friluftsliv is not dependant on organizations: it is possible for
  individuals to choose their own time and place for practising it.

Interestingly, in addition to the Norwegian tradition of friluftsliv, we
can also see that the international leisure activity culture in nature has
spread in Norway. These international "outdoors activities" are first and
foremost activity-motivated and tied to facilities in nature. The activities
are most often organized and are set up through commercial interests or
institutions that run education programs or short courses. This leisure
activity culture is often a part of the commercial travel industry and
organized as long trips, expeditions or "adventures." They sell as experience packages.

The international activity culture has gained much of its inspiration from well-known persons who have made widely-known expeditions. Central to Norway are the role models of Fridtjof Nansen and Roald Amundsen as known through their Northwest Passage and Polar expeditions. This type of approach to nature has also gained inspiration from military survival practices and from travel writings based on canoe expeditions through, for example, Canada's deep "wilderness" areas.

It is unfortunate, but understandable, that those universities and colleges with a special responsibility for arranging individual Norwegian day trips and celebrating friluftsliv, have let themselves be taken in by the international leisure activity culture. Likewise, leisure activity culture and "expeditions" experienced through the education of teachers have been taken deeper into the state school system. Under the theme of friluftsliv, ski days are arranged with Telemark skiing and snowboarding, as are "expeditions" with canoes and sleeping in snow caves in the mountains. Is this the way to learn the key elements of Norwegian friluftsliv tradition?

What is worrying the institutions protecting friluftsliv, is that more and more of today's young people than before are missing traditional friluftsliv and instead are participating in the international leisure activity culture. To what degree this concern is based on qualified research results or only on a feeling of a situation is somewhat unclear. The leisure-time patterns of youth must be systematically mapped as youth patterns function differently in different communities and cultures. What is possible to assert is that children who have been socialized in the ways of Norwegian friluftsliv return to this tradition when they themselves have established families. This is true whether they were only partly or even not engage in friluftsliv during their youth. Let youth be allowed to have their own activity culture for, as the Nordic expression goes, "they do not forget mother's milk so fast."

The most effective way to maintain Norwegian friluftsliv tradition will be to ensure that children are socialized within traditional friluftsliv while they are at an age when their leisure time is spent together with their parents. Traditional friluftsliv is open for all and can be practised throughout one's lifetime.

The patterns of friluftsliv demonstrated by the Norwegian people have been constant and are still relatively stable. It is still the simple foot tour and ski trip based on motives of enjoying nature, health and camaraderie, and on developing nature interests that are strongly dominant. "The people's friluftsliv" is still highly alive, but a lifestyle with stress has meant that some people's practice of friluftsliv has been substantially reduced.

Pressure on the traditional patterns of friluftsliv has been great in past decades. The general development of society and the introduction of new activities and varied leisure time are some of the more important reasons for this. But pedagogic institutions have also worked to create new forms of friluftsliv activities. A "sportification" of friluftsliv has occurred. In the competition for students, colleges, folk colleges and sports institutes have needed to target themselves at youth groups. They have chosen to emphasize new trends in outdoor activities and "adventure" tours, even ones to foreign countries.

Despite this, throughout the country, the pattern of friluftsliv has shown itself to be relatively stable. This can be explained by the fact that the youth groups have never been and are not currently a decisive factor for Norwegian friluftsliv. It is the age groups before and after adolescence that are dominant and decisive in friluftsliv. Friluftsliv is an activity form that is practised from birth to the grave.

What is the "Knowledge Status" for Norwegian Friluftsliv?

That friluftsliv still has a large following in Norway can first and foremost be explained by the fact that it is deeply established in the common culture, where the practice of friluftsliv "tacit knowledge" is still passed on from generation to generation. Additionally, our settlement structure is relatively continuous. Even at the beginning of this new century, all Norwegians still had a very short distance to travel to nature and to cultural landscapes where friluftsliv can be practised.

We have accumulated a great deal of experience in pedagogical work with friluftsliv over the last thirty years. Different pedagogical methods, such as the following, have been tried. "Conwaying" is defined as sharing the experiences of free nature (nature possessing its own original rhythms) in accord with the patterns of thought and values of the Norwegian tradition of friluftsliv. This happens, in the main, in smaller groups where the emphasis is on the joy of identification with nature as well as inspiring the finding of a route in modernity toward a lifestyle where nature is the home of culture.[2] Conwaying has become a useful term, and in many ways represents its own culture within friluftsliv. Conwaying represents its own "school" in friluftsliv pedagogy that has been shown to function very well in certain pedagogic situations such as guided outings. Perhaps the use of conwaying should be differentiated to a greater degree for different target groups.

The "conwayers" position in too many instances has been too dominant in guided learning situations. Participation in the practice of friluftsliv demands a fundamental education, a resonance with nature that requires a free and independent development over time. The core of this development as a sounding board for nature is the experience of "being in" a rich natural and cultural landscape. We must create a good "learning room" for friluftsliv, not a guide-centred approach.

Outdoor Life: Based on Whose Values?

The Norwegian outdoor life tradition has given us the understanding that outdoor life leads to good health for most people and develops an enduring relationship to nature that contributes to the taking care of and improving the "earth's health." Using time and money to bring forth more research results to support this experience, with the objective of winning over the "doubting" voting politicians and bureaucrats is both meaningless and, with respect to research, problematic. Efforts should be made instead to find ways to carry out stimulating initiatives that make it possible for more people to practise an outdoor life that is healthy both for them and for the earth.

In this respect it is important to accept the fact that Norwegian's leisure-time use of nature takes different forms and is based on different traditions and values. Norwegians' use of nature in their leisure time can be separated into three primary forms: nature life, outdoor life and outdoor activities.

The concept of "nature life" comes from the Norwegian country culture. One reaps nature's surplus without using it up, but at the same time outings provide positive experiences of nature and opportunities for social fellowship. Outdoor life is perceived as a form of nature use that is traditionally tied to urban people's leisure time and to tourists who wander in and climb Norwegian mountains. As noted earlier, the motives for practising outdoor life are often a combination of experiencing nature firsthand, the joy of being out in the fresh air and the benefits of social fellowship.

The value of nature life/outdoor life is, first and foremost, that it leads to a knowledge of and the feeling at home in nature. Thus, for small children, youth and adults, this type of life experience will be an alternative form – an experience of the simple life that develops that ability to manage with natural and simple forms of food, clothing, light and warmth. In this way, nature and outdoor life will help lead to lifestyles characterized by greater harmony between nature and humans, and to developing responsible and well-rounded people with the ability to co-operate in the local, as well as the global community.

Outdoor activities are often motivated by pleasure in activities and social interaction. Many forms of outdoor activities do not have a long tradition in Norwegian society. Often these are play and sports activities that are practised in nature and oriented to the surroundings on the participant's premises. The activities are of a positive character for the individual and can be positive in a societal connection but can be problematic from an ecological perspective. Outdoor activities, such as thrill-seeking hand gliding and risk-taking white water paddling, are different from nature and outdoor life and unfortunately are often a result of a consumer society. These activities are strongly concerned with equipment and physical performance.

In extreme examples the "risk takers" strive for media attention in order to satisfy their heroic self-image and sponsors. Unfortunately, they often are successful in a world with a growing group of journalists who are more concerned with their own personal goals than their responsibility for the development of society. This "symbiosis" between nature acrobats and narcissistic journalist creates an extremely uneven picture of the Norwegian people's outdoor life habits, and represents a strong threat for socialization in the traditional outdoor life.

Identifying with and focussing media on extreme variants of outdoor activities, together with the growing disappearance of nature areas in local areas and the increased organization and bureaucratization of outdoor life, are perhaps outdoor life's most difficult challenges.

Socialization Towards Outdoor Life

For me, contact with nature, participation in sports, and friluftsliv were a natural part of growing up. I first learned to see friluftsliv as something to be taught through my studies at the *Norges Idrettshøgskole* (Norwegian University of Sports). There I met my advisor, Nils Faarlund. As a result of our initial meeting I saw for the first time the link between friluftsliv and the ecological situation that dominates our globe. Since then, I have tried, through teaching friluftsliv, to foster an interest in friluftsliv.

My studies in biology helped me to understand some of the negative ecological effects of outdoor recreation, and left me determined to find ways to prevent them. From time to time I have found it difficult to balance the use of the outdoors in an eco-philosophical way (best described as "the way is the goal," where the way is to maintain harmony with nature) against my misgivings about exposing plant life to more damage and increasing disturbance to wildlife, both the result of increased traffic.

Because I recognize that humans are part of nature, and also because I have come to understand that there is a connection between taking action to protect nature and experiencing the joy of being in nature, I remain committed to using education as a means for bringing friluftsliv centrally into peoples' lives, for promoting socialization into friluftsliv and for encouraging active protection of nature.

Taking a historical view of the factors that influence an individual's involvement in friluftsliv and of the opportunities for socialization into friluftsliv, we find that things are very different from even one generation ago. Today, the simplicity of friluftsliv is challenged by a higher standard of living and by the amusement-park-like repertoire of outdoor offerings. Socialization into friluftsliv as a normal part of everyday life can no longer be taken for granted. We can no longer assume, for example, that families go for walks on Sundays, as was the case during my childhood; today there are many alternative leisure activities.

Friluftsliv can be reinforced in these changed circumstances through the realization that these changes have gone too far. More and more of those now living apart from nature have a sense that something is missing in their lives, as if life without nature affords less meaning. This remains a premise of friluftsliv. In this situation the greatest challenge is to find and implement effective ways to socialize children into friluftsliv. There are two key questions to guide us: Which measures directed to which groups effectively socialize into a form of friluftsliv that stimulates the desire to protect nature?, How can we implement these measures with the means we have at our disposal, taking into account practical circumstances that may both help and hinder?

With the intention of finding such measures, and in the hope of implementing and evaluating them, I began a project that was financed by the Directorate for the Protection of Nature, a Norwegian government institute. The project centred on the relationship between socialization into friluftsliv and local nature conservation.

Interestingly, the project used tourism as an agent for developing an ecologically sustainable local community. In many ways tourism is a threat to the friluftsliv, but at the same time reflective eco tourism can help conserve local culture and contribute to creating economic sustainability in the local community. This basic idea has so far proven to be both an effective strategy and technically defensible. The development of a system of locally built mountain huts for both tourist and local use created many beneficial community spinoffs. It has opened dialogues with groups previously unconcerned with friluftsliv, not least of which are business and industry, both crucial to any attempt to move toward ecologically and economically sustainable development.

Key Findings of the Project

Increased involvement of the local population in friluftsliv and in the protection of nature and culture is essential. Local attitudes – indicated by locally stated priorities and views expressed on specific local cases – necessitate this strategy. My research found that while 96 per cent of the local population practises friluftsliv, only about one-third of the population (the highly active group) practises it in such a way that it is part of their everyday lives. This highly active group is sufficiently involved in nature to enjoy significant health benefits.

The highly active group articulated an interest in environmental problems and indicated a willingness to be engaged in environmental action. While this suggests a positive correlation between practising friluftsliv and active engagement in nature conservation, a link has not been documented at this stage. However, it is possible to establish that those who are active in friluftsliv during their upbringing, remain loyal to friluftsliv throughout their life. Correspondingly, the less active group reported being less affected by positive influences during their upbringing.

Diverse motivations are evident for socialization into friluftsliv. There is a strong connection between nature and health and one or more nature-associated interests (dogs, boating, photography, hunting, fishing, berry/mushroom hunting, birding, botany, etc.) An interest in friluftsliv tends to be enduring.

In the evaluation of motivations, it is important to pay attention to hindrances to involvement in friluftsliv. In so doing, it is possible to find that "weak" groups either lacked the upbringing or training that could have socialized them into friluftsliv, or faced genuine obstacles to involvement in friluftsliv. Disproportionate numbers of people who are married, are full-time workers, are women and who have children, report "lack of energy" as a reason for their low or non-involvement in friluftsliv.

If community involvement in friluftsliv and nature conservation is to be increased, it is necessary to understand what these broad motives and hindrances mean in actual practice, and to delve deeper into the different motives. "To experience nature" is the frequently stated motive, but experiencing nature is a complex concept. It includes, for example, aesthetic experiences, serenity and stillness. SFT (the Norwegian environmental protection authority) has conducted a descriptive study entitled "Serenity as a Quality."[3] Further work is needed on the relationships between experience of nature, knowledge, and empathy.

More Findings of the Study

There was a clear statistical correlation between the level of activity a person has currently and the level of activity he or she had as a child with one or both parents. Analysis of the data shows that activity level of the father, mother and the individual themselves during their childhood is the main influence in determining the level of involvement in friluftsliv in later life.

On the other hand, it does not seem to be of great important that the family was active in friluftsliv as a family; that is, they did not have to take walks together. This may be explained by role theory. The father and mother are seen as friluftsliv role models both in childhood and adulthood. Primarily, it is the mother who takes the children on walks and has the greatest socializing influence in friluftsliv. Perhaps when the father occasionally joins in he serves as a role model.

There are other relationships/factors that positively affect lifelong interest in friluftsliv. In decreasing order of importance these are as follows:

- parents' relationship to friluftsliv,
- distance to suitable areas,
- friends' relationships to friluftsliv,
- a hobby/interest that leads "out into nature,"
- a family access to a cabin or summer home,
- owning a dog.

In closing, it should be pointed out from this study that all of the relationships/factors that could be described as "educational measures" – instruction in middle school, high school, college, and courses/memberships in non-profit organizations that deal with outdoor life – are collectively about as influential as owning a dog.

Conclusion

Friluftsliv should continue to be available to all. The individual's physical condition and personal wealth should not be deciding factors for participating in friluftsliv. With the development of sport in mind, all attempts that could threaten the "daily walk friluftsliv" or "vacation friluftsliv" should be opposed. Friluftsliv must not be for the elite. A "sportification" of friluftsliv will be destructive; let friluftsliv avoid becoming a spectator's sport.

It is important to undertake frequent critical evaluations of our own activities within administrative, organizational and pedagogical institutions that work with friluftsliv. There should be a continual dialogue about what is the core of traditional friluftsliv and examination of this core in relationship to our own activity. Without a clear understanding of friluftsliv's core content, it will be difficult to develop effective socialization and recruiting strategies and learning programs for a friluftsliv that is to adapt to the new challenges that will always be present in a changing society.

CHAPTER 2

Friluftsliv as Slow Experiences in a Post-modern "Experience" Society

Hans Gelter

Introduction: Three Outdoor Experiences

"The fractal dancing of the flames from my fireplace slows my mind into a trance. I sit alone by the fire at my favourite place, the Falcon Cliff. Behind me from an old pine, a lonely male redstart desperately tries to attract any stray female with his melancholic song. I feel a strong sympathy with the lonesome bird and his half-hearted attempts this late in the season. From the bogs below I hear a crane pair giving their majestic greeting calls, accompanied from a distance by the bubbling evening displays of black grouse. At the horizon in front of me, I see the distant archipelago islands of the Baltic Sea flooded by the Subarctic midnight sun, and I shiver with the pleasure of the intense moment. My mind expands and merges with the more-than human world around me. I merge into a natural part of the landscape and its drama."

"The rubber on my right shoe is slowly gliding off the rock and my left leg is starting to tremble like a sewing machine tanking up on lactic acid. Desperately my right hand is probing the cliff above me, while at any second I am likely to fall off the wall. Just when I am giving up, my fingertips find a crack allowing me to hold my weight and push myself up to a stable position. My adrenalin level is peaking and the dopamine/endorphin cocktail flushing my brain kicks me into a state of euphoric happiness. I take a quick glance at the spectacular landscape behind me, look down at my buddy who responds with a 'Right On' and I continue for the next challenge."

"I prepare our morning coffee having just crawled out of our tent and been greeted by the dazzling mountain landscape flooded in the morning sun. Getting in the mood for a great day I hear the first humming in the distance. After an annoyingly long time this disturbance increases to an inferno when three snowmobiles nonchalantly race past very close to our tent, leaving a stinking petrol trace in their wake. Behind us on the slope they start to challenge the steepness of the mountain by driving up as far as their strong engines can manage, making one loop after another on the up-to-that-point untouched snow. After what seems like an intense eternity, the snowmobiles give up their play and their sound fades away. We have just recovered from the stress when a new sound reaches us from the distance. While we are finishing our breakfast, a snowcat, dragging a dozen young snowboarders up the mountain, appears from the valley. With great enthusiasm for their mountain adventure and the untouched snow the kids race down the slopes and the snowcat slowly returns back down. In the same moment the first heli-skiing tour of the morning passes above us. We prepare for our departure."

My three outdoor experiences just described above characterize different aspects what we in the Nordic countries call "friluftsliv."[1] The first experience outlined represents the original interpretation of friluftsliv as a way of life in relation to nature, where the interconnectedness and immersion in the natural setting is central, a low key activity I have called "Genuine Friluftsliv.[2] It is a philosophical experience of human interconnectedness with nature with roots in the romantic "back-to-nature" movement in the 18th century. Its essence is not unique to only the Nordic countries and has been described within environmental philosophy as well as by early naturalists such as John Muir, Aldo Leopold and others.[3] What is unique for the Nordic countries is that friluftsliv has become a way of everyday life for most people and part of the national soul. In 1921, the Norwegian explorer Fridtjof Nansen talked about friluftsliv as a philosophy to co-operate with nature's powers and as an alternative choice for youth to avoid "tourism," the superficial acquaintance with nature.[4] Nansen believed that free nature[5] was our true home and that friluftsliv is the choice and the means for making our way back home. Also, the Norwegian philosopher Arne Næss described this personal interconnectedness with nature, often associated with strong emotional and spiritual experiences, as essential for developing his deep ecology philosophy.[6]

New Forms of Friluftsliv

Friluftsliv has, however, through organized activities of early tourist and outdoor associations and through recent commercialization, moving from an original way of thinking to today's focus on the activities per se, as illustrated from my first example vis-à-vis my third, been altered considerably. The result is a more superficial conceptualization of friluftsliv that I call "Post-modern Friluftsliv." Today, there usually has to be a reason to visit nature such as: experiencing nature as a working place of work; exploring natural resources (fishing, hunting, picking berries etc.); collecting natural artefacts (minerals, plants, bird observations etc.); building a collection of names of places that have been visited (nature tourists); learning about nature (scientists, school excursions, etc.); aesthetic exploratory trips involving nature (photographers, painters); searching for sacral experiences (meditation, reflection, etc.); escaping from urban life; or consuming nature as an arena or playground for recreation and sport activities where nature functions as a big coulisse for competition and personal challenges. Today, many of these outdoor activities are included in the general concept of friluftsliv.

The most expanding field of outdoor activities, and included by many in the concept of friluftsliv, is the increased use of nature as a playground for motorized recreation such as snowmobiles, Ski-Doos, water-scooters, motor boats, 4x4s, etc. Illustrative of this reality is that in the last twenty years the number of registered snowmobiles in Sweden has increased from only 20,000 to over 262,000 today. This can be compared with about 570,000 such vehicles in Canada.[7] Traditional outdoor activities such as hiking are increasingly being replaced by motorized outdoor activities and contact with nature has evolved from a low-tech slow interaction to a high-tech-based fast activity.

Friluftsliv as Slow Experiences

This change in the Scandinavian relationship to outdoor life reflects the rapid change in our western society. Our human culture has evolved through several transformations from a hunting/gathering society to our present-day post-modern society. This cultural evolution has resulted in increased complexity as expressed by the many labellings of our contemporary society, such as the information, communication, knowledge, post-modern and experience society. Also, the speed of the transformation of the society has increased, and having just entered the realm of the experience society, with its demands for experiences as personally staged memorable sensations, we already talk about the coming "transformational society" with its demands of "makeover" and personal changes of appearance and lifestyles.[8] This new post-modern society with its never-ending search for all-consuming experiences and quick fixes has fundamental implications for our relationship to nature and to outdoor life. Today, urban people generally spend more than 90% of their time indoors and visit nature more rarely then previous generations. They mainly experience nature and the outdoors through media such as television.

In addition to being flooded by information, speed has become the icon of our time, determining both our behaviours and consumption patterns. All our technological development is oriented towards increasing speed and "saving time," resulting in an ever increasing quickening of the pace of life. This trend is one reason for the increasing popularity of motorized friluftsliv as people feel the need to race through nature in search for experiences. This speedy life has resulted in a longing for an alternative to such a hectic life, a search for "slowness," for an opportunity to get a break to breathe and regain energy. Besides the recent trend of the mass popularity of yoga and other meditation techniques, a new global counter-trend has emerged – the "Slow Movement" where "slow environments," "slow products," "slow design," "slow food" and "slow cities" are dedicated to promoting an alternative to ever increasing faster urban conditions.[9] Urban stressed-out people are searching for "Slow Experiences" designed to temporary "stop the speed" of the hectic everyday life. People are complementing the urban quick-meal with a "Slow Food" experience where the time waiting for and consuming the food is the essential experience, searching for *flow* experiences where time ceased to be – a reference to a well established international and popular concept originating primarily from the scholar Csikszentmihalyi. Interestingly, the Greeks talked about a dual time concept, where Kronos – the Greek word for the linear time that now rule**s** our lives – meant the chronological ticking of time to create order in chaos and facilitate our interpretation of the past and planning of the future. In contrast was Kairos – the Greek word for vertical time or experienced time, "the right moment" that makes time stand still, as in the optimal moments in the flow experiences.[10]

To test the concept of Slow Experiences within friluftsliv, I conducted a pilot-study (unpublished) to test if a Slow Experience through contact with nature can affect the mood of the mind. Within the context of a number of field trips, 221 adults were to have a short solo experience, and silently sit down in the natural setting. After ten minutes of silence in nature, individuals members of the trip group would gather together and each participant was asked to write down his or her thoughts and feelings during the experience of silence in nature. Most (96%) expressed a positive feeling towards this encounter with nature. The most common reflection (66%) recorded by the participants dealt with their mood, as expressed through such terms as calm, relaxation, stillness, quietness, peace, harmony, recharging the batteries, etc. Almost as common were comments on new sensations – to see, hear, feel and smell the surroundings and be more aware of details. A third type of response expressed feelings of gratitude, dauntlessness, happiness, freedom etc. This study confirmed the "common sense knowledge" that contact with nature is a positive experience. It puts one in a relaxing positive mode, extending one's senses to rediscover details within the surroundings, allowing one's thoughts to wander freely, forgetting everyday life issues and getting into a state of relaxing flow, where Kronos-time evaporates and Kairos-time puts one in a state of absorption of the present. This type of experience can thus be called a true "Slow Experience" and is the essence of Genuine Friluftsliv.

It is interesting that only ten minutes of close encounter with nature can alter one's mental rhythm and time sense. Rhythms are central to our experiences and daily we are ruled by social rhythms, working rhythms, media rhythms, indoor-leisure rhythms and technological rhythms violating our internal biological rhythms, seasonal rhythms etc. This disharmony of biological and technological rhythms can result in people feeling inharmonious. Even our thoughts have their rhythms affected by external and internal rhythms, where rhythmical movements such as walking stimulates our creative thinking. Looking at the rhythms of a fireplace, or at the ocean with the rhythms of the waves, and the rhythms of the sparkling lights of sun reflections on the water may affect us in such a way as to trigger feelings of infinity, with a rhythm with the frequency of zero. Such zero-rhythms are Slow Experiences, and are essential to Genuine Friluftsliv in contrast to the post-modern urban rhythms and the fast Post-modern Friluftsliv.

Understanding Friluftsliv as Different Experiences

To understand the diversification and complexity of contemporary outdoor leisure, we can look at friluftsliv as having four distinct experience realms: entertainment, education, escape and aesthetics, based on the type of activity and environmental interaction.[11] The basic way to understand different expressions of friluftsliv is to engage in the experience; this is the first dimension in the approach to the four experience realms. At one end of the involvement spectrum is passive participation where the individual does not directly influence the events in the experience, but rather is an observer. This form characterizes Genuine Friluftsliv as illustrated by my first example where a person just by being passively in nature may experience emotions and moods, which can interconnect one with the place, the landscape and nature as a whole. At the other end of the spectrum, lies active participation where the individual vigorously affects the events and creates a personal experience. This type characterizes most forms of Post-modern Friluftsliv such as illustrated in my second and third Friluftsliv experiences. Although Genuine Friluftsliv may involve outdoor activities such as canoeing, it is not the activity per se that is the focus and reward of the experience, but rather the being in the landscape and interacting with the forces and rhythms of nature.

The second dimension constituting the four experience realms is environmental, where absorption of the experience comes through the attention given to bringing the experience into the mind like a sponge absorbing water, as in a learning situation. At the other end of this dimension lies immersion, the ability to "go into" the experience deeply, such as when powder-skiing down a big mountain and immersing oneself in the alpine snow landscape. Both attention and immersion are essential for Genuine Friluftsliv and Slow Experiences.

The first realm of entertainment within friluftsliv is illustrated by my experience of the fractal dancing flames of the fire, which involves my passive absorption of the experience through my senses, an essential component of Genuine Friluftsliv. The second realm of educational experiences is also fundamental to friluftsliv. As alienation from nature increases in our post-modern society, we need positive environmental education as an aid in restoring human interconnectedness with and active engagement in nature. A variety of educational programs and curricula have emerged to educate the post-modern human to be aware of, understand and engage in environmental issues.

Genuine Friluftsliv has the same ultimate goal as many environmental education programs, but does not use any curriculum and is not about teaching and lecturing or being on excursions. The only educational aid is being in nature itself. Genuine Friluftsliv is thus not traditional outdoor education with its specific learning goals

of place (natural environment), subject (ecological processes) and reason (resource stewardship).[12] Rather, it involves learning the ways of self and place in the more-than-human world and developing an interest in the ways of every creature and phenomenon you meet on your journey through life. It links natural history and philosophy and connects the knowledge of oneself and one's surroundings with an understanding of the world. Traditional environmental education and natural sciences enrich and deepen the experiences of friluftsliv, that is to say one comes to understand the song of the redstart, but the goal is not to become an expert naturalist or a skilled adventurer. Although friluftsliv is on the curriculum of educational systems in Scandinavian and elsewhere, its goal in such an educational context has often become that of outdoor education with its focus on mastering different outdoor activities, but rarely on the deeper philosophical mission of Genuine Friluftsliv.

The third experience realm of modern friluftsliv is that of escape, requiring complete immersion and active involvement in the experience, and often resulting in a sensation of *flow*. Contrary to passive entertainment experiences, in escapist experiences the individual becomes the actor, affecting the actual performance often based on adventures and playful interaction with the environment and its elements. Staged adventure experiences, where the real risk is minimized and apparent risk optimized to create fun, active and challenging opportunities, could be called

"Adventuretainment" to distinguish them from serious and often very high-risk adventurous expedition experiences. When rafting or hiking in the wilderness, one can become deeply immersed in the environment and through this escapism completely forget everyday life at home. The post-modern individualisation and commercialisation trends have made this adventurous escapism from modern life a very popular form of friluftsliv, a new "active post-modern Friluftsliv." Although Adventure-tainment is most often performed in groups, it is still strongly focused on individualism through personal performance and development as described in my second experience story.

The fourth and final experience realm of friluftsliv is the aesthetic, where you immerse yourself in an environment while having little or no effect on it. Such experiences include visiting nature scenery where the main goal is not to learn as in the educational realm, or to behave as in escapist experience, or to sense as in the entertainment realm, but just to be there, being passively immersed in the experience for its own sake. Such esthetic experiences of nature often have a touch of spiritual or existential experience combined with strong emotional effects, and can be called "Contemplatainment." When aesthetic nature experiences involve a restorative escapism from urban life, they can be conceptual-ized as passive post-modern friluftsliv and become important parts of the Slow Experiences of Genuine Friluftsliv.

Restorative escapism into nature is not a new concept. Nansen's "way home to nature" from urban life was adopted early during the emergence of organized friluftsliv and early nature tourism for the urban working class in Scandinavia and elsewhere, to "strengthen the working people." New today is that this urban escapism has been individualized as a per-sonal way to cope with post-modern speedy urban life. This quest for Slow Experiences to de-stress and regain power, to "detox one's mind," is an important concept of Genuine Friluftsliv. Nature's power as generator for "mental energy" and well-being is now empirically and theoretically well-documented and constitutes a solid theoretical basis for Contem-platainment. Such searches for Slow Experiences through Genuine Friluftsliv and Contemplatainment will probably increase in the future as the urban population grows and urban speedy-life escalates.

Conclusions

I have shown that Nordic friluftsliv in today's post-modern society can be conceptualized in several ways. Genuine Friluftsliv is the original interpretation of a way of life in relation to nature, where the interconnectedness and immersion in the natural setting is at the centre of a philosophical experience of nature. This original low key "Genuine Friluftsliv" has the potential to become an important Slow Experience in the contemporary, global Slow Movement. Secondly, we have a post-modern conceptualization of friluftsliv where the activity is in focus and where learning and improving one's outdoor skills are in focus. High-tech equipment is an essential part of this increasing active post-modern friluftsliv as well as the need for play and adventure, an experience realm I call Adventuretainment. Thirdly, there has emerged a second post-modern conceptualization of friluftsliv as an escape from urban speedy life and stress to "detox the mind" and regain power through a quest for deep and slow experiences. Nature's power as a generator for mental energy and well-being is well documented and constitutes the foundation for this Contemplatainment. The need for well-being through nature will increase as the urban population grows and urban Kronos-life gets out of hand. Through the understanding of Genuine Friluftsliv as a different experience realm, basically being a "slow" experience with educational, escapist, entertainment and aesthetic components, the concept of friluftsliv can then become an important tool for understanding outdoor life and be applied globally for management, planning and organizing leisure and tourism based on the outdoors.

CHAPTER 3

DESERVING THE PEAK:
WHEN NORWEGIAN FRILUFTSLIV MEETS THE WORLD

Jo Ese

Friluftsliv has traditionally been seen as an intrinsic part of Norwegian culture. As this anthology exemplifies, people from other parts of the world look to Norway to find inspiration on how to behave in nature, and to learn from the friluftsliv approach to life in the open air. Here I will turn the gaze, and look at how Norwegian friluftsliv is being influenced by other countries.

In recent years, the way Norwegians behaviour in nature has been affected by international trends, especially from America and southern Europe. As a result of this, traditional behaviour in the Norwegian open air is now subject to change. A possible consequence of such change is that public conception of the term friluftsliv is undergoing change as well. In the following, I will summarize the research I have done on how this meeting between the specifically Norwegian and the global is taking place, with particular emphasis on different forms of practice that have developed in the Norwegian outdoors.

Before I started my research, I had to clarify what traditional Norwegian friluftsliv is. Heidi Richardson presents a thorough discourse analysis of excerpts of over one hundred years of friluftsliv-related literature.[1] Based on this, she singles out three core values that she finds in friluftsliv.

These are:

- use of simple equipment,
- simple or no accommodation or facilities,
- skill and experience among participants.

I set out with the assumption that these traditional friluftsliv-related values are being challenged in Norway today. Subcultures emerging from activities like freeride skiing and snowboarding, surfing, river kayaking and mountain biking have become influential, and these subcultures bring with them elements that not always cohere with the strict demands that Richardson describes. This possibility of conflict between the traditional and the new trends has also been described in former research, by both Alf Odden and Øystein Aas and by Anette Bischoff and Alf Odden.[2]

With these assumptions in mind, I wanted to look further into what cultural differences can be found between traditional Norwegian friluft-sliv and the "new," and to try to answer the following question: Is conflict taking place between traditional friluftsliv and new outdoor trends in the Norwegian open air?

I started by interviewing informants who were active participants in different parts of the Norwegian outdoors milieu. The informants were quite different with regard to their approach to life in the outdoors, ranging from purist traditionalists to brand-sponsored snowboard terrain park youth. In 14 qualitative interviews, all quite thorough, I asked questions about a wide range of themes, for instance, how their outdoor activities are conducted, how one feels about controversial issues like widespread use of helicopters and snowmobiles, and what values they believe are connected to life in the outdoors. These interviews are too few in numbers to give my research any quantitative statistical significance. Still, according to principles of qualitative research, my findings can be transferred to other situations, as long as the same set of premises are apparent.

In the following I will look at some areas where I found that conflict is, to some extent, apparent today, and where conflict might escalate in the near future.

Three Forms of Practice

When I started my research, I believed I would find two quite distinct groups of users in the Norwegian outdoors, one group of users that prefer the old traditional ways, and one group that wanted to explore the newer activities. This belief was based on former research (see Note 2), the quite frequent media presentations of the subject and on my own perception of the field. When I started analysing my interviews, I found that a division into three forms of practice was a more correct way to describe the user groups. I named these three the traditional, the freeride, and the freestyle. I came to this conclusion by developing two dimensions that describe the agents' practice in the field – activity and understanding of nature.

These dimensions are divided into two opposites, traditional and new, constructed to point out the difference between the forms of practice. Traditional activities have been performed a long time in Norway. New activities are the new outdoor activities inspired by international trends such as off-piste skiing and snowboarding, river kayaking and mountain biking. The other dimension, understanding of nature, is divided between practical and abstract. It focuses on how the form of practice indicates an understanding of nature – if it looks upon nature in abstract or practical terms. The abstract intellectualizes and idealizes nature and the landscape, and gives them symbolic value as an abstraction that is something more than the mere physical structure they consists of. Each has value through what it is, not through what use it can be put to. This means that landscapes untouched by humans have value even if the onlooker, i.e. the agent, is not experiencing it first-hand. The mere knowledge of the existence of such landscapes is considered valuable for agents with an abstract understanding of nature. The practical focuses on functionality or what use nature can be put to. When it has no use, it has no value. The practical does not see the idea-based values that the abstract sees. Still, agents with a practical understanding of nature see value in landscapes untouched by humans. For instance, if a river is subject to industrial pollution and there is no fish in it, it can no longer be used for fishing. This would be perceived as negative from both abstract and practical points of view.

This division between the abstract and the practical is based on two cultures of experiencing nature, as presented by Ketil Skogen.[3] In his research, based on quantitative interviews with Norwegian youth, he finds a connection between class background and position on the abstract-practical axis. Agents with a middle or upper-class background have a tendency to perceive nature in an abstract fashion, while agents with working class backgrounds have a more practically oriented view of nature.

As mentioned, I named the three forms of practice identified as the traditional, freeride and freestyle. Within the new subcultures in the Norwegian outdoors there is a difference between freeride and freestyle based activities. These are international words that have many different meanings. In snowboarding, for instance, freestyle is a terrain park-based activity, where the focus is on tricks and jumps, while freeride is a more general all-terrain use of the whole mountain, including off-piste. The words are mainly used to describe different ways of using equipment, but in this article I will use the words to differentiate between ways of understanding and experiencing nature. I choose these specific words because they already exist in the field and thus will be recognized.

Table 1 shows where the forms of practice are placed according to the dimensions activity and understanding of nature:

| | | ACTIVITY | |
		TRADITIONAL	NEW
UNDERSTANDING OF NATURE	ABSTRACT	THE TRADITIONAL (Richardson)	FREERIDE (Bischoff & Odden)
	PRACTICAL		FREESTYLE (Skogen)

Table 1

The Traditional Form of Practice: Traditional Activities – Abstract Understanding of Nature

This is the typically Norwegian friluftsliv way of behaving in the outdoors, with simple equipment and a good knowledge of life in the outdoors, in accordance with the earlier mentioned core values found by Richardson. The respondents I interviewed that belong to this form of practice told me that nature as untouched by humans as possible is the ideal. The experience is ruined if it is affected by disturbing elements like roads, power lines, ski lifts or air traffic. Life in the open air should be spartan, and the agent should go through trials of endurance before reaching her goal and getting her reward. A sample of an interview follows:

> Respondent: "Well, everyone can ride a snowmobile to the top of a peak, right? Or ride a cable car like in the Alps. And then go tell your friends you've been to that peak, right? But you really can't do that. Because you haven't walked there by yourself. And what's the point of being there when you're there with a bunch of Americans that came in the cable car with you?"
> Me: "So it ruins the experience, then?"
> Respondent: "Yes absolutely! At least, that's not the way I want to experience the open air. You get a much more intense feeling of nature when you kind of have to work with it." [my translation]

You have not been there if you have not walked there yourself, the respondent says. You do not deserve the peak if you do not climb to the top. This tells us that the trials of the experience are an important part of the traditional form of practice. The respondents that fit into the traditional form of practice are seemingly very positive towards new outdoor activities. Some of them even do things like off-piste skiing or river kayaking regularly. But when confronted with problematic aspects of the new, they are quite clear on their stands. An employee in DNT (*Den norske turistforening*, the Norwegian Trekking Association, Norway's biggest outdoor activities organization) tells me:

> Respondent: "Yes, we definitely try to recruit people doing those things. We want them to come to our cabins and use their snowboards there. We are very clear on this issue."
> Me: "But if they want to drive to the cabins on snowmobiles, would that be OK?"
> Respondent: "Well, our cabins are situated in the middle of national parks, so that would of course be impossible. It just won't be possible." [my translation]

When I spoke to my respondents about such subjects I found that they were sceptical towards many elements of the new forms of practice. The use of new equipment is fine, but it has to be used in accordance with traditional values. The aversion starts when something contradicts the second dimension from the table above: the traditional understanding of nature. A snowboard tied to a backpack carried to the top of a peak is innovative friluftsliv; a snowboard carried to the peak by a lift is not.

Freeride: New Activities – Abstract Understanding of Nature

The agents that fit into this form of practice perform new activities like the freestylers but share the abstract understanding of nature with the traditionalists, with one foot in each camp. They use snowboards, mountain bikes, kites and river kayaks but prefer to use the new equipment far away from disturbing man-made elements like roads and ski lifts. As a consequence of their understanding of nature, they are opposed to recreational use of helicopters and snowmobiles, the building of large alpine skiing areas or large cabins in the mountains. They feel that their outdoor experiences will be ruined by too much cultural contamination.

At the same time they feel that they belong to an international subculture connected to the activities they perform. They read the magazines, watch the movies and wear the clothes connected to these subcultures in the rest

of Europe and America. Because of this they tolerate and use, for instance, ski lifts to a greater extent than agents that belong to the traditional form of practice. But their favourite experiences are when they are situated in untouched nature, unaffected by civilization. A respondent telling me about why she prefers to walk to the top when skiing off-piste, illustrates this:

> Me: "What is it then about walking to the top that makes the experience so much better?"
> Respondent: "Well, I don't know … you notice the mountain a lot better if you walk to the top. You don't get the same perspective when the only look you get is from the lift. It's better to ski back down when you've struggled for every metre." [my translation]

Thus, the form of practice ends up as a mix of traditional Norwegian friluftsliv and international trends. Because of its abstract understanding of nature, it is to a great extent accepted among the traditionalists as part of the Norwegian way.

Freestyle: New Activities – Practical Understanding of Nature

> Respondent: "Well, it's really odd that it isn't legal. Just think of all the cool mountains in Norway, and we can't use any of them! I think every boarder wants to try heli-skiing … that's like the dream … the mountain is like yours alone, you know, you can just cruise for half an hour. It's like the biggest thing you can do … for me any-way." [my translation]

The activities performed in the freestyle form of practice are quite similar to the ones performed by the freeriders. The agents use the same equipment, often in the same areas. The difference lies in the way the agents understand nature. The freestylers have no interest in spending time walking to the top when what they want to do is to ski down. They see no point in the struggling and spartan ways of the traditional or the freeride forms of practice. For them, there is no reason why for instance heli-skiing should stay prohibited in Norway. They have a practical understanding of nature and do not mind physically adjusting the terrain so that they can get the most out of it. One of my respondents said:

> Me: "So you don't care that much about the environment?
> Respondent: "No. Of course it's a good thing if people care, but I haven't bothered getting into it."
> Me: "So if Hemsedal [a downhill ski area] expands their lift system and environmentalists are giving them a hard time …"
> Respondent: "I don't care at all. They can cut down all the forest they want if it's up to me. Well, it ruins it a bit for us that know our way around there. It's better to have the forest like it is now, with people riding off-piste there. But it's not concern for the environment that makes me say this. I don't care at all about the environment." [my translation]

The respondent looks at nature as a playground that he can form the way he wants. He is opposed to cutting down the forest because it gives him challenges when he is snowboarding, not because he wants to preserve it. There is an obvious connection between these statements and the practical understanding of nature.

The Conflict: Who Deserves the Peak?

The question I wanted to answer when I started my research was whether or not a conflict in the Norwegian outdoors exists. Through qualitative interviews I found an indication that this is the case, and that it is linked to how the agents understand nature, and how they approach it. Internationally, new activities like snowboarding and off-piste skiing are associated with the use of helicopters, snowmobiles and the growth of large resorts in the mountains. The people with a traditional form of practice that I interviewed expressed clearly that they were opposed to such development in Norway.

If one should try to predict the development in the field, one should consider that agents in the traditional forms of practice have considerable power in affecting regulations in the field. Organizations like DNT and *Friluftslivets fellesorganisasjon* have influence in questions concerning legislation, and are quite clear on their attitude towards helicopters and snowmobiles. On the other hand, research made by Odd Inge Vistad and Marie Skaar indicates that parts of the Norwegian population, especially in rural areas, are in favour of more liberal legislation on the use of snowmobiles.[4] In addition, Marit Vorkinn, Joar Vitterso and Hanne Riese finds that young people in Norway are positive to allowing heliskiing.[5]

My material indicates that some people adapt elements from international subcultures to fit better with the Norwegian traditions (the freeride form of practice). The question for the future is, as I see it is: Can one make these forms of "Norwegianalized" activities become the norm? Or will the international trends be fully integrated into Norwegian outdoor life without adjustment? If the latter takes place, my prediction is that this will not happen without dispute.

CHAPTER 4

DEFINING FRILUFTSLIV

Nils Faarlund

What? – Friluftsliv is a Norwegian tradition for seeking the joy of identification with free nature.[1]

Why? – The emphasis on identification with free nature in accord with the Norwegian tradition of friluftsliv has intrinsic value, as well as an approach to challenging the patterns of thought, values and lifestyles imposed by modernity.

How? – Through conwayorship, a sharing of the experiences of free nature in accord with the patterns of thought and values of the Norwegian tradition of friluftsliv in smaller groups for the joy of identification, as well as for finding in modernity routes towards lifestyles where nature is the home of culture. What follows are key terms chosen to explain in English, the what, why and how of the Norwegian tradition of friluftsliv.

Free Nature

When we speak about identification with nature as the essence of the Norwegian friluftsliv tradition, we need to define the term "nature" as meaning the home of our ancestors at the time of the birth of this tradition as well as humankind's home through the ages.

For ages, the lifestyles of humankind were inspired by a "touch the

Earth" philosophy. The natural rhythms of the plants – seasons, diurnal rhythms and growth rhythms – were not gravely abused until the onset of the Industrial Revolution. Thus, humankind grew up on a planet with free natural rhythms, which obviously left deeply rooted patterns in us. As the terms "untouched nature" or "wilderness" imply, nature is not the home of culture. The term that best complies with the friluftsliv tradition is free nature (nature possessing its own original rhythms).

Paradigm
The paradigm or patterns of though spelled out in the 16th century by René Descartes, reducing nature to a mechanistic system (*res extensa*) by use of instrumental thinking, and the natural science approach based on a fundamental doubt rooted in the maxim *cogito, ergo sum*, gives sovereignty to abstract thinking.

Modernity/Post-Modernity
The breakthrough of the natural scientific paradigm led to Descartes' *l'homme est maitre et posseseur de la Nature* and to Bacon's "knowledge is power" (over free nature) mentality. In retrospect, this turned out to be a divide in human cultural traditions.

The aggressive use of instrumental thinking led to the success of the so-called Industrial Revolution. This accordingly led to a belief in an ever better future, which was followed by traditions more obsolete, leaving us in the desperate situation of producing an ever-changing conspicuous identity to match the frenetic changes of modern culture – modernity/post-modernity.

Tradition
Whereas tradition in the paradigm of modernity represents the obsolete solutions and useless rituals of cultures of the past, experiences made in the mountains, the woods or at sea, where the natural rhythms are still free, ensure that free nature never becomes obsolete. On the contrary, only by paying attention to the experience of generations past may we eventually develop our abilities to familiarize ourselves with nature.

Identification

Instrumental thinking, making up the basis of the paradigm of modernity, "has the bad habit" of describing reality in such a way that, according to Arne Naess, "it leads away from concrete content towards abstract structure." Through the imperative of not "getting in touch," we are resigned to the role of the observer. Identification is made impossible. Modernity knows many diagnoses for crisis that arise from the lack of ability to identify, feel at home, and create friendship. Identification is the basic condition to meet the existential urge for confidence.

Values

The instrumental thinking of modernity denies free nature intrinsic values due to the reductionist paradigm view as *res extensa*. As friluftsliv in the Norwegian tradition originates from the 18th century protests movement towards modernity, the basic values of friluftsliv are the core values of the European Deep Romantic Movement, which had the general goal of a restoration of nature in one's life to curb the forces of modern life.

Joy

Conwaying includes finding words to share the many aspects of identification with free nature, eg: to qualify experience into connaissance of weather, snowbirds, etc. and contrasting the natural sciences, meteorology and ornithology with more field studies/ awareness approaches.

Although joy must be said to be the driving force of friluftsliv, according to the Norwegian tradition, it isn't possible to adequately spell out its meaning in words.

Whereas we may exchange connaissance of snow after having agreed on the adequate words when sharing the experience of snow, joy belongs to the intangible, which hardly may be shared out of context. We certainly have to rely on artistic skills. What we may comment on are the obvious basic conditions for joy in the friluftsliv experience – free nature, confidence and awareness.

Daring to comment on joy, it must be pointed out that we try to speak of a quality of life that is archetypical to humankind. It is not related to modernity's shallow "fun" or "high sensation seeking" and thus exposed to being pulled down in the turmoil of modern life. Joy is an all-embracing experience, absorbing and deeply moving, according to Baruch de Spinoza. In the language of Henri-Louis Bergson, we have to do with *les domnées immediates* – that, which is immediately given, that which is not conveyed by a medium. Although joy in friluftsliv might result from great efforts, it is an experience of tranquility. This tranquility is not a passive attitude. It inspires serendipity and the confidence to act in accord with personal values, even when the initiative might be against mainstream thinking.

Serendipity
Studying pre-modernity Norway we come upon the strange character of Espen. The Ash-Lad – the hero of the fairy tales of "the noble savages." His brothers Per and Paul did not appreciate "the good helpers" whom the Ash-Lad made his conwayors. These were the wise animals represented by the bear and the fox (symbols for the teachings of free nature) and elderly people (symbols for the teachings of traditional culture). When the brothers were put to the test, only Espen had the awareness, confidence and creativity to pass. What he had in common with the three princesses of Serendip was serendipity.

Serendipity, as understood by modernity (i.e. Per and Paul) is the ability by good luck to stumble over the solution to unsolvable problems. Espen was thinking by patterns; in contrast, Per and Paul limited themselves to thinking by rules and thus were unable to master the situation (a master relies on extensive connaissance, feeding a creativeness, which is not controlling but complying).

Friluftsliv's Meeting with Nature, As a Road to a Life in Harmony
Nature meeting for all does not only demand access to free nature for all.
Because three-quarters of the Norwegian population now live in urban
areas, many lack the knowledge of nature and the skills needed in order
to manage the "doorstep mile" to near nature/near friluftsliv. We therefore need an active public effort in order to make guidance in friluftsliv
available to everyone.

Guidance in friluftsliv must be accessible to everyone, in order to
make organization unnecessary, which means:

i)   Access to guidance throughout the country – preferably
     in the family, among friends, at work or in the neigh-
     bourhood, or through volunteer organizations, professional
     or public institutions,
ii) Access to qualified guidance according to friluftsliv's
     traditional knowledge and value of nature – a friluftsliv that
     awakens human values and nature values,
iii) Access to guidance in all forms of nature can be found in the
     areas in which there are traditions to travel, that is, long
     established understandings of a culture of travel,
iv) Access to guidance for everyone – old and young, trained and
     untrained.

Guidance in friluftsliv attempts to enliven the meeting with free
nature in the steps of the traditions of the cultures that are close to
nature. The guide works along with the natural grandmother/grandfa-
ther role. Children who do not get the chance to play in the rich diversity
of free nature become strangers in life. Play is important for life. Play in
nature is the road to the understanding that the nature is the home of the
culture. The human value, as well as the nature value is lost without the
play in the free nature. With friluftsliv, the game of nature meeting can
continue as a lifelong experience.

The Trantjern Seminar (FOR-UT's 5th working seminar 1979), held in
Nordmarka, north of Oslo, concluded that a guide in natural friluftsliv
takes on a three-way responsibility:

i) Responsibility to stimulate the values on natural friluftsliv,
ii) Responsibility for life and health of the participants (during the guidance, but also afterwards!), and
iii) Responsibility for the free nature where the guidance takes place.

As a result, a qualified guide in natural friluftsliv must therefore:

i) Have good knowledge to free nature, desire, and skills to conduct forms of friluftsliv that do not harm the nature's life, and
ii) Participate in society with the major interest in working for a greater harmony in the relationship between nature and humans, as well as between humans.

In conclusion, let us consider the words of C.W. Rubenson from "On The Peaks Friluftsliv," written in 1914:

Those who have felt what life is like among the peaks
Or can be like for humans,
Do not need to read about it,
And those, who have never felt this,
Will nevertheless never understand.[2]

CHAPTER 5

What is Friluftsliv Good For? Norwegian Friluftsliv in a Historical Perspective

Björn Tordsson

Among the Nordic countries, Norway is probably the one where friluftsliv has the strongest standing in terms of culture and daily lifestyle. Norway has a limited and widely spread population and easy access to rich and varied nature.

However, the position of friluftsliv in Norway also has historical and ideological roots. In the development of modern Norway, friluftsliv was given roles in the main social projects. Thereby, the friluftsliv tradition has been packed with different ideologies, descending from the many different socio-cultural contexts from which they once evolved. When such ideologies become established in society, they also produce patterns for how the individual "spontaneously" experiences and interprets meaning in meeting with nature.

By studying friluftsliv during different periods, we get a survey of its qualities as they have been considered from time to time. From this we can look for intrinsic values of friluftsliv and ask ourselves what "questions" exist in today's society that friluftsliv could give "answers" to.

Friluftsliv and the National Project: Nature and Nation

During the 19th century and up to the end of the Sweden–Norway union in 1905, the national issue was the most important. The task was to express a pronounced and common understanding of natural and cultural characteristics and to build a modern nation on that foundation. The privileged classes looked at wild nature and uncivilized culture with an open mind: What did the different parts of the country really look like? Where can one find the most spectacular mountains, the most impressive waterfalls and the most characteristic life patterns? And where in Norway is the most typical Norwegian nature to be found?

Since the middle of the 19th century, landscape painters had shown dramatic vistas from the romantic and expressive Norwegian landscape. Following in the footsteps of the painters, tourists looked upon nature as pictures, and selected regions and places became attractive destinations.

The first tourists had to use the same means of travel as in medieval times – at best in a carriage, more often on horseback, in boat whenever possible, but mostly on foot. Travel by itself was mainly considered as distances of transport or as physically stressing hindrances towards aimed destinations. As modern means of communication were introduced, people found that different ways of travelling also meant different ways of experiencing the landscape. Now a new form of aesthetics developed, advancing a physically and sensuously active relation to the landscape. Friluftsliv was separated from common tourism, and people were told that a real northern dweller ought to experience the landscape in an active and engaged manner.

Tourism and friluftsliv resulted in the meeting of urban and rural culture. On one hand the Norwegian peasant was ideal according to romantic ideas, since identity was formed by uncivilized culture grown in harmony with the natural landscape. The urbanized traveller had to strive to attain such

genuineness by actively becoming familiar with nature. On the other hand, the educated man from town saw, as his obvious duty, the selecting of particular features in folk culture that were typically Norwegian, and teaching the rural population how to polish their manners. The peasant should not be entirely occupied with the utilitarian aspects of nature, but should also be able to appreciate the shimmering light at sunset or the atmosphere during a stormy day.

The national project became very successful. The nation managed to establish a mutual and all-embracing picture of Norway. Bridges were built over cultural differences, and an image of traditional Norway laid a foundation for modernization. Friluftsliv pointed out a way to develop an identity for both the individual and national, through joyful experiences in the Norwegian landscape. This construction of national identity related to nature is in many ways still valid. The tours in nature are still highlights of the year. Seventy per cent of Norwegians have access to a country cabin, and are often more strongly bound to that than to their urban street address.[1]

National Identity or Heritage Preservation

The expression "national identity" might have an undertone of aggressive defence of established domestic culture against foreign influences. Nowadays, we prefer to talk about cultural heritage. Rather than drawing a line against others or assimilating minorities into the common standard, cultural heritage has to do with contributing to fellowship among peoples and cultures.

In a globalized world, local and regional multiplicity tends to lose ground due to the impact of powerful commercial forces. But the fact that new trends and products are launched does not prove that they represent something better. (The farmed salmon outclasses the wild one not because of quality and fitness but because of artificially produced numbers.) Culture can be regarded as accumulated knowledge and experience transformed into life patterns, and heritage preservation as protection of that knowledge.

The aim of friluftsliv, however, is not to try to return to patterns of life from former times. In friluftsliv we can appreciate our cultural heritage as a genuine part of the modern world, without being lost in nostalgia. The traditional sail/row boat is "built around the body" and adapted to wind, waves and shores, and is excellent for friluftsliv. By using elements and practical skills from earlier times we can let heritage meet our own time, teaching us that contemporary terms for human life are not the only valid ones.

Nation, Nature and Identity

The understanding of national character implied that all Norwegians, even those living in towns, fundamentally belonged to nature. Here you could experience your true identity. The mythology of nature and nation is different in other countries. In the United States, for example, one important conception is that each part of the land was once a frontier between the settled area and the Wild West. The immigrant from Europe dealt with the unknown and had to develop "American" virtues: energy and drive, power to meet challenges and improvisation to overcome hindrances. When you discover new land, you also explore your own hidden abilities.

This might explain why "challenge," "adventure," "risk activities" and "achievement" still are emphasized in American outdoor life. If nature is regarded as something alien, a great many tasks become challenging – even sharing a tent with others or eating sitting on the ground. Here we are speaking of pronounced conceptions rather than measurable cultural differences. But the different mythologies might be a starting point for pedagogical thoughts. The American concept stresses the fact that nature can teach us to accept challenges, both mentally and bodily, as a necessity for human growth.

This element is, indeed, not unknown in Norwegian friluftsliv. But here nature should not represent something we have to conquer. It is on our side – the side of life. In Norwegian tradition the ideal is to respond to delicate and risky tasks with a smile, with elegance and full security. You can seek demanding challenges – as long as you have the skills that make it natural to do so.

Emotional Life and an Open Mind to Cultural Values

Nature is a rich storeroom for fantasy, emotions and aesthetic experiences. It holds abundant sources of expressions, symbols and qualities that interplay with our inner life. By obtaining this immaterial treasure the individual life can be ennobled and sensibility developed.

This concept has deep roots in the philosophy of romanticism. Nature and Spirit were understood as two sides of the same coin and open correspondence between the human soul and the expression of nature were stipulated. The emotional experience, not rationality, was seen as the main way to a true understanding of nature.

As a philosophical theory on how the world is composed, this might be of historical interest only, but the basic attitudes are still valid. To "experience nature" is to open oneself up for all its qualities and values. As life's susceptible artists, we receive the impressions from nature and tune them into correspondence with our emotional life.

The contradiction emotion-rationality is still subject to disputes in education. In schools, friluftsliv is often used to give an emotional understanding of nature as counterweight to the dominating theoretical approach. Experience could provide a more committed and personally integrated comprehension than a one-sided focus on theoretical understanding. But why either – or? Could friluftsliv be a bridge between these ideological contradictions: sense/emotion, subject/object, knowledge/experience? Is it not reasonable to listen to your emotions and add the sensibility to make use of your rational ability?

Friluftsliv Between the Wars: The Social Project

The ideology that formed early friluftsliv was individualistic. Members of a new elite meant that nature brings forth originality and independence. Mirroring the individualistic ethos in modern competitive society, the ideal was to be alone in the wilderness.

During the interwar period this changed. Characteristic for the time was a concern for society – a fear that it might fall apart and be divided into contradictions between those more privileged and a growing labour class

in industrial areas. The labour movement rejected the individualistic ideology. Being a worker, you had few chances to choose a career in life. Workers should rise as a class, in solidarity. Also the nationalistic ideology was
rejected. That ideology did not include the worker who had no real native
country but were brothers and sisters of the same class in all nations.

But another road led the worker to the friluftsliv tradition. Town and
industry became symbols of capitalism, oppression and unworthy conditions. In contrast, nature was seen as liberation, uplifting and a way to a
decent life – physically, spiritually and socially. Nature itself was considered both as a critic of society and as an effective cure for social distress.

The first reform the labour movement struggled for was the reduction
of working hours. Leisure time was understood as a lever for improve-
ment, time that should be used in an active way. The social and human
life, distorted in urban living, should be restored in nature – in open air,
with sunlight, clean water – together with others, to develop virtues of
solidarity and the ability to achieve something in fellowship.

The labour movement worked hard in order to save natural areas near
towns and cities, to open means of communication to nature, to arrange
summer camps for poor families and to build vacation cottages owned
by the union. Thus, public access to nature became a politically potent
issue. Here the users' needs confronted the owners' powers – symboliz-
ing the main contradiction in capitalistic society.

At the same time deep economic crises characterized the period. Many
people understood industrialism and urban life as a "blind road" in history and expected a future characterized by handicraft, farming and fishing from small vessels. In this context, friluftsliv could be regarded as the
first step towards a new "green" society. In this period thoughts from
modern "reform pedagogics" influenced friluftsliv. The boy scout/girl
guide movement – formed to integrate youth from different classes by
developing "citizenship" – adopted methods like teamwork, learning by
doing and project-based learning. School camps were initiated where
young people were to learn directly from nature through their own experiences, thereby developing creativity.

The social project was successful too. As the workers grew more
acquainted with the land, they also gained a native country. Legislation

was initiated to guarantee public access to nature. All forms of "free nature" were regarded as worthy goals for friluftsliv.

Friluftsliv as Means to Social Development

To be on a hiking trip together with others is a form of sociability often regarded as distinctive for Nordic culture. It seems that urban entertainment, restaurant visits or mingling at public events is not the genuine Nordic way of keeping company. Real friendship grows at the cabin, in the sailboat, when skiing or around the campfire... .

The idea that nature brings forth social virtues has brought about a variety of professional methods in the field of social work – as resocialization of juvenile delinquents and therapy for drug and alcohol addicts. This practice is well established.[2] It is remarkable, though, that little is documented regarding the effects of, or concise theories on the socio-pedagogical values of friluftsliv. Why should living together in free nature easily develop social abilities?

In friluftsliv we must show more of our personality than in many other situations in life. Hidden sides of our personality will be apparent. In friluftsliv there is – in the long run – no other durable authority than that built on true competence and the ability to contribute to the group as a whole. We can relate to each other according to personal qualities rather than to preconceived roles. Human differences can be valued as qualities when they contribute to variety in the group. In friluftsliv you can get a direct response to your acts. We constantly put our understanding and ability to the test when solving small or large problems together. Pressure and demands from the outside can create inner unity.

In friluftsliv it is often impossible to solve problems without letting disagreements be obvious. Walking away from each other is no solution. We have to work ourselves through disagreements.

Such qualities (of course found also outside friluftsliv) should be understood more as potentials to be realized through conscious work than as obvious truths. However, in our time, the ideals of individualism, independence and self-government are often over-emphasized. The opposite ideals ought to be stressed. People are social beings and good fellowship can also create the best possibility for the maturation of the foremost of our traits of character.

Friluftsliv as a Concrete Form of Cultural Criticisms

The worker in the interwar period in particular could experience an "alternative identity" in nature. This was neither something like a philosophy nor a particularly deep form of criticism, but rather the experience of contrasts between values in friluftsliv and everyday life. In nature one could experience life as it really should be, and these experiences should be guidelines for the building of society.

Is this critical aspect relevant in our time? It ought to be. Our effort to develop an educational friluftsliv must not mean to adjust our work in relation to those attitudes in society that we want to work against. Rather than rigid organization, time-effectiveness and pre-conceived total solutions, we must make room for spontaneity, unexpected events and the inherent possibility of each situation.

The 20th century was a period of great social visions, something we often lack in our time. The idea that people create their conditions of life together with others through ambitious political work seems to diminish. Could we create warming and illuminating "fireplaces in life" for talks around what really is important, and how to make worthy the newly gained individual freedom? Perhaps in the process we can become pathfinders for others.

The Postwar Period Modernization Project

Industrialization and urbanization accelerated during the postwar period. The new society was characterized by a growing state administration, universalistic solutions and the scientific approach. Welfare and leisure time increased, while the program for leisure time as a guide for future community weakened. Now vacations and holidays should compensate for the deficiencies of urban life, thereby increasing health standards and thus benefiting productivity.

However, sport, rather than friluftsliv, was chosen as an instrument for modernization. The inherent features of sport are closely related to modernistic ideology – achievement, progress, self-discipline and competence. It was more difficult to link the values of friluftsliv – enjoying the qualities of free nature – to the modern project.

Not until the 1970s was friluftsliv accepted in the modern project. One discovered then that many more people were involved in friluftsliv than in sport. The authorities of the time began to develop the tools of modern society to secure friluftsliv. Investigations and statistics, classification of needs, compilation of plans, rules and standards, central and regional management plans, all came into prominence. Permanently marked footpaths, parking places, established campsites and systems for dealing with hygiene and litter are all examples of the results achieved.

Friluftsliv and Health

The sedentary life of our time has caused "welfare diseases" such as diabetes, obesity and heart disorders. The number of people asking for medical treatment grows faster than the available resources. A change of lifestyle seems to be the only way to deal with the causes rather than treating the symptoms.

But should friluftsliv be used as a treatment for a sick society? Will a one-sided focus on body and health turn intrinsic values into duties and transform nature into a regulated training ground? On the other hand, if even a slight experience of uneasiness sets limits to effort, life shrinks. We risk amplifying the bad circles of discomfort. Well-being has to do with overcoming uneasy feelings and even to endure pressure and pains – being able to handle the strains of life.

An important question is to what extent should the landscape be adjusted to suit leisure life? General planning will be needed in order to save open areas for friluftsliv. But we definitely don't want nature to be changed into a type of outdoor gym, or see an expansion of the road network. We wish to interpret nature as an open address and to choose our projects ourselves.

Friluftsliv as an Alternative to Dubious Leisure Activities

As leisure time increased in the postwar period, people became aware that this could also cause problems for the young generation. Should they not be helped to avoid negative influences? Friluftsliv was looked upon as positive activity that could meet young people's desire for adventure and autonomy. Similar thoughts are behind the use of friluftsliv as an educational and sociological method for treatment of youth in the "danger zone."

Wouldn't the idea of friluftsliv as a positive alternative be valid also today? Without shame, the commercial culture legitimizes itself as profitable. Shouldn't each activity demand ethical legitimacy: Is this good for youth? Why are commercial forces set free while works based on ideological thoughts are described as "moralizing"?

There is, however, a risk that friluftsliv will become dominated by "those who know best." Adventure and challenge can be transformed to controlled, routine and standardized activities. Professional education in friluftsliv can act in the same direction. Let us ask again: How can friluftsliv be a real youth movement, managed and conducted by young people themselves, rather than activities governed by adult leaders? How can adults encourage the young generation to develop their own life instead of buying ready-packed sensations?

The Eco-Social Project: A Society In Ecological Balance

At the end of the 1960s, reactions against the postwar welfare society were expressed in a new and radical way. Relationship to nature was not a question of "subtle spiritual experiences" but regarded as fundamental for the survival of mankind. Pollution, lack of resources and ecological crises were not just insignificant side effects of modern society, but results of fundamental errors in the ideology of growth.

Unpaid bills were received for what was mistaken as "free goods": Dead waters in lakes, acidified forests, black snow on hillsides. Ecology could explain why this happened – and gave the basis for understanding nature as a fundamental order with inherent interests. But as modern society demands increased production, and as the resources are limited, sustainable development prerequisites radical change.

Friluftsliv was tied to these perspectives and was legitimized by far-reaching ambitions as a rich life with simple means, which inspires to a less materialistic lifestyle. It generates knowledge of nature as a living totality rather than as a site of resources to exploit. Friluftsliv shows a picture of the good life (both joyful and morally good), which can inspire to changes in society. When friluftsliv became part of the curriculum at schools and colleges, such ambitions and ideologies had to be underpinned theoretically, (and thereby the degree of gravity increased).

Is this program relevant also today – or is it tied to an idealistic and over-ambitious radicalism of the past? Some sociology studies have statistically shown that we now are less concerned about the environment than some decades ago.[3] Predicted sudden ecological breakdowns have not yet occurred, although radical changes in society and lifestyle have not been made. Did doom watchers create the anxiety about the environment? The respected World Watch Institute concludes that we are further away from a sustainable development than ten years ago.[4] The problems will soon return, but in a more severe form.

A New View of Nature

Even if the environmental problems would be technically "solved," one educational task remains: to convey to new generations an understanding of nature that will not result in a repetition of the mistakes.

Ecological Identity

A fundamental task for modern man is to maintain self-esteem in the balance between inner capacity and outer conditions. At the same time, identity has to do with relationships. When we identify ourselves with something, we include it in ourselves. Nature can contribute to a deeper identity.

A Rich Life with Simple Means

The ideal of a simple personal lifestyle must not build on arguments from the puritanical heritage in society but rather from positive visions of the good life. Choosing what is most valuable in life implies dropping things that prevent us from reaching fundamental goals.

A person who is accustomed to complex, expensive and refined means is vulnerable, not free. Experience of quality in your own actions results in a more genuine self-esteem. This treasure can be found in every human being, but can be difficult to discover and develop. Friluftsliv is a simplification of means and an experience of meaningfulness in plain actions. For a time we can manage with the contents of our backpack ....

Friluftsliv Today: Individualization and Global Trends

Friluftsliv has fortified its position in contemporary Norwegian society. More people are skiing or hiking in the mountains than ever before (although participation of the young generation seems to diminish).[5] There are also new trends:

- More welfare. When basic needs for food, clothes etc. are satisfied; consumption takes on a symbolic function. We buy the advertisements rather than the product.
- New forms of outdoor activities: on snow, in running water, in the air etc. Through media these are related to concepts such as youth, action, recklessness, opposition. Leisure time, more than work and daily life, is the sphere of life where you express your identity.
- High speed, quick changes. We imagine that we are short of time for adjustment to nature's "slow time" and compensate for it with higher intensity. The "risk seeker" shows how desperate the search for the dramatic and intense can be.
- Media-created reality, global trends, values and ideologies. Changing family patterns and a growing leisure industry has weakened the traditional, informal aspects of friluftsliv and strengthened the commercial. The role as a customer having paid

for the goods, dominates over the role as a member of the team with duties corresponding with rights.

This review has shown how friluftsliv has become meaningful in relation to the main challenges in different periods. Our task is to make it meaningful in our time: Letting people experience situations with inherent qualities, and using them as a starting point for meaningful reflections about challenges in life.

Can friluftsliv be more than a sector in life where we "play" freedom? Can it confirm a more fundamental freedom in a period where there are no marked trails for life? Can it inspire us to a joint future vision of a good society? Here we can choose, from ethical considerations, rather than surfing on the trend waves or being the pipe through which the spirit of the time blows.

CHAPTER 6

NORWEGIANS AND FRILUFTSLIV: ARE WE UNIQUE?

Odd Gåsdel

Norwegians appreciate the outdoors. According to Odd Frank Vaage,[1] the only recreational activities that consume significantly more of our time than friluftsliv are TV watching, reading and social visits or gatherings. Some years ago an opinion poll performed by the research institute FAFO[2] indicated that friluftsliv tops the list of activities we would pursue more often if we had time available. Later surveys[3] have provided similar, although not quite as striking results. Are we (Norwegian's) special, and if so, why?

Several Norwegian friluftsliv enthusiasts, including Nils Faarlund[4] and Tove Nedrelid,[5] believe that our kind of outdoor recreation is unique and that our relationships to nature are closer and more "natural" than those of other European language-speaking people. Official accounts of the subject have grown more temperate over the years, as can be seen from a comparison of the 2001 "Report on Friluftsliv" to the Storting (Norwegian Parliament) with the corresponding 1986 Report. But despite a glaring absence of other documentation than subjective impressions, many Norwegians still conceive of us as a nation that has discovered greater values in nature than other nations.

To the extent that they/we really are different, our leisure preferences may originate from easy access to nature areas or traditional rural utilization of uncultivated areas. But one might also speculate that they are caused by our relationship to each other and to our political and religious history. I therefore believe that our understanding of friluftsliv and society in general might benefit from a closer scrutiny of how leisure and other aspects of social life etc. are associated in Norway as compared with other nations. This article is a modest start to such an analysis, but modesty has not prevented me from committing the sacrilege of replacing the concept of friluftsliv with "outdoor recreation" in instances where a common word is needed to designate that which is similar in Norwegian and non-Norwegian outdoor activities.

What Differences Are There Between Norwegian and Other Nations' Outdoor Recreation?

Our information on motivation is limited, but in 1992 FRIFO, an alliance of Norwegian friluftsliv organizations, conducted a random sample survey of Norwegians' motives for recreational walking/hiking.[6] The survey questions are strikingly similar to some of the items Beverly Driver used in a series of North American surveys.[7] They thus give us an opportunity to make a crude comparison of Norwegian and American motives.

The answers to Driver's questions depended on who the respondents were and on what kind of activities they pursued. But those who were hiking in designated or undesignated wilderness areas tended to rank enjoyment of nature as their most important motive, with physical fitness in second place alongside stress reduction and attainment of peace and quiet. Attainment of control and independence, company with family, spiritual experiences and consideration of personal values received a lower rank but were still listed far ahead of achievement and risk-taking.

For some reason FRIFO did not ask how much the enjoyment of natural environments mattered to Norwegians. The motives they did ask about, however, were ranked fairly similarly by Norwegians and Americans. Peace and quiet came out on top followed by social motives (company with family or friends) and physical fitness. Spiritual experiences were somewhat less valued than these, but the Norwegians agreed with the Americans in putting the longing for spiritual experiences markedly ahead of achievement and excitement.[8] Thus, the idea maintained by Nils Faarlund[9] that the FRIFO survey proves Norwegian outdoor recreation to be completely different from its American counterpart seems curious.

But surely we pursue such activities more frequently than other nationalities. The 2000/2001 general survey of adult U.S. residents' recreational activities[10] reveals that more than 80 per cent participated in recreational walking during the last 12 months. This is on the same level as the Norwegian 2001 and the Swedish and Canadian 1999 participation rates as documented by Vaage,[11] Statistics Sweden[12] and the study conducted by (Canadians) Craig, Cameron, Russell & Beaulieu.[13] It is difficult to compare hiking and backpacking participation rates because the activity groupings are different in American and Scandinavian statistics, but we note that 33 per cent of the U.S. respondents claimed that they had been hiking and 10 per cent that they had been backpacking. The 2000 Alberta Recreation Survey[14] indicates that the corresponding numbers in the province of Alberta, Canada were 35 per cent and 7 per cent respectively. Among the Norwegians and Swedes 73 and 78 per cent claimed to have been walking in forest areas, while 47 per cent and 10 per cent had been walking in the mountains. (The lower rate of mountain walkers in Sweden is clearly due to topographical causes.) Estimated hunting participation rates were about the same in the United States as in Norway (about 10 per cent), a little lower in Sweden and Finland[15] and about 6 per cent in Alberta, Canada. More Norwegians (48 per cent) than Americans (34 per cent), Swedes (32 per cent) and Albertans (24 per cent) had been fishing. But the Finnish numbers were almost as high as the Norwegian (43 per cent). So, the picture is a mixed one. The Norwegian overall participation rates may be higher than those of the other countries, but there are no clear indications that Norwegian outdoor recreation tastes and habits are entirely different from those of all other nations. On the contrary, there seems to be many similarities between our outdoor recreation patterns and those of people in some other countries or regions of countries.

Causes

But why do these people visit nature areas to acquire peace and quiet, social company, spiritual experiences and deeper meanings? And why are these goals so popular in the first place?

Let me start with the obvious. Most people need access to nature areas relatively early in life to develop an interest in outdoor recreation. In some parts of the world most people live in metropolitan areas where wilderness is out of easy reach. In other places trespassing rules, fences and cultivated fields prevent access, or people are struggling hard to earn their daily bread. None of these conditions further the development of a passion for outdoor recreation or friluftsliv. (However, Anne Wallace[16] refers to some indications that even the impoverished mid-nineteenth century English agricultural workers regretted the lack of common lands for recreational walking.) The situation is different in Norway but not entirely. Norwegian urban residents often experience everyday natural area access opportunities that are similar to those experienced by other urban dwellers. A large proportion of what Norwegians count as friluftsliv actually takes place in green areas on the urban fringe, i.e. in areas that are quite similar to the green belts and designated recreational areas that are available to urban residents in other countries. The Norwegian "green belts" may perhaps be wider or wilder, but most of those who go there don't move far from the car park or the public transport stop anyway.[17] The Norwegian *allemannsrett* or public right of access is also an important factor. But we share this right with our neighbouring countries. Participation in outdoor recreation may be easier for us than for many others, but this difference is just a matter of degree. It still does not provide a full explanation of why so many of us actually use nature areas for these purposes.

Perhaps the explanation resides in old rural traditions? Norwegian rural residents used to combine agriculture with extensive use of backcountry and wilderness for subsistence and economic purposes. Some of these activities conveyed a sense of freedom, and people often kept on pursuing them after they had lost much of their economic importance. This interest was often spurred by visiting English aristocracy who brought with them centuries-old traditions of recreational hunting and angling. But Norwegian peasants were not the only peasants who made use of uncultivated lands for subsistence. Moreover, some of the activities they pursued, such as hunting and fishing, are equally popular in other countries too, whereas the most popular Norwegian activities, hiking and walking for pleasure, have few obvious predecessors in Norwegian peasant society.

Walking pursued for its special inherent qualities seems to be a modern phenomenon. According to Rebecca Solnit,[18] it started in the renaissance when nobles in parts of Europe no longer needed to engage in warfare and physical labour at home. Instead, as a substitute for other physical activity they took up walking for health's sake. They built walking galleries, gardens and parks, which, in eighteenth-century England. came to look more and more like natural countryside landscapes. Therefore, when state authorities eventually made roads safe, recreational walkers did not hesitate to step out of the park and into the countryside proper. Likewise, city parks became popular in the first part of the nineteenth century much because of their supposedly positive effects on health. When friluftsliv became fashionable among the broad strata of our population between the two world wars, its advocates put particular emphasis on its beneficial health effects.[19] As FRIFO's survey shows, exercise is still one of the main motives for Norwegian recreational walking. But we have no reasons to believe that Norwegians are radically more interested in physical exercise than other people. An obsession with health and exercise can be found in many other developed countries as well.

Norway is distinguished by its short history as a sovereign nation and by its relative lack of other national symbols than meagre soil, deep fjords and high mountains. With few recent military or cultural achievements to commemorate, nation builders began celebrating what continental critics of civilization had already attributed to us in terms of wild landscapes and uncorrupted closeness to nature. These developments were, however, foreshadowed by similar processes in pre-unification Germany.

As early as in the fifteenth century the idea emerged that the unspoiled German "savage," who once had sprung directly from the country's forest soil, was still resting there ready to be reawakened for new battles against Italian and Papal decadence. This idea survived with deistic undertones until the age of romanticism when local bourgeois celebrated domestic nature and took up solitary walking in protest against the French-inspired decadence of the court nobility (for more background, see Simon Schama[20] and Gudrun König[21]). No wonder that large numbers of Germans still go on pilgrimage to the mountains and forests of their even more savage Germanic brethren in the north. But we should also take notice of how this idea once revealed its darker sides and took the shape of Nazi ideology under the slogan of "Blut und Boden" (blood and soil), which signified the exclusive right of people of German descent to live on German soil. Combinations of deism, other religious ideas and patriotic protest against the decadent city life and European civilization can also be found in the young American nation's recurrent worship of simplicity, naturalness and wilderness as documented by Roderick Nash[22] and David Shi.[23]

In spite of its political aspects, Norwegian friluftsliv has a predominantly private character. During the interwar period, Norwegian Social Democrats, like radical nationalist or socialist movements in other countries, practised and promoted collective hiking and camping. But while the radically nationalist Israelis according to Tom Selwyn,[24] still boast of the genuineness of their own collectivist hiking habits, Norwegians nowadays mostly prefer to walk alone or in small private groups. One of the main motives for these activities is, as we have seen, peace and quiet or withdrawal from the hustle and bustle of urban life. It is not just the physical noise that bothers them. The demands that individualistic societies put on people to plan for the future and make the best of their lives may evidently be experienced as stressful. Social mobility and the fear of losing class positions may add to the stress. Private outdoor recreation or friluftsliv offers an opportunity to become master over one's own time and body, to reflect over one's own social trajectory, and, hence, to gain a sense of spiritual and physical wholeness and control in the midst of social turmoil. Some may also seize the opportunity to indulge in romantic dreams about membership in a more natural and moral order of friluft-sliv – people high above the lowly life of ordinary people as epitomized by the tragic I-figure in Ibsen's poem "Paa Vidderne" (in which the word friluftsliv appeared for the first time.) But according to Nicholas Green,[25] similar although less flamboyant feelings could be found among Parisian bourgeois several decades before Ibsen wrote his poem. And according to Anthony Giddens[26] and other theorists of modernity, the problems of identity formation that people (presumably) try to alleviate through soli-tary walking are endemic to all late modern societies. Still, one might speculate that Norway's particularly egalitarian type of individualism makes social encounters more anxiety laden than such encounters are in other more hierarchically organized modern societies, thus creating a higher demand for social escape.

But if these are the personal problems that Norwegians try to solve, then they definitely do prefer the friluftsliv solution to alternatives such as psychotherapy or meditation. Why is that? Maybe some of us prefer friluftsliv because the exhausting and ascetic practices of long, lone walks accord well with the pietistic religious traditions of hard work and sim-ple living we once inherited from Lutheran Germany. The religious fer-vour has waned, but delight in self discipline and hardship still flourish among many friluftsliv enthusiasts. This may sound unappealing but could also be viewed as a much preferable alternative to other far more self destructive attempts to escape social confusion and identity crises such as self-starving and self-cutting, which now occur at an almost epi-demic scale in many modern societies.

It is against this background of pietism and nation building that we should contemplate one of the perhaps more truly original traits of Nor-wegian friluftsliv, namely the strong ideological impact that was won by a group of enthusiasts headed by Nils Faarlund in the 1970s and 1980s. As documented by Björn Tordsson,[27] these people to varying degrees com-bined eco-philosophy with anti-capitalist nationalism and a belief that the ascetic Norwegian-style of friluftsliv is a particularly genuine kind of life, more true to mankind's psychic and biological needs than any other kind of modern life. This strange brew of thoughts seems to have had a lasting impact on Norwegian education in friluftsliv, and may thus have made its own conception of Norwegian friluftsliv's particularity come true post hoc. But, of course, most people still carry on their deplorably conventional and non-ascetic outdoor activities in semi-urban woodlands, or on beaten trails, prepared ski tracks, and crowded beaches, just like before.

Conclusion

Thus, my preliminary conclusion is that we may be different from other nations, but the difference seems to be one of degree and to reside more in the combination of attributes than in any particular trait of Norwegian outdoor recreation or society; and it is not entirely obvious that other nations should copy all the traits that contribute to the furtherance of outdoor recreation in Norway. But there are still plenty of tasks to take on for those who are interested in pursuing comparative studies of recreation and society.

CHAPTER 7

THE ASH-LAD:
CLASSICAL FIGURE OF NORWEGIAN ECOPHILOSOPHY

Sigmund Kvaløy-Sætereng

About one-third of the vast collection of traditional Norwegian fairytales and legends has one special figure that dominates, Askeladden, the Ash-Lad. Strangely, this peculiar figure hardly appears at all in the tradition of Norway's Scandinavian neighbouring countries, Sweden and Denmark. He is also largely lacking in the German fairytale collection of the Brothers Grimm.

Up until recently, the Ash-Lad has been regarded somewhat as a central symbol of Norwegianism – a character describing Norwegian identity. Instead of striving and strafing in the outer world, he sits by the fireplace, stirring the ashes and watching the ever-changing flames of the fire. He is fascinated by the process, how nothing is constant, and how he can kindle and re-kindle the process but never control it. But he learns a lot of what can be useful – if he only is attentive and open to everything happening around him in nature and in society: He follows the "watchfulness of the flame" when he leaves home and wanders off to experience the complex and creative process that is the world. Here is a retelling of one version of the Ash-Lad stories.

The Ash-Lad has two brothers, Per and Paul. They live in a kingdom where the king has a problem with his daughter. She never laughs; she has never so much as displayed a smile. So the king announces that whosoever can make her laugh shall have her as his wife and shall inherit half of the kingdom.

Immediately, Per and Paul start practising for the contest. Per achieves mastery in a very intricate form of military march; it contains an unusual limp. Paul imitates a priest who is renowned for reciting liturgical masses at breakneck speed. Paul doubles that. Ordinary people would find both these performances both impressive and comical. But the princess does not even smile. Throughout her life at the royal court she has seen too much of regimental though ornate drill!

In contrast, the Ash-Lad shows no interest in this competition. He keeps watching his flames and wonders about the unplanable process of the world. But his mother scolds him and urges him to go out and hunt for a career [my interpretation in terms of our current world.] Getting tired of his mother's nagging, the Ash-Lad leaves home and starts on a path in the general direction of the royal abode. But instead of being directional and goal seeking, he is observant and fascinated by what presents itself along the road. The world turns out to be a fantastic realm, full of new information. All this information changes the original goal [if it existed! – This approach reminds me of Gandhi's process thinking: "The goal is the road, and the road is the goal."]

In our story, the Ash-Lad on his road has experiences that Per and Paul just missed, being fixed on a prefigured point in a future – the future as an already made map. For the Ash-Lad there is no map, but an ever-changing, complex challenge. He picks up objects that to most people are trivia, like a rounded stone and a dead bird, but to him they are wonderful and idea-giving [in one version of the Ash-Lad adventure they are used to stop the princess' haughty erudition]. He shares his meagre food with hungry old people, sits down with them and learns things that expand his grasp of the world's possibilities – all things that Per and Paul missed. He finally arrives at the king's castle – seeking work, not the competition. He is lucky and gets employed by the chief cook to carry firewood and water. He immediately sets off to haul water from the local well. It is like a pond, and in it swims a many coloured, shiny fish that no one before had noticed [again, the story stresses the point that the Ash-Lad is more attentive than most.]

Diligently, the Ash-Lad catches the fish in his bucket and starts carrying it homeward. Then he meets a lady with a golden goose. They agree to trade. The lady gets the fish and the Ash-Lad gets the goose. Now the lady reveals that there is something strange about this goose. If someone comes over and touches the goose, and if the goose's owner – in this case, the Ash-Lad – then cries out, "If you want to join, just hang on!" that someone will get stuck to the goose, his hand like glued to the bird. Of course, the Ash-Lad is delighted. He tries this out; it works, and not only that, it turns out that anyone touching someone who is attached to the goose gets caught in the same way.

The first case of this is a blacksmith who runs up with a pair of pincers and pinches the back of a woman who is attached to the goose (he has an old grudge against her). The Ash-Lad reacts quickly, crying out: "If you want to join, just hang on!" Immediately, the blacksmith gets hooked to the woman through his pincers. Similar things happen to several people on the way down to the royal castle. All these suffer unexpectedly from a new situation they cannot master: Being attached on one side, they are forced to move (downhill, helped by gravity). So they stumble along, falling, getting up, and bumping into each other. Being members of the environment of the well-ordered royal court, they have never experienced a challenge like this and chaos breaks out.

Finally, they are in front of the castle balcony, where the princess stands watching this Ash-Lad spectacle. Seeing well-known members of

her normal entourage in a chaotic state, she laughs! The Ash-Lad has revealed to her the artificiality of the regimental court life and how it fails when confronted with real life. They are rigid, lacking the elasticity of adapting to new rhythms.

My interpretation here is inspired by the French process philosopher, Henri Bergson. The title of one of his books is *Laughter*. His idea is that we tend to laugh when observing someone who reacts mechanically when nature requires rhythmic elasticity. Bergson thinks this is an old survival measure. In new situations, requiring a break with previous regimentation, laughing at our stumbling is a signal to relax and get in step with a rhythm adapted to current demands – or more generally – to the rhythms of nature. In this Ash-Lad story, the royal court presents a machine-like structure, as we would say today, in contrast to nature as a creative process.

The Ash-Lad has been the hero of Norwegian youngsters for hundreds of years. Why didn't the children of Denmark and Sweden have a leading figure like this one? My explanation has to do with historical and political circumstances. Norway was occupied and trampled under foot by Denmark for 400 years up to 1814, and thereafter forcefully brought into union with Sweden for another 100 years (ended in 1905). Throughout this time, especially under Denmark, the majority of the Norwegians were poor, surviving only through an intimate knowledge of nature, inventive resourcefulness and a highly developed ability to improvise. These qualities came about as the answer to naked necessities under harsh, often unpredictable natural conditions. (We see the same qualities developed among materially poor people elsewhere in the world.) They (the Ash-Lads) saw resources where the Danish (Per and Paul) overlords just marched by ignoring their environment.

It should also be noted that in this period most Norwegians were farmers and fishermen. Their properties were tiny but quite independent entities; they were not surfs under a feudal system, as were the lot of farmers in Denmark and Sweden. Although the Norwegians were heavily taxed by the Danish kings, they had their "Ash-Lad" methods – and their children learned survival by being told the stories of a poor peasant boy who won over the rich and mighty through nature knowledge and cunning.

In contrast to Norwegian agriculture – crawling up mountains and creeping along fiords – Danish and Swedish food production happened in vast fertile plains, – the kind of landscape that furthered feudalism. The majority of people were caught up in a system tantamount to slavery where any "Ash-Lad" method would have had no chance. Additionally, the vast flatness of Denmark and southern Sweden, gave the feudal overlords easy opportunities to reach out quickly and strike down any embryonic uprising among the surfs. The craggy Norway offered few opportunities of this kind.

And a Norwegian tradition of cherishing local and national independence and distrusting foreign regimentation has survived among the majority of people to this day. An illustration of this is Norway's saying "No" to joining the European Union (at two referendums, 1972 and 1994) while both Denmark and Sweden said "Yes" and are both union members – imprisoned as many Norwegians see it.

In 1960 an American psychiatrist, Herbert Hendin, was looking through statistics showing the rates of suicide in various countries. He was surprised to see an enormous difference between the three Scandinavian countries: Denmark had the world's highest rate (together with Japan), while Norway was at the very bottom. Sweden was also high. Hendin's reaction was that since the differences were so great it must signal a basic difference in culture. This view was, of course, in conflict with the standard opinion that the three nations more or less shared the same culture. Hendin's scientific curiosity was raised so much that he went to Scandinavia and spent four years there, learning to speak Swedish and Norwegian and doing research. In 1964 he published a book, *Suicide and Scandinavia*.[1]

To make a long and complex story short, Hendin's one main conclusion was that children in Denmark and Sweden were brought up under a pressure of regimentation and career pursuit, producing a number of persons unable to live up to the demands, thus viewing themselves as failures. In contrast, Hendin found that such pressures were weak in Norwegian families, children were allowed to roam around and experiment, while taking part in farming and fishing – "leaning by looking and participating," not by being instructed. In a relaxed way, self-reliance was built up, thereby avoiding feelings of inadequacy and failure.

Interestingly, Hendin also took note of the differences in the historical backgrounds of the three countries and, connected to that, the differences in the kind of stories told to children. Actually, he is the one who made me notice the prevalence of Ash-Lad tales in Norwegian tradition, in contrast to those of Denmark and Sweden. The heroes in Danish and Swedish fairytales win out in contests through magic and miracles, while the Norwegian Ash-Lad wins by his own knowledge-seeking and inventive actions. In other words, the Ash-Lad is an ideal model, inspiring practical and self-reliant activity and a concomitant distrust in higher spirits as helpers in difficult situations.

The Ash-Lad type of approach was still the living star in Norway during the German occupation of the 1940–45 World War. Hendin compares the different reactions to the German expansion in the three Nordic countries: the Danes gave in, the Swedes protected their neutrality, while Norway's mountains sheltered guerrilla resistance. Actually the resistance movement strengthened the Ash-Lad ideology. It also inspired the rebuilding of Norway's industry, farming and fisheries in the two decades after the war. Professor Sigmund Borgan at the Norwegian University of Agriculture has shown that the surprisingly quick restoration of Norwegian industry following the war was made possible through a workforce recruited from youngsters with backgrounds in small-scale farming and fishing. These individuals shared the "Ash-Lad approach," and in many cases solved problems through advising practical short cuts where the academically trained engineers had become stuck in theoretical deliberations. However, these youngsters participated in building a trap for themselves and their children, as soon as Norwegian industry reached a sophistication and size of interest to the international capitalist markets. Stressing the principle of "compete or die," Norway's economic structure changed its character. Today, small farms and fishing hamlets have lost their "rationality," and grand scale centralization and urbanization is happening. The mass media and the schools are preaching individualistic competition as the way to the future. Small-scale farming and fishing is being replaced by a tourist economy where exotic folklore on abandoned farms is taking the place of food production and computer games are replacing real games. It should be of interest to note that exactly in parallel with this development, the rate of suicides has grown tremendously in Norway, now being one of the highest in the world.

However, some of the Ash-Lad mentality lingers. We still have a majority saying "No" to joining the European Union – and the present shift in the world climate might soon change all priorities, bringing the Ash-Lads back.

CHAPTER 8

THE RIGHT OF PUBLIC ACCESS: THE LANDSCAPE PERSPECTIVE OF FRILUFTSLIV

Klas Sandell

The landscape perspective is a crucial element of the Nordic tradition of "friluftsliv." If compared with the traditions of outdoor recreation in other places, for example, North America, it could be argued that this, the "mental landscape" of nature-based recreation found mainly in Sweden, Norway and Finland, involves less of "wilderness" and more of a cultural landscape. The so-called *allemansrätt* (the right of public access to the countryside) is a vital basis for this landscape perspective, and there are numerous examples of the central role it holds for outdoor recreation among the general population. This is true both with regard to daily outdoor recreation close to home, and vacation visits to landscapes such as the high mountain region or the archipelagos. Therefore, the following presents the landscape perspective of friluftsliv as focused on the right of public access in Sweden. As an introduction about the content of the right of public access, we could quote from a brochure titled "Common Sense and the Right of Public Access," published by the Swedish Environmental Protection Agency: "Do not disturb, do not destroy – that is the basic principle of Sweden's right of public access."

But before digging a bit deeper into the right of public access, this chapter will start with a few more general reminders concerning access.

Thereafter, the Swedish right of public access will be presented, followed by a brief effort to compare this perspective with the situation in British Columbia, Canada, to try to further illustrate the character of the right of public access. The chapter closes with a brief discussion of future challenges and with the presentation of some ideas about changes that may be necessary for the right of public access to play a key role in the future of the Nordic tradition of friluftsliv.

Some General Reminders Concerning Access

Even though in a modern urbanized society the question of public access is generally related to leisure, tourism and the outdoors, it is important to remember that, fundamentally, access involves very basic human-ecological factors concerning resource use and identity. With regard to leisure aspects of our current industrial society and the struggle for sustainable development, there is reason to believe that environmental education and opportunities for people to be in contact with nature are of utmost importance. A well-known characteristic of modern industrial society is a tendency to keep separate the spaces we use for living, for working and for recreation. Moreover, we are spatially separated from (and thus largely unaware of) the origins of those things that meet our most basic needs, such as food and clothing. It could be argued that this makes nature-oriented recreation activities and public access to the countryside crucial for urban dwellers' perceptions, attitudes and activities with regard to developing a sustainable human-nature relationship for tomorrow. Therefore, basically the role of the uncontrolled elements and processes in our environment – our relation with something greater than man himself – and the interlinkages with urban dwellers' recreation, could be seen as the point of departure for this chapter. In short, the out-of-doors and public access to the countryside form important elements in the human ecology and the environmental history of industrial society.[1]

It is important to remember that "access" is a richly nuanced and very dynamic phenomenon, and there is a broad scale of different access perspectives that will meet each other in the physical landscape: perspectives that involve basic perceptual and socio-cultural dimensions such as mental, legal, social, physical and economic access.² It could be argued that public access is basically a question of the extent to which people feel that they have the type of access they want to a landscape they want to access. Out of this comes the understanding that it is essential not only to look for the type of access issues traditionally discussed by planning authorities and the like (conflicts, regulations etc.), but also to look for general patterns of underlying landscape perspectives involved in the debate.

The Swedish Right of Public Access

During the 20th century in Sweden, paralleling the rise of the welfare state, the idea of outdoor life and contact with nature was emphasized as fostering goals of different kinds. "Nature in Sweden" and "the nature-loving Swedes" became important rhetorical clichés in shaping the modern Swedish nation. Around the turn of the century (1900), the rapid industrialization and urbanization processes formed the background to a great interest in physical leisure activities. With higher material standards of living, gradual shortening of working-hours and the Compulsory Holidays Act (1938) in Sweden, it became possible for the broad mass of the people to have, and make use of, leisure time. Tourism, recreation and outdoor life established themselves as important economic, regional and professional fields of interest.

The "Swedishness" of this form of dealing with nature must not be over-emphasized. But, there is still reason to talk about a Nordic outdoor-life tradition characterized by simplicity and popularity. The *allemansrätt* (the right of public access to the countryside), which means that everyone has the right, within certain restrictions, to move freely across private land holdings, pick mushrooms, flowers and berries etc., is a basic element in the Nordic outdoor tradition. The Swedish right of public access is traceable at least back to the county laws of the Middle Ages and aspects of this right can be regarded as a "tradition" deriving from pre-industrial society. The tradition is one of being able to move about the countryside undisturbed, provided that one does not disturb or damage the property of local inhabitants. Generally, one has not been entitled to take away or damage anything of economic value, for example trees, crops, birchbark or acorns (used to feed the animals). This also means that, basically, hunting and fishing are not included in the right of public access, although fishing with hand gear has more recently has been allowed in some areas. The survival of this right is probably largely attributable to the fact that Sweden is sparsely populated. Also, the tradition of freedom for the farmers and the Germanic tradition of legislation, as opposed to the Roman, are conditions referred to in support of the public right of access in the Nordic countries today.[3]

Preservation and conservation ideas borrowed from Germany and North America were added to the limitations of the right of public access from the turn of the 20th century – even though these were often motivated at least partly by recreation interests. Those rights that were "left over" according to the previous discussion of damage and disturbance – picking flowers, berries and mushrooms, or making a campfire and staying overnight, etc. – became part of a "free space" and are now collectively referred to as the right of public access. Mainly during the 1930s, as a parallel to the development of a modern recreation politics, the term and the approach of *allemansrätt* became an important element of mass recreation in Sweden.

Today, there are a wide range of management methods used in the case of outdoor recreation and the case of conservation of nature, but the right of public access continues to hold a strong position in Sweden, both culturally and in practice. For example, a recent survey among a random sample of the adult Swedish population showed that a total of 96.1% agreed (86.1% in total agreement and 10.0% in partial agreement) with the statement that it is important to defend the right of public access. This could be compared with the 61.7% that rejected (41.1% totally and 20.6% partly) the statement that the landowner should have increased ability to restrict the current right of public access.[4] From this it could be argued that the right of public access holds a very strong public position in Sweden today, which means that any discussion concerning changes – especially with regard to limitations – has to take this into account. With regard to public access there are similar, but, from the point of view of outdoor life, sometimes more restricted situations in Norway and Finland. Norway has a special law regarding the right of public access centered around the difference between the earlier village commons, where public access is the basic rule, and the fields and meadows that, in the pre-modern society, were privately owned ("utmark" vs. "inmark"). In Denmark, or farther south in Europe or in North America, for example, it is hardly possible to speak of a right of public access similar to the Swedish model.[5]

In modern times the tradition of the right of public access has to some extent been bolstered by legislation. Instances include: the obligation of the landowner in specific circumstances to make arrangements to let people pass through his fences; the prohibition of new constructions along shorelines; the inclusion of matters of conservancy and responsible use in legislation concerning agriculture and forestry and a special law prohibiting the driving of motor vehicles off-road for recreational purposes (which is important from the point of view of non-mechanized outdoor recreation) if there is no snow on the ground.

In summary, the right of public access in Sweden is in common law and can be seen as the "free space" between various restrictions, mainly: (i) economic interests; (ii) people's privacy; (iii) preservation and (iv) the on-going utilization of the landscape, such as for agriculture, forestry and infrastructure. For example, camping for no more than 24 hours is generally allowed; traversing any ground, lake or river; swimming, lighting a fire, etc. are permitted wherever the restrictions mentioned above are not violated. Also, it should be noted that as long as the participant does not threaten the boundaries of the "free space" (see i-iv above), both organized and commercial activities could use the right of public access. However, especially since the late 1990s when new environmental legislation was passed, these activities face more strict demands with regard to the need for consideration, good knowledge, suitable selection of place and sometimes the duty to announce plans to the authorities, and also perhaps to adhere to certain restrictions from them.

A Comparison with British Columbia, Canada

Together with the geographer Erika Daléus (previously living in Vancouver), a brief comparison of public access to nature in Canada, mainly British Columbia, and Sweden was carried out.[6] Of course various problems are involved in such a comparison, but nevertheless we believe the figures below (Fig. 1 and Fig. 2) summarize the general situations in Sweden vs. British Columbia. The most striking difference is the situation of no basic right of access except in combination with managed outdoor recreation in British Columbia vs. the situation of a basic right of access in Sweden (even though today's outdoor recreation in Sweden, to a very large extent, is influenced by conflicts and management efforts similar to those in British Columbia). Conflicts in both places arise due to a heavy demand for access close to urban areas and in attractive areas along coasts and high mountains. This situation gradually evolved during the last century, and in Sweden was always in one way or another related to the right of public access. It is important to note in Sweden the lack of direct influence upon the utilization of the landscape stemming from the right of public access, as mentioned above. This is in contrast to the management perspective (in Sweden as in British Columbia); there, the landscape being looked upon from a perspective of outdoor recreation, is the point of departure.

A major difference between British Columbia and Sweden, with regard to natural features of the landscape, is the limited physical access in British Columbia. The landscape of British Columbia is often very difficult to traverse due to terrain and vegetation. Sweden, on the other hand, is to a large extent a cultural landscape with many small roads and paths in managed forests and shows more "pastoral" agricultural features. Industrialization and urbanization of the landscape decrease physical access in both areas.

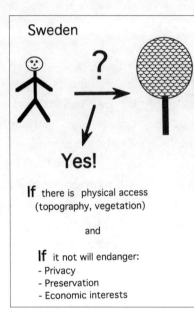

Figure 1. (*left*) Public access to the rural landscape in Sweden as based upon the "free space" of the right of public access (see Note 6).

Figure 2. (*below*) Recreational access in British Columbia, Canada, illustrated by the conditions of land tenure related to degree of access as constrained by topography and management strategies (see Note 6)

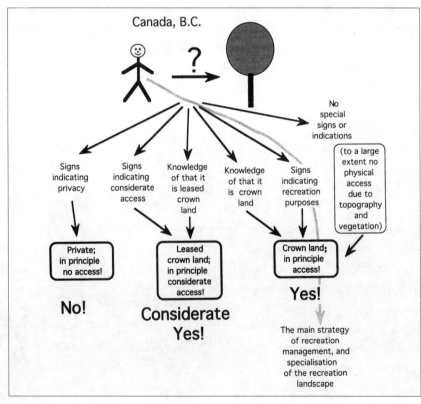

Some Current Challenges to be Discussed

There are, of course, various aspects that are important to discuss with regard to the right of public access in the future. In short, I want to argue that there are two basic aspects that are of utmost importance with regard to such a discussion: (i) the fact that the right of public access is to be read in the landscape; and (ii) the question of how it is possible to anchor a tradition in a dynamic landscape. Both must be addressed.

In the context of a multipurpose-use approach to landscape, it is important to note that a prerequisite for the right of public access is that you can "read" the landscape. It is "the landscape" that tells you what is – and what is not – allowed. For example, the way the land is being used may indicate how sensitive it is for people walking on it, and the weather tells you how safe it is to make a campfire. Also, it is important to note that the current right of public access in Sweden, even though mentioned in the constitution, is not defined in the law apart from the "left-over" perspective mentioned. Therefore, the position, content and role of the right of public access clearly are linked to habits, socialization, education, etc. Of course, this is an aspect that could be very tricky in a more and more multicultural society with increasing mobility and tourism. In other words, more diverse landscape perspectives will meet each other in the physical landscape, and sometimes they will have very different views of what may be seen as reasonable to be included in the free space of the right of public access.

As mentioned above, the "free space" left for the right of public access is restricted not only by what is not allowed – that is, the restrictions of economic interests, privacy and preservation – but also by the current physical landscape, and its utilization must be seen as a prerequisite for the content of the right of public access. With a few exceptions the right of public access does not include any right to make demands about how the landscape is used or transformed by, for example, forestry, agriculture or infrastructure. The value or content of this free space could be reduced or altered by factors such as noise, crowding, resource exploitation, etc. Also, the increasing "industrialization" of agriculture and forestry makes it physically more complicated to traverse a landscape on foot and often less interesting to do so. The further specialization of the landscape (including special areas set aside and arranged for recreation purposes according to management perspectives outside the right of public access tradition) will probably form an increasingly important framework for the future situation for the right of public access, and therefore also of the general perception of nature and environmental issues.

Out of the above – the importance of reading the landscape and the dynamic and cultural nature of the right of public access – it is necessary to discuss the need for further investigation, clarification and legislation with regard to the future situation of what many in Sweden today think is a very valuable tradition. Perhaps, for example, the following suggestions should be discussed:

- In law, define the core of the right of public access,
- Introduce an insurance against damage for the landowners paid by the tourism industry,
- Exclude the combination of organized and commercial use from the right of public access (but continue to make it possible for organized non-commercial use),
- Try to link the "size of the free space" of public access to residence, giving the locals more access than, for example, tourists
- Make it easier to contact and make deals with the landowners collectively when necessary (e.g. with regard to nature-based tourism),
- Make it easier to "read" the landscape with the help of better maps, temporary local restrictions and GPS-based information systems,

In closing this chapter, I want to highlight a broader perspective of public access to recreational landscapes. Often it is argued that there is a close linkage between the "sustainable development" approach and a more "local" and "territorial perspective" (e.g. "deep ecology," "eco-development," "another development," "alternative development," "eco-regional strategies," etc). In democracies, public understanding, motivation and inspiration are crucial for a long-term acceptance of effective environmental policy. Also the importance of traditions and local contexts with regard to civic community, locality and democracy illustrates the need to take both a spatial and an historical approach into consideration. Out of this, it is important to raise the question as to what extent territorial affinity is a mental prerequisite for environmental engagement? It seems reasonable to believe that, here, the type of and extent of public access to what type of landscape, plays a crucial role. Or, in other words, it is important to highlight the role of the right of public access (to what and for whom) for a sustainable development in a democratic society.[7] The basic element of a considerate multipurpose landscape perspective as the right of public access could also be seen as an important linkage to other policy discussions with regard to "commons."[8] It is useful to investigate further which features are important for a territorial feeling and for a comfortable relationship to nature and/or the local landscape, and how this is linked to environmental aspects and out-of-doors – a question dealing with basic aspects of democracy and sustainable development. One way of tackling this field of investigation would be to use a cross-cultural perspective, for example by comparing different countries, regions and traditions. Such an exchange would, of course, also involve the Swedish and Nordic tradition of the right of public access and its linkages to the Nordic tradition of friluftsliv.

CHAPTER 9

THE VALUE AND NECESSITY
OF TUMBLING AND FUMBLING

Aage Jensen

When I was boy a bit younger than I am now, I grew up in the middle of Norway in the 1950s. My home was in the Norwegian countryside close by the sea or the fjord, but the woodlands and the mountains were also within ready reach. (Because of being so far north and so close to the sea, the tree limit is about 150 metres above sea level. We could say that we were high up in the mountains when we were only 200 metres above sea level.)

Along with going to school, now and then, together with my friends we had a wonderful time living in this landscape throughout summer and winter (we had excellent opportunities for both skiing and skating) – and throughout spring and autumn. And as the different seasons changed, we always found new opportunities for new activities, whatever the weather! Even if it was raining cats and dogs, we would grab the opportunity to be out-of-doors.

Among a lot of different activities, we had a particular fondness for climbing about in trees. It is difficult to say actually why we loved it, but the best answer is perhaps that it was just a natural part of our life. But this raises a new question? Why was it a natural part of our life? It is difficult to come up with a definitive answer to that question, but I do think this activity was very important to our discovery of ourselves – to find out who we were and what qualities we had. We didn't do it just to seek a special kind of adventure. (It is very important for me to say that we did not look upon tree climbing as a dangerous project.)

Another day, and I remember it as if it has been yesterday, I was climbing around in a Rowan tree close to my home when suddenly I started to think, "What would happen if the branch I was standing on or grasping suddenly broke?" Again, it is not easy to answer this question in a simple way, because normally this situation should never occur. During our "climbing life" we found out exactly what kind of branch we could place our foot on or grasp, and we knew without hesitation that this branch would not break. In our climbing life we found out which branches were strong enough to bear our weight. We knew what such a branch looked like by observing various qualities of the branch – colour, angle from the truck, thickness, species, whether it was wet or dry, etc – and we knew for sure how far or close to the trunk we should place our foot to avoid breaking the branch. Sometimes we could tell why it was safe to stand on; sometimes we could not tell the reason why, but we just knew it was safe. And we developed this kind of wisdom because we had been tumbling and fumbling around in many trees in our lives.

What I have described so far is a bit about how we were playing or, better, how we were living. We did not talk so much about playing at that time. We would say we were playing when we were busy with a special activity, such as football or soccer. But when we were roving around in the woods, wandering in the mountains, skiing or skating, this was our way of living. Today, I would say that we were tumbling and fumbling through life.

It is easy to consider both tumbling and fumbling and trial and error as two synonymous concepts, but this is not the fact. When you are tumbling and fumbling, you may be close to making a mistake, but you can always find a way to go back before you end up in a dangerous situation or have an accident. There is always (and I want to emphasize this), always an aspect of security built into tumbling and fumbling. That fact leads us to another important part of conwaying leadership[1] – security and safety. That point of view gives meaning to the slogan we often use:

"A tour according to your abilities." That is why we dislike words like "emergency" and "crisis."

These should never arise in friluftsliv where the ultimate purpose is to yield to nature instead of opposing it. But you need to be an experienced conwayor (leader) to handle such a situation.

Tumbling and fumbling is the beginning of the conwaying process but also a continuation of the playing process we practised as children, or, as I like to look at it, a continuation of the free life we were living as youngsters. I guess that today there are only a small number of children in the industrialized world living the way we did. All normal children are, of course, playing and I look upon it as a good thing to take care of them and give children every possibility to play. I have tried to explain that we were also playing as young boys and girls, but we did not just play; we did something more. It is important to differentiate between playing and the free life we as children were living in close relationship with nature. That life is more or less disappearing in the industrial world and, as I look at it, it is more important than ever to have the opportunity to live in this way. Through friluftsliv, a way of living, we still have that opportunity.

It is impossible to talk about tumbling and fumbling without mentioning the Norwegian word *kjennskap*.[2] The term, *kjennskap*, refers to the kind of wisdom you gain through tumbling and fumbling, and it is one of the most important keywords in conwaying.

The result of tumbling and fumbling is that you acquire more and more *kjennskap* and are developing the ability called "serendipity." *Kjennskap* is a way to recognize, come close to, get used to, look and listen, touch and taste – using all your senses. *Kjennskap* is a way to understand life, and that wisdom can only be obtained by "being in reality." It is that kind of wisdom which characterizes the Ash-Lad character known from the Norwegian fairy tales. Through his tumbling and fumbling, he becomes able to solve questions, particularly those without obvious answers.

When we were climbing trees we participated in another important and typical aspect of *kjennskap* – we shared our experiences. It is relatively difficult to climb a birch trunk without any branches to help you. But we managed it and, among ourselves, discussed different techniques of how to do it. We shared our *kjennskap*.

The connection between tumbling and fumbling and *kjennskap* teaches us to take care not only for ourselves, but also even more importantly, for nature. We develop a unique awareness of nature that endows us with attitudes towards life and norms of behaviour. This wisdom is normative and "tells" us how to live with nature. It is through this process that we develop new patterns of thought and discover more about those patterns we have gathered earlier. It is more important today than ever before to give people (both young or old), the possibility to tumble and fumble through friluftsliv and through the provision of nature as a "learning room."

Conwayors (outdoor educators) today have to help participants find nature "learning rooms" – space in nature where they can be given the possibility to tumble and fumble. People need the opportunity to develop positive relations and attitudes to nature. The ultimate purpose of conwayorship is to change our way of living to a lifestyle of harmony between nature and ourselves. To my mind, in today's world, it is more important than ever to do this.

CHAPTER 10

How Modern Friluftsliv Started: Fridtjof Nansen, Instigator and Model

Gunnar Repp

It is a prerequisite to the attainment of a satisfactory understanding of the cultural phenomenon known as friluftsliv to have some knowledge about Fridtjof Nansen. The purpose and idea here is to introduce Nansen himself and his understanding and concept of friluftsliv, together with some links to the understanding of the practice of friluftsliv in Norway and the rest of Scandinavia.

A Young Man Amply Supplied with Experience

In all likelihood very few Norwegians, if any, have been written about more than Nansen. Even if we say Scandinavians, the theory might still be right. Just as interesting is the fact that he also produced an extraordinary number of books, articles, short stories for children, speeches, letters and scientific works. As well, Nansen has an international reputation because of his humanitarian work, his Nobel Peace Prize, his adventurous crossing of Greenland from east to west and the quest of reaching the North Pole when he let his unique ship, *Fram*, built for the purpose, freeze into the ice north of Siberia in the autumn of 1893 and then drift with the current towards Greenland.

Together with Hjalmar Johansen, he left his ship at 84° 4' N and pushed across the ice on skis, with kayaks, sledges and dogs, reaching the highest latitude achieved up to then, 86° 14' N, on April 7, 1895. Not less impressive was the return trip of the two men back to civilization with their overwintering in Franz Josef Land. A very simple improvised shelter on the northeast coast in the group of islands turned out to be sufficient for survival of the Arctic winter. This example is only one instance out of many as to how the friluftsliv experiences of these men became useful, and even vital to their existence.

One of Nansen's essential ideals and principles was the importance of simplicity because it offers independence. Simplicity allows the individual more freedom in choosing where and when to go. One of his greatest ideals was to live a very simple life in nature, totally free from all kinds of superfluous equipment. In his lifetime, he maintained that everyone should be able to manage – at least in summertime – to survive in nature in a good and proper way with only a few matches and a fish line with a hook.

The rest of his life bore the imprints of his experiences as a youth in the Nordmarka nature area outside Oslo. He could live there for weeks in the summer. With their parents' farm at its doorstep, his elder brothers showed him how to fish, hunt and survive in the wilderness. Thus, Nordmarka became the entrance for Nansen's ventures and explorations of the mountainous regions found in many parts of Norway. His love of and affinity for nature developed in the direction of practical as well as intellectual challenges, and even artistic interests. The practical everyday experiences were crucial to Nansen. He admitted that he chose to study zoology because of its closeness to nature. Becoming a zoologist, he anticipated many opportunities for his own "friluftsliv." In a book about Nansen and his wife Eva, written by their daughter Liv Nansen Høyer, we can read that her father thought it unthinkable to be locked up by a job or a profession away from the free, unrestricted man's life to which he had become accustomed to up in the mountains and in the deep woods, beyond Oslo (Christiania).[1]

Nansen loved to investigate and discover. Searching into the unknown was part of the core of his personality. This can be exemplified by the following tale. In the Greenland crossing expedition, the group of six

Norwegian explorers realized very soon after they had reached Godhåb that they would have to spend some winter months there waiting for a ship in the spring. The acknowledgement prompted some mixed feelings. Nansen, however, decided not to waste time. Early on, he had admired the Inuit people who were so well adapted to their environment. With their knowledge of nature and all their skills and local experiences, they certainly must have lessons to teach guests from abroad. To begin with, he decided to learn as much about the culture of the Greenland people as possible, as well as their language. And so he did. According to Ernest Shackleton's writings, Nansen was unusually clever at learning the language of the people. After only six-and-a-half months he could understand almost everything said to him and they could easily understand him.[2]

Secondly, he wanted to learn how to build kayaks and how to handle them. While earlier visitors had seldom ever, or never, shown interest in the Inuit's vital skills, tools and traditional knowledge, Nansen has been praised for his wisdom and ability to be interested in the people and their livelihood as well as their country. To Shackleton's way of thinking it was quite significant, "… that Nansen and the other Norwegians learned to handle kayaks, the importance of which, for exploration, had not till then been appreciated"[3] (In the British explorer's opinion the kayak was to be the key to success in Nansens's later Arctic experiences.)

Examining the Map for its Blank Spaces: The Adventure of Discovery

We need not mention Nansen's most heroic deeds to characterize him as an explorer – quite the contrary. The curiosity to know, to find out and to solve problems, were integrated and important parts of his personality. He was fascinated by most varieties of nature, by mountains as well as the forests and the sea. But he was no climber or mountaineer. Ascending the highest and most difficult mountains required peak fitness and expert mountaineering skills and was of little importance to him personally. In a broad friluftsliv perspective, it is of interest how Nansen personified the strong character, the professional, the genuine, as well as determination and capability of action. At the same time he also praised and favoured interdisciplinary approaches together with practical as well as theoretical interests, supported by qualifications on a high level. Trying to interpret and understand his main motivation concerning friluftsliv assumes an interest in and the capability to probe into many of his approaches to life.

In the autumn of 1887, Nansen defended his doctoral dissertation "The Structure and Combination of the Histological Elements of the Central Nervous System" in Christiania. At the time, this work was considered to be neither remarkable nor pioneering. However, in our time this has changed and Nansen has now been viewed to have been ahead of his time. He has even "… secured his place among the founders of neurology."4 In 1987, at the University of Bergen, there was a celebration – The Nansen Symposium on New Concepts in Neuroscience – on the 100th year anniversary of Nansen's dissertation. In the same year the report, *A Centenary Commemoration of Fridtjof Nansen's Contribution to Neurobiology,* was published.

Nansen was a researcher. He became a university professor, but soon he abandoned neuro-anatomy in favour of other challenging tasks. One of these was oceanography in which he became a pioneer. He also developed an intense interest in geology. Nobody should be surprised that the explorer also would become an innovator of polar equipment. He designed and constructed a sledge that later bore his name.

Nansen became a person with encyclopaedic knowledge. He has been called one of the very last polyhistors (a person having a general knowledge spanning many fields). But, first and foremost, the focus here will be on the explorer's attitude, a man with curiosity and creativity in thinking – a wondering Ash-Lad (see Kvaløy-Sætereng's chapter in this anthology) being absorbed by the unknown. What might there be to discover behind the distant hills?

In the following section I shall focus on Nansen's thinking and ideals concerning our relationship to nature, as friluftsliv is about human beings establishing, forming and believing in a friendship with nature. This starting point will, accordingly, also make possible an introduction to his own reflections and writings about education and pedagogy in general; but also more specifically guidance, instruction and experiential learning in nature.

Practitioner and Theoretician: The Legend and His Ideals

Fridjtof Nansen, born in 1861, obviously gained an unusually wide experience in nature that began in early childhood. There is an unanimous opinion among European authors that his "nature-life" – his friluftsliv – while growing up at the edge of Nordmarka, a huge area of hills, forests, streams and waters, with plenty of opportunities for fishing and swimming, was important in forming his character and individuality. From early childhood the nature of Nordmarka met and challenged the very young explorer, Fridtjof Nansen. His much older half brothers were important, playing a major role as motivators and instructors for his ever-increasing experiential meetings with nature. Many of his later ambitions, deeds and attraction to nature can be viewed against that backdrop. This perspective is important in the discussion about friluftsliv serving an educative and didactic process. Obviously, Nansen also saw nature as an arena of alternative life experiences focusing upon educational values, experiential learning and adventure education. His reflective approaches might also lead to discussions about his critiques of modern civilization and his ponderings on ecological problems or nature's diversity as concern for all people.

Why can Nansen be described as a legend? With his hidden depths, what were the capacities he possessed to qualify for epithets like legend, great hero, the first among sportsmen, statesmen, explorers, humanitarians and researchers?

More than a century ago Nansen urged that an alternative approach to the rearing of youth should emphasize traditional knowledge and develop a sense of joy in being in nature. And because of his own joyful meetings with nature, he also threw himself into the breach for Norwegian sport (specifically skiing) – a sport strongly influenced by our friluftsliv tradition for generations. Nansen and his collaborators, however, fought a losing battle in terms of sport and joyous encounters in nature. Under the influence of British ideologies of sport, many Norwegians chose competitions and sport for the sake of the activity itself. Increasingly, young people came to regard sport activities as important irrespective of utilitarian considerations concerning education, health or military preparedness. However, Nansen himself held competitions and specialization in sport as an abomination.

After traversing Greenland on skis in 1888, Nansen gained his first international reputation as skier and explorer. At the same time skiing's role as an instrument of national consciousness increased. However, in all probability the real skiing pioneers in Scandinavia had lived at least four thousand years earlier. Nevertheless, Nansen played an important role for in the year 1888 quite a sensational account spread across the world – Fridtjof Nansen on his skis had traversed Greenland in 40 days. The whole world was suddenly keenly interested "in the long wooden pieces."[5]

In fact, the skis were much more than a good and practical device. Skis simply belonged to the notion of Nansen's adventure. They played a prominent part in his approach to nature – his friluftsliv and his expeditions to unexplored nature. By means of his skis Nansen was able to explore nature's richness and diversity, and experience the freedom of the hills in winter.

Nansen was eager to fulfil his plans and expectations. He hated superficiality and worked hard and to develop the skills necessary for the challenges which lay ahead of him. His incentive was not one of personal ambitions for power and wealth, but rather he was searching for something special that he often called "adventure." His speeches and writings about adventure really are lessons about his dreams and calls from nature and his reflections upon ideals, values and the possibilities of life. His famous speech, "Friluftsliv," made to young people in Christiania in 1921, is about their own community – a city that he describes as an assembly of houses in rows, closely packed, where crowds of some odd creatures always are in a hurry, scurrying from one house to another.[6] He voices his criticism of modern civilization on many other occasions. Such concerns leads us to conclude that Nansen perhaps was in advance of his age, with thoughts and theories about ecological problems and challenges. There is no doubt that he studied Ernst Haeckel's writings – and Charles Darwin's as well. But we cannot feel so confident that he knew the speeches and books of people like Henry David Thoreau and John Muir. In any case, Nansen did not concern himself about organizing protests for nature protection as an activist. The defence of nature through resolutions, demonstrations and other forms of serious environmental activism belonged to the future, even more than a generation later. However, Nansen's other messages about nature would turn out to be of great value. Let us examine them.

Many of Nansen's writings, speeches, drawings and paintings communicate a strong delight in and identification with nature. He often talked and wrote about *"det store rum"* – the great room. This, probably, implies some transcendental experiences in nature. Part of it is difficult to explain or describe and put into words. Therefore, many of the friluftsliv values he espoused have to be experienced, to really give deep meaning. This in itself is not so remarkable, Americans Henry David Thoreau and John Muir, as well as Norwegians Peter Wessel Zapffe, C.W. Rubenson and many others, express similar relationships to nature.[7]

His deeply rooted love of the Arctic mood, sometimes a solemn atmosphere, at other times a cold, windy, very demanding nature – physically as well as mentally – made him obsessed by a strong passion for nature. Ice studies with the *Fram*, crunched by the ice; the sky, birds, polar bears and other animals of the Arctic world and the unusual examples of the human species – all were central themes. His sketchbook was constantly in use and he photographed incessantly. As many scientists did at that time, Nansen also learned relevant techniques for illustrating his books and scientific reports – sketching, watercolour painting, pastel and pen-and-ink drawings. His artistic output even included lithography. Nansen's art was motivated by friluftsliv and nature. L. Øestbye tells us why. He is underlining "the contrast between the matter-of-fact scientist and the man easily moved by feelings, possessed by a passion for nature and profound love of poetry" According to Oestbye, Nansen was "… a truly gifted, even a creative artist."[8] Nansen's "great room" was explored via travel, friluftsliv-inspired sport, sketching, prose and poetry.

Nansen's artistic approach might also be considered in another interesting, reflective perspective. Nansen's ideal was a friluftsliv marked by simplicity, responsibility, curiosity, hands-on experiences and first-hand meetings with nature. Developing love of the silence, of the loneliness and the magnificence in nature was also a part of it. Nansen encouraged young people to have at least one hour daily by themselves for concentration and for realizing their capabilities. First and foremost, he believed that young people should improve their ability to come close to nature "to see the hidden things," to be open for "the call of the unknown" and to indulge themselves in "the longing for the Land of Beyond." Put differently, his main message to our generation is to develop the ability to see the simple elemental things, to try new trails, to run the risks and to dare the unknown.⁹

Now, let us look at the consequences of his work from the perspective of education and pedagogy. According to Nansen, three "deities" are of the utmost importance to take us to our goals: courage, independence and the spirit of adventure. These deities will be explored in that which follows.

Fram, the name of Nansen's ship, means "Forwards." That seems well in accordance with one of his greatest beliefs – burn the ships and blow up the bridges behind so as to concentrate on the road ahead. He was strongly criticized by many national and international authorities for, in their view, irresponsibility and inexperience. But one of his main messages to youth was always to develop the ability to stand alone and to have confidence in their own plans and judgments. However, at the same time they were told to beware of obstinacy and foolhardiness. Nansen emphasized that people will always have to take risks to attain achievements – to gain their ends. But certainly there should be some proportionality between what is ventured and what can be attained within reason. Experiential learning had convinced him that in order to be successful in reaching his goals, he had to regard nature with respect, meet her open mindedly with love, and live and work with nature, not against her. In the act of co-operating with nature, there is an essential assumption of living there without courting danger and accidents. How far did Nansen succeed in that? He was fairly successful, indeed. But sometimes we will have difficulty in deciding whether it was because of high personal proficiency or owing to strokes of good luck.

Obviously, Nansen was a very experienced friluftsliv man as far as the basic skills and "know how" is concerned. He was an accomplished skier and certainly undaunted like few others, both physically and mentally. But on the other hand, he had little or no climbing experience, and there were some narrow escapes in the ice falls on the east coast of Greenland because of the men's lack of knowledge about glaciers and crevasses. On their way to the North Pole five years later, frozen in the ice with *Fram* north of the New Siberian Islands, they discovered that Nansen was not an accomplished dog handler at all. He was deeply humiliated making his first attempt at driving dogs solo.

There is, therefore, some clash of interest between this quality, his idealizing of usefulness and versatility, and his leaning towards being too scattered among many demanding and interesting challenges. His life was, in this way, coloured by ambivalence and contrasts. Sometimes he praised patience, while on other occasions he spoke in glowing terms about vigour and the ability to get on. He worked hard to be an expert and a specialist, but he criticized specialization and records in sports and early on became convinced that competitions and records were bad things. But it does seem likely that his expeditions – as well as his plan for the Antarctic – to a considerable extent was also about prestige, about competition and being first – the winner. He enjoyed his triumphs and seldom came up smiling when he had lost a fight.

A comparative study of two epochs has turned out to be interesting and inspiring in the challenge to understand and to explain better and more deeply the phenomenon of friluftsliv – the first part concerning the epoch of Nansen's friluftsliv and the second one that of our generation. Actually, the belief has become quite firm that it has been quite necessary to shed more light upon the differences and similarities between the basic values and ideals of friluftsliv of our time compared to those of Nansen. What was Nansen's friluftsliv philosophy and how did his friluftsliv and his thoughts about nature and values exert influence on the national friluftsliv of our generation?[10]

Is Nansen the "archaic" ancestor of our generation's friluftsliv people? To what extent are written formulations and their thinking behind them concerning friluftsliv today reflections of the values and ideals of

Nansen? Why did the explorer and Nobel Prize winner also become a model and idol of our generation's outdoor life of friluftsliv?

The conclusion here is that the opinion appears correct, the friluftsliv of our generation is a heritage from Nansen. At the same time, however, it is neither mischievous nor lacking in consequence or respect to go on asking questions as to whether his significance is still overemphasized, and which basic views of nature and friluftsliv do his writings really reflect? What are the values implied? However, if I adhere to what I called a "formulation arena" for our Norwegian, or Nordic friluftsliv, one of the most central and often quoted persons is still Nansen.

When death came to Nansen, on May 13, 1930, to many people "… it seemed almost unbelievable that this man of untiring action and superb physique was no more. The truth, however, was that Nansen had worn himself out with his tremendous activities and that, during the last years, he had not been able to spend sufficient time in the open air to get necessary exercise, so great were the demands upon him."[11]

We should, however, also be fair to generations before Nansen and recognize that from certain angles of view, friluftsliv has a far more distant history than that of Nansen alone. But then we should have to write another story, an account about another kind of connection to nature. That story would also be concerned with a strong delight in nature and identification with her. It might deal with transcendental experiences in nature as well as love of the silence, of the loneliness and the magnificence found in nature. It would certainly discuss a more traditional and historic relationship to nature, focusing on a daily life, close to nature, but one often that was demanding and hard. This life might be described by words like experiential learning, everyday understanding and personal and tacit knowledge, together with social mutuality as well as independence and self-reliance. Nansen proves to be a bridge between those generations and that of our own. As famous explorer, citizen of the world, gifted artist, humanitarian, and every-day friluftsliv enthusiast, Nansen remains with us still today.

CHAPTER 11

Nature Guidance and Guidance in Friluftsliv

Svend Ulstrup (translated by Hans Fransson)

Denmark is a small country in the Scandinavian context, lacking snow-covered mountains, infinite forests or streaming rivers. What we have in Denmark are fjords, bays and islands with a total coastline of more than 7,000 kilometres. We have through time been a people where different parts of the country have been connected by water. This connection to the water has been a part of the daily Danish culture that now is on its way to disappearing.

The Danish people's relationship to nature has not been any different from that of other people. It is a dependent relationship involving getting a roof over one's head, clothes on one's body and food in one's mouth; this is universal. When we, like others, have a place to live, have warmth and full stomachs, we then can look out over the landscape and search to meet those needs that are other than the elementary physical ones.

Each child responds to the surrounding world into which she/he has been born and absorbs it naturally. What else? No one can deny one's origin; in one way or another we will be connected to it for the whole of our lives. The expression "Love of the Mother country" was a reflection of this understanding – meaning "love of nature." Today, however, this phrase has lost its meaning.

The Danish folk soul is turned into poetic form in *The Danish Folk High School Song Book*. The significant value that nature has to the Danes is expressed here. Of course, the tone is romantic, but the conflicts that have occurred during the development of the nation and its change into a modern country are also clearly mentioned. When nature's blessings of clean water, clean foodstuffs and clean air are no longer natural, every sensible creature will feel robbed and uncertain of the future. That is why the problems of pollution, environmental devastation and the destruction of natural areas are on the world's agenda. The answer to this dilemma could be the horror version of Goethe's *Faust* – "You can get everything back again – if you want to pay for it!"

To those of us in the educated world, who do not celebrate the principles of the modern market economy as the basis for an appropriate pedagogical method, is the solution not simple? We already have the experience of strong qualities in the simple friluftsliv approach to nature, qualities that can enlighten, acknowledge and influence our way of life.

Forms of Guidance in Nature and Friluftsliv

Guidance in nature and guidance in friluftsliv are not pedagogical contradictions: they are actually basic to each other. It may, therefore, seem mysterious as to why these two parts have not realized the necessity of mutual co-operation. In reality, it is non-existent. The nature guide's task is to teach people about nature. The friluftsliv guide's task is to teach people to enjoy being in nature.

When guidance in friluftsliv as a pedagogical model received inspiration from Norwegian and Swedish friluftsliv, the Danish friluftsliv authorities looked towards Scotland to find a model and method of how to teach the Danes about their own nature. Probably with strong influence from the academic environment, biologists and others with higher education filled the positions as nature guides. They worked at nature schools, which were supported by government and municipalities.

With offers of more or less free nature guidance, the potential to reach a large group interested in nature was created. With support from the municipalities, the school children could visit and receive education at no cost, at the nature schools. From the authorities' point-of-view, the organization of nature guidance became a big success. In, addition, the Danish Board of Forests and Nature created its own educational program, but those who wanted work with friluftsliv were left to find education possibilities in Norway and Sweden. In Denmark there were various private schools and many institutions of higher education offering education. But it is just since the early 1990s that the Danish College of Physical Education has been able to offer a program including friluftsliv defined as higher education.

Nature guides are typically well versed in biology, which they skilfully apply in the field with participants, essentially conducting an outdoor biology class. Groups are most often taken on excursions, meaning that the time they have to spend outdoors is limited and specific. In contrast, the friluftsliv guide's tool is that of hiking. A hike often stretches over more than a day and includes an overnight stay. The goal is to teach people to feel comfortable and enjoy nature. Besides having knowledge of the area being used, the guide arranges permission to enter the area and sets up the overnight stay.

As often as possible the hike is made as a trip by land and by sea. Excellent opportunities to use sailboats, canoes and kayaks along our coast mean that the guide must be especially skilled when it comes to practical and safety matters, and must have a thorough knowledge of rules of the sea as well as the legislation concerning traffic in low water areas, and possess a sound understanding of the local culture.

The simple life in nature is about, for example, feeling joy in finding a spot to stay overnight, putting up a tent, eating, sleeping and getting

dressed to welcome the next day. When this becomes routine, we open up to the experiences and opportunities that nature offers. However, before we have reached that goal, the road may have been cold, wet and windy and we may need guidance in elementary areas such as the selection of clothing and food, the appropriate equipment and tools may be required. It is clear that these two realms overlap but strong differences remain.

Teaching in Friluftsliv

I was a high school student in the 1970s and received an invitation to visit Norway from a Norwegian friend. He wanted to show me the Norwegian ski opportunities, so we registered in a course about ski joy/snow joy. One of the teachers was very occupied with what friluftsliv meant to ordinary people. His name was Nils Faarlund. Convinced by his presentation, I formed the impression that all Norwegians worshiped friluftsliv as a holy passion and a duty – a movement that connected friluftsliv with engagement in society and a concern for nature.

Young and naïve, I went home and organized a seminar about friluftsliv at *Gerlev Idraetshojskole* (sports school) and spoke about these Norwegians. There was no doubt but that there was a curiosity for the subject and those who already went regularly to Norway to ski could not deny that it was as much about enjoying nature as being physically active. By shifting the focus from sports to the experience of nature, the body, as a pure moving machine, also became a receptor of emotional and aesthetic feelings. In the years following, increasing attention was given to the concept of friluftsliv, a development that was met with such varied responses as anxiety, irritation and smiles.

When friluftsliv appeared as a subject in the Danish high school, it spread with a speed that cannot be explained. At the high school level, outsiders considered friluftsliv as a holiday and a time for pleasure, so they were hard pressed to take the subject seriously. Comments were often patronizing, equating friluftsliv with scouting. The mistrust reached even greater heights when forest owners were asked about the possibility of students staying overnight in their woods. The answer was a resounding "No." The landowners were wary of what we were up to. While several hundred orienteers had been running around in the forest for some time, our group of ten people was rejected.

We were not scouts; if we were, we would automatically have had almost unlimited permission to do as we pleased. The scout movement was, in fact, actually offended and quite irritated by our activities. From their perspective, we apparently had stepped into their domain, and they repeatedly refused our invitations to discuss with them the dimensions of friluftsliv. The adding of politics into the friluftsliv debate was something the scout movement did not understand, and therefore refused any efforts at early dialogue.

Starting in the early 1980s, friluftsliv became a concept that all high schools, schools of continuing education, and youth schools are still using to this day. There was no doubt about the fact that something "new" was going on and it wasn't long before all free schools had "friluftsliv" on their program as a hugely popular subject. The popularity and power of these friluftsliv inroads into schooling seemed unprecedented to many – and this without teachers having any formal education in the subject.

In 1982, I founded Naturlivsskolen (Life in Nature School) and offered courses in nature life and friluftsliv, outdoor skills, and art and craft. The stream of people attending was steady and the schools were enthusiastic. The only groups I could not get along with were the authorities governing nature and forest domains. The situation was that my main employment was as a forest worker and my superiors were not interested in "having people running around in the woods." Their attitudes were that people from the outside would only make noise and play military games in the woods. The fact that this inappropriate behaviour could be prevented through good guidance about being in nature did not occur to them. Even today I find it difficult to condemn those who behave inappropriately in nature. How can you expect the public to behave perfectly when they have never learned how to be in nature? When I made clear my intention to continue with my school, I was fired from the forest authority.

What is special about friluftsliv is the possibility of going for a hike, being outside in nature, and spending a night under the stars. The joy in the participation and the understanding it promotes are the key goals. The technical part in that education is lighting a fire, putting up a tent, having appropriate clothing, packing the backpack, biking, hiking, kayaking or canoeing and sewing an anorak and other accessories, and generally developing the skills needed to become a participant.

But the problems are lurking around the corner and Danish friluftsliv is slowly getting seduced. In the educational system there is only an allowance of one week of education away from the school area each semester. That means inexpedient planning. Taking a group out into nature is becoming problematic and requires a lot of preparation concerning the gathering of the necessary formal permissions. Staying overnight is only permitted in certain places that are not always appropriate for education about "free nature." Overall, the general attitude toward experiencing the Danish landscape is unfriendly. As a result, the huge longing after the freedom that friluftsliv offers in comparison to one's daily life results in national emigrations to other countries.

Nature guidance and guidance in friluftsliv can both be ways to create an environmental engagement, but it would be extraordinarily naïve to imagine that we can achieve such results alone. School children learning about consideration towards nature, environmental responsibility and ecological preservation must get quite frustrated by sitting in a classroom, getting to know that life is about good education, a good job and, with that, a good economy – this is the way your life becomes nice and safe. But is it? Unless the whole school system proposes that all teachers integrate questions about preservation of nature, life quality and the values of life in education, being optimistic on the behalf of humans and nature could be a challenge. People between 16 and 30 years of age are steadily more occupied with experience in nature, but it is a group that extends their activities into a more or less exotic direction.

The desire to engage in particularly advanced challenges is rarely hand-in-hand with the reality of peoples' experience base. The trend has grown toward challenges that push the limit. This can be seen as a consequence of the general absence of experience with nature, so when it, at last, is possible, the dose must be extra powerful. Added to that, the visual media and the newspaper/magazine coverage focus on experiences far away from daily life and on the other side of the world (adventure trips) and depict nature as a practice-course simply there for pleasure, instead of as a fundamental basis for deeper insight and understanding of other cultures and their relationship with nature.

I gladly admit that nature guides have an important function, but I do not find their work more important than guidance in friluftsliv. I stand by my age-old conviction that people aged 16 to 30 are beyond the nature guide's range. This is an active time in life "when something must happen" – it is exactly the age group that friluftsliv guides are well equipped to handle. It would seem that now, more than ever, is the time for nature guides and friluftsliv guides to meet in mutual respect and develop an approach that combines the qualities of both of their disciplines.

CHAPTER 12

FRILUFTSLIV WITH PRESCHOOL CHILDREN

Britte Brügge

Friluftsliv is a word with many definitions. From an international perspective it mainly includes hiking, canoeing, rock climbing and other adventurous activities. Swedish friluftsliv is this as well, but it is also more and more frequently associated with experiences that bring people closer to nature. Seen from a child's perspective, friluftsliv can be seen to venture into the school's immediate surroundings from just outside the school doors. It is here that the feel for, and knowledge of, what is outside the room begins. For small children the act of climbing a boulder can be as pleasure-filled and exciting as for an adult climbing a mountain.

A few generations ago many people still lived outside the cities and encountered nature on a daily basis. In those days, children often spent more time with adults who then could share their knowledge and experience things together with their children. Nowadays, we live in cities and many young people follow a predictable pattern of movement: home – school – mall. Today, people from different parts of the world, with different traditions and different experiences from the outdoors, frequently meet and exchange ideas. Among them can be found the many reasons why we should teach children to play and to discover the many possibilities of nature and to feel safe when in the outdoors.[1]

Healthier Children

Preschool has not always been a place where priority has been given to consciously working towards equipping children with a natural attitude to that which is outside the school walls. Many preschools have focused on indoor activities. Now, research has shown the importance of outdoor activities – children who spend much time outdoors are healthier than those who are indoors a lot. Playing in a natural environment also benefits their motor skills more than if they are playing in a planned environment. Children today spend more time in front of the TV and the computer, almost totally inactive physically and largely deprived of sensuous experiences. Also, today's children weigh more than they used to in former years. Many schools and preschools have been paying attention to this and are working to shape "active" children who spend more time outdoors.[2]

Changing one's focus to " what can we do outdoors that we usually do indoors?" is not always easy, but it is necessary to adapt one's teaching methods to the outdoors. Swedish teachers can find support for outdoor education in their Preschool Curriculum. One recommendation is that children should be able to switch activities during the course of the day. These activities should provide scope for engaging the child's own plans and supporting imagination in play, and for learning to occur in the indoors and the outdoors. Time spent outdoors should provide opportunities for play and other activities to take place in both a planned and natural environment.[3]

The Significance of the Location

Anne Lenninger and Titti Olsson show that the immediate surroundings of the preschool is of great importance to the child's development.[4] Schools are designing an attractive outdoor environment to give both older and younger children opportunities to experience new things and to receive training in dealing with emotions and developing motor skills.

This type of environment includes grass instead of asphalt, and plants, along with natural opportunities for climbing and finding different smells and places like labyrinths, sandpits, water areas, and neat places for "just being." Many of Sweden's preschools can use green open spaces that surround the school, and Swedish law allows everybody to access private land. Children can explore nature for themselves and create their own favourite spots.

As a rule, small children's friluftsliv only includes the school's immediate surroundings, but when they grow to be four to five years old, their world expands. It may be the adjacent forest that attracts them with its paths, fallen trees, big rocks, or perhaps the park with its natural features. Here, with adult guidance, the child can use imagination and gain new experiences. Most children, given the opportunity, can develop here. A child who is timid, shy and cautious gets to encounter the unexpected in a familiar environment. For a child who needs a lot of space and physical challenges, there is opportunity for that as well. And everybody needs peace and quiet and a place to be alone sometimes. With friluftsliv there are many opportunities for solitude beneath the branches of a tree or beside the shelter of a big rock.

If the outdoor environment is to be confined to the schoolyard, it is important to regard the five-to-six-year-olds need for movement, for being able to work in groups and for a place to be by themselves. By adapting the schoolyard to meet these expectations, it is possible to meet many needs.[5] Many schoolyards have a spot suitable for making a fire. One can make a fireplace on asphalt or sand as well. A supervised fire can become a natural meeting point and a place where both children and adults can reflect upon and share their thoughts.

The Positive Effects of Friluftsliv

The "frilufts-activities" are mostly focused on providing children with opportunities to develop their own activities and games. This scenario is when the outdoor environment is fantastic. Here everything a child could want can be found; the only obstacle is imagination. Initially, not all children have the ability to create their own activities. It then becomes the teacher's role to encourage initiative, acting and daring to try new things. For the children to feel that they are allowed to climb and run is important. Through physical activity on natural ground, both fitness and co-ordination can be strengthened.[6] Also, limits can be stretched. The child can make an independent decision as to how high to climb. The act of balancing on a stump requires great concentration. Next time the stump might be a bit higher... Friluftsliv is a method for achieving better condition, increasing muscular strength and stimulating motor development. Friluftsliv also creates opportunities for learning sensuous experiences, and experiencing joy and better health.

Play, Learning and Responsibility

Friluftsliv in preschool is mainly about playing. Playing is learning for children. Through games they can process events, build their social skills, gather new knowledge and discover life! With nature as their playground they will also notice and come to understand that which they cannot change. The whistling wind, birds singing, the warmth of the sun, raindrops falling, frosty branches, slippery roads and all the things that are there if you allow yourself to feel and look.[7] Friluftsliv in preschool is full of surprises. As a teacher one always has an anticipated outcome as part of planned activities, but one has to be prepared for the possibility that anything can happen. A teacher always has to be able to change plans and respond to the moment. Obviously, one cannot concentrate on leaves when a cat is nearby and willing to be petted. Instead, the children's questions about cats are answered and knowledge about cats is explored. Working with the environment and friluftsliv creates opportunities to tie theoretical knowledge to what is encountered in everyday life. It is about finding possibilities and connecting experience to knowledge.

Reflection in connection to outdoor activities is important. The children are often so engaged in what they're experiencing that they do not realize that they are learning as well. At the moment of reflection, one looks back on what has been done and what learning has taken place. Often it is surprising to discover that many different things have been learned. Children want to receive confirmation of having acquired new knowledge and are proud of their achievements.

Through the habit of spending time outdoors, the step towards working consciously with learning is not a long one. Many preschool teachers believe that teaching is easier outdoors.[8] Actually, many things done inside can easily be shifted outdoors. Colour and shape are concepts that can be worked with all year round, inside and out. During seasons without snow, there is the possibility of bringing colours outside to paint exciting pictures. When doing nature pictures, one can use nature itself in addition to the colours. When there is snow, the watercolours are brought back out again, and the works of art are created on the white surfaces of the papers. Finding exciting shapes or looking for geometrical figures trains observation with the eye and mind. There are plenty of circles, triangles and squares outdoors if one only puts on the "glasses of the geometrical figures." In the wintertime, geometrical figures are exercised by shaping snow into three-dimensional shapes: a cube, sphere, and pyramid. The experience gained outside can be used to advantage indoors.

In the schoolyard many group games are played to develop social skills and encourage good spirits. One can also practice co-operation, motor functions, body awareness, and ability to co-ordinate, by daring to stand in front of the group. But one must show consideration and wait for one's turn as well. Many of the games have old traditions and playing them is a way to carry the culture of play on to the next generation.

The preschool yard is the place where "freedom with responsibility" is practised. When conflicts occur outdoors, it is easier for the children to solve them by themselves. This is an opportunity for them to learn how.

A Rainy Day with the Smallest Children

It is raining. In front of me is a group of little two-to-four-year-olds dressed in red, green, yellow and blue rainwear. A couple of them are squatting, shovelling water and sand into a small bucket, which they then turn upside down, and are rewarded with a "Splash!" The bucket is filled, over and over again, and it is turned upside down again just as often. Three other children have discovered that they can catch the raindrops from the roof in their mouths. Cheerful noises can be heard from the group far away. It is exciting to jump in the small pools and experience how far the water splashes. They are all so occupied with what they are experiencing that nothing else exists. The sensuous discovery of rain and water is exciting learning. What can it help with in the future? Is it a first step towards enjoying spending time outdoors?

Circus Adventure with 4–5 year olds

"Tra-la-la-la-la ... Stop!" The children place themselves in pairs behind each other. "The person in front, crawl backwards between your friend's legs!" – a difficult task to perform with a backpack on your back. When everybody has finished this activity, the walk and the singing continues until the teacher once again calls out "Stop" and gives the children another task. Tra-la-la-la ... The children are on their way to the "big forest," some 300 metres from the preschool. To make the walk exciting, the teacher plans to include songs and activities that practise the concepts of behind, in front of, under and over as well as enhancing motor skill development.

They gather by the "Secret Rock." The small backpacks are put down beside the rock and everyone knows that it is "Explorer time." They also know that they must stay within eyeshot of the rock or the teacher. Three of the boys climb onto the "elephants back" (a boulder) and immediately more children are involved in the game. Two girls are balancing on a branch that is lying on the ground (not a very simple thing to do as it keeps rocking from one side to another). Some others are playing "circus dogs" and walk on their hind legs, putting out their "paws" and "barking" the number of times the dog trainer tells them to. A true circus performance is growing into existence. Suddenly. a character appears with moss as a hat on his head and decides, "It's time for a break!" Everybody is eager bring out sandwiches, fruit and lemonade from their backpacks.

After lunch they start to explore the surroundings. The moss on the stone where the sun shines attracts everybody's attention. "Wow, it's so soft." "This one is much greener than that one!" "Oh – a spider." "1, 2, 3, 4, 5, 6, 7, 8 legs – it's a real spider!" The teacher instantly picks up on the idea. "Let's make our own spiders!" The children do not have to be coaxed, and as a result of the improvised drama workshop a great number of fantasy spiders, all with eight legs, are created.

The children radiate with joy. With this activity they have, amongst other things, practised motor skills, co-operation and mathematics. They are familiar with this area as their preschool teachers often take them outdoors.

Before they go back to the school they form a circle. Now it is time to reflect on what they have done during the day and more importantly, what they have learned. The answers vary: a spider has eight legs, moss smells good in the sun, and we have to help each other to be able to climb onto the "elephant" … To wind up the day, they sing songs about spiders. This moment of reflection is good for allowing the children to take in what they have experienced, confirm that they have learned something and preparing them for the return trip to the school.

Fire and Food: Favourites of Five-Year-Olds

This is the day of the week when they cook outside. The five-year-olds eagerly stuff a half litre of water and a vegetable (potato, carrot, Swedish turnip or leek) into their backpacks. A plastic bag, with dough for bread, is, with some effort, tucked in under the children's shirts, directly over their stomachs. The body heat will make the dough rise. Two girls are responsible for a big pot while each of the others carries a log of wood for the fire. Everyone has an active part in preparing food. Under adult supervision, two of the children are in charge of the fire and of adding more firewood to it. Experiencing newly baked goods and vegetable soup together with scents of the forest is very special; it is a memory for life.

The above description is of an ordinary day in a preschool. Outdoor education has become a natural part of the curriculum. By being outdoors every day for either the entire day or shorter periods, the children create their own feeling of security and safety. Such benefits mean it is important for the preschool staff to learn about the values of friluftsliv. The basics of good friluftsliv are to keep warm, dry and having enough to eat, while obtaining knowledge through experiences in the outdoors. This knowledge contributes to building the sense of security that is important for feeling the pleasure and joy of being out of the safe indoors.

For those interested in working with friluftsliv and outdoor education, here is some useful advice:
- Explore your immediate surroundings to find suitable locations,
- Determine what changes might be made in the schoolyard to make it more suitable,
- Make it a habit to go outside: it is better to do it a short while every day than one entire day every semester,
- Let the children experience things themselves and provide opportunities for using their imagination. Encourage challenging activities!
- Once you are comfortable in the outdoors – use it as a resource when you teach,
- Use theory as well as experiences when you teach,
- Reflect on what can be done outdoors that is usually done indoors? Go outside and try!
- Use all senses,
- Be prepared for the fact that not everybody is going to be positive towards outdoor activities from the very beginning. The children and parents as well as the teachers must have an opportunity learn that preschool activities can take place outdoors and that these activities provide multiple benefits, and

• Dare to try! Both children and adults will gain from new experiences.

Today there are courses in friluftsliv and outdoor education to improve the quality of outdoor activities. Internationally, the importance of outdoor education has been discovered and the European Union (through the Comenius Project Outdoor Environmental Education[9]) adds to this by giving European teachers the possibility to learn about, and participate in, some of the outdoor activities that can be used to increase their understanding of the method. Over the last few years, teachers from European countries have participated in week-long courses in Sweden, Czech Republic and Scotland.

CHAPTER 13

The "Oslomarka" Greenbelt: Protection and Use in Friluftsliv

Oddvin Lund

"Oslomarka" consists of partly separated areas surrounding Oslo and encompassing a total of 1,600 square kilometres. Nineteen municipalities share the areas. On the regional level these municipalities belong to five counties. Developed since the 1930s, the Oslomarka greenbelt is a "no growth zone" with a defined border, and as such a pioneer area in terms of conservation.

Natural History and Forestry

Most of the areas lies between 200 and 600 metres above sea level, the highest hills being just above 700 metres above sea level, Oslomarka is a forested land dominated by the narrow-leafed spruce and pine trees, with birch and other broad-leafed trees mixed in. As most of the land is subject to forestry, there are only very small pockets of land that can be called virgin forest. Still there are old growth tree populations in all parts of Oslomarka. Many of these are found within protected areas.

Along with the forests are numerous lakes and waterways. Many of the largest lakes have dams that were created for the floating (transportation) of timber. This activity was abandoned about 40 years ago, but the dams have been maintained since the lakes are important to the water supply of Oslo. They represent a stable part of the ecology and they are important in recreational use.

Conservation

The first proposals for a protected greenbelt were made more than 100 years ago. At the time, labour unions were politically active, since the areas were important for recreation, fishing and the gathering of wild berries and mushrooms. The main threat to the greenbelt came from the upper classes wanting to parcel the areas for the building of private cottages. The first "no growth" borders were mapped in the 1930s.

The NGOs within recreation and conservation have since then asked the municipalities to avoid development of the greenbelt areas, but it was not until 1986 that the government forced the definition of the greenbelt upon the municipalities. A defined border and specific management regulations were adopted within all the municipalities in the subsequent years. The main regulation stipulated that only construction activities related to agriculture and forestry are allowed. The exception to this is that construction necessary for the development of friluftsliv and sports activities are allowed.

The municipality is the formal area-planning unit, but in the greenbelt we now have a formal regional "planning tool." If a municipality wants to change the no growth borders, this has to be accepted by the regional government representative (county) or by the Ministry of Environment, should there be a dispute.

Every fourth year the municipalities can change their area-use policy and hence redraw the no growth border. This means that greenbelt conservation is an ongoing battle. In the recent years, however, those NGOs fighting for conservation have found very strong support in other aspects of area planning. It has become evident that traffic congestion and pollution problems cannot be solved if urban sprawl is to continue. Efficient use of the already designated development areas and of urban renewal schemes is now being intensified.

There have been major disputes between the NGOs and the forest industry. Modern forestry methods (clear-cut and replanting) have been seen as the main threat to nature conservation. These methods are still the dominant ones, but there are some restrictions. Clear-cutting units of more than three hectares near the city, and five hectares, elsewhere are not allowed.

Law against forestry and other economic activities protects about 6% of the areas. These conservations areas are mostly situated the central parts of Oslomarka, the largest being about 21 square kilometres.

There is an ongoing debate between the NGOs on how one should go about trying to protect nature while still encouraging people to utilize the areas in recreation. Without allowing heavy use of the areas in recreation, we cannot expect major support for the greenbelt conservation in the long run. Luckily, the greenbelt environment is not brittle in the ecological sense. Wildlife seems to cope well, in spite of some disturbance.

An act for the long-term protection of Oslomarka was proposed in 1981, but was set aside after a change of government the same year. Following the national election in 2005, an act for the protection of Oslomarka, and other city forests, are once again being discussed.

People of the area have a passionate and supportive relationship with their surrounding forests, though this **is** not always expressed in public. On occasions, however, when news papers monitor opinions, this thoughtful support is clearly manifested. Any development in Oslomarka for housing projects is, for instance, strongly opposed. In this way, the informal public notion of the no growth zone is strong, and indeed constitutes the political force for the protection of Oslomarka. People do expect that the elected politicians will look after and care about the protection of what is important to them, namely Oslomarka and the possibilities for friluftsliv.

The Economic Use of Oslomarka

Forestry is the main economic use, but some agricultural land is also situated within the greenbelt. Other economic activities, in general, are not permitted.

There are only a few thousand people permanently living in the greenbelt. The NGOs have expressed some concern about the drop in the

number of residents. Farming and other traditional activities are important factors in the conservation of landscape features and to some degree
act as service establishments for hikers and skiers.

   About 80% of the greenbelt area is privately owned by nearly 2,000
owners. A large proportion of the private land is in the hands of only a
few land owners. Municipalities own most of the public land. To a large
degree this is land that was purchased to secure attractive forested areas
for the friluftsliv movement. Even though land ownership is basically
irrelevant to the users of Oslomarka, there are differences in the way
forestry has been practised, and this has had effects on the landscape and
how it is perceived by all users. The large, more "professional," landowners have relied more on industrialized forestry than the municipal forests
and the small-scale forest owners. Regardless of ownership, the *allemannsrett* principle applies – people are free to ski, hike etc. in the forests,
and in the fields when the ground is frozen.

Recreational Use

Hundreds of thousands
of people use the green-
belt for their recreation,
putting the greenbelt in
heavy use throughout the
year. The total popula-
tion in the Oslomarka
surroundings   exceeds
nine hundred thousand.
   In 2004, the munici-
pality of Oslo investi-
gated the recreational use
of its own forests, the

most used forest areas in the vicinity of Oslo city. It was concluded that
81% of Oslo's population use the forests for recreation at least once per
year and that nearly 75% of the population use the forests weekly or
monthly on the average throughout the year.

The most popular days for friluftsliv in Oslomarka are the typical ski Sundays of mid and late winter during the months of January, February and March. Many skiers drive their cars to the edge of Oslomarka, with the result that all parking spaces are filled. Others use trains, the subway or busses, or ski more or less directly from their homes. Skiforeningen operate a bussing service every Saturday and Sunday during ski season. With as many as 27 buses from a bus-out-ski-home service, the area can regularly be filled with skiers during popular weekends.

The NGOs have signed, marked and mapped about 2,600 kilometres of ski tracks (The Association for the Promotion of Skiing, Skiforeningen) and about 1,600 kilometres of summer trails (Norwegian Mountain Touring Association, DNT, local chapter). About two-thirds of the ski tracks are groomed by machines or by snow scooters. Cyclists mostly use the web of forestry roads. There are about 50 establishments that sell food and drinks to those involved in recreation (hikers, skiers, cyclists, fishermen), but less than half of them are open daily. A few offer overnight facilities.

There are some conflicts between users, for example, between bikers and hikers, or skiers and dog owners. This is most likely to occur along some of the more frequented forest roads or ski tracks. There are hardly any officials around to enforce the law, hence people are expected to use their common sense and otherwise obey the principles of the friluftsliv act. These state that you are free to practise your *allemannsrett* as long as you do not harm the interests of fellow recreationalists or the land owners legitimate economic use of the area. Quarrels and heated discussions do occur. This can be seen as a positive phenomenon – people care about their friluftsliv.

Conclusion

The management of the Oslomarka greenbelt is an example of how natural areas near cities can be conserved at the same time as one tries to encourage people to use the areas actively in recreation. Directions and regulations are enforced on landowners and municipalities in order to ensure nature conservation and the preservation of attractive recreation areas.

Oslomarka, with its history and use in friluftsliv and sports, enrich the lives of hundreds of thousands inhabitants in the Oslo area. The politics of conservation and management is based on popular support for the protection of the forest environment. Strong traditions in friluftsliv and sports prevail. Even stronger long-term protection is likely to be developed under the current political leadership in Norway.

An Experience in Oslomarka:
Bob Henderson, Simon Beames, David Taylor

We were three Canadians who met in Oslo for a Hut-to-Hut ski tour. During our Oslomarka trip, just outside of Oslo, we were repeatedly asked, "You came to Norway just to ski?" People seemed astonished we would come all this way from our Canadian winter to experience simply another winter across the ocean. Why Norway? Why Oslomarka? Well, let us explain, but first a thought that came to mind as we were questioned – "I'm always astonished that people are not more astonished" borrowed from C.K. Chesterton.

We Canadians were astonished at the extent folks there seem to take the superlative – defining Oslomarka experience – for granted. For us, ski touring in Oslomarka would be (and did prove to be) an exotic and rewarding experience. The wealth of trails and enticing huts with a variety of services, and the healthy active skiers of all ages, not to mention the bakery/drink stops along the way and the mix of groomed tracks and off track options. All came together to make Oslomarka a place of skiers' astonishment.

Sure, we in Canada have similar ski destinations linked to large cities, such as the Gatineaus north of Ottawa and the Laurentians north of Montreal and not forgetting Skoki and Mt. Assiniboine Lodges in the Canadian Rockies, but it's more than just good tracks. There are cultural issues that intrigued us. With our ski tour in Oslomarka we were glimpsing experientially into a skiing culture – a culture of Nordic people that actually embrace the winter season. As Canadians anywhere stretched across the land, "being a Nordic peoples who embrace our core season of winter," is not something we can say with confidence. Rather, at best, we

Canadians are a "semi-Nordic" peoples who tend to deny our winter season, which should be a defining, core to our Nordic character, but is not. Saddened by this, rather than escape to Florida for a few weeks, we went in search of our Nordic soul amongst fellow skiers. A Scandinavian friend once told me the comic story of a classic cultural confusion on arrival to our Canadian winter. He had heard of "snowbirds" (folks who leave the Canadian winter for the American South for the sunshine). He had assumed snowbirds were keen recreationalists heading north for winter fun. Hmmm, we supposed we might call ourselves true snowbirds.

Thanks to Oddvin Lund with *Skiforenginen*, (the Association for the Promotion of Skiing), we had an itinerary in hand when we arrived. We met Oddvin at the Sognsvann train station February 17, 2003, and headed out directly into the hills for four days. First stop was the Skjennungstua bakery. The place was so full of skiers' ambience and a long tradition of all the joys of friluftsliv, all wrapped up into one place, that we were – well – astonished. This start was totally confirming that Oslomarka was a good place for us to be. We believe that "places" are created out of space, when experience infuses a landscape with meaning. The many people buzzing around the bakery/rest stop and the many happy faces at the lunch tables obviously familiar with the setting have long created "place" as they have so filled this particular landscape with meaning. The joy of it all was contagious.

Next onto Turvann and a single Alpine ski run on the tow before the long downhill to a bus stop at the shores of Bogstadvannet. The bus took us to Skansebakken where we continued on skis to the Smedmykoia DNT hut. We could have planned our own first day in Oslomarka but not this day. Oddvin, our guide, planned a brilliant first day experience.

The next morning while in the hut, Oddvin received a cell phone call (none of us own cell phones back in Canada). We are being asked to approve the dinner menu at Kikutstua, which looks a long way away on our map. We were elated to approve the menu – any menu – and headed out that morning feeling happily a long way from home. Back home the cell phone experience is never connected to our travel, but seemed so matter-of-fact here. What would Kikut bring and would we ever get there?

There was major variety to this day two. Groomed trails, off-track skiing, some road ski travel, a charming lunch amongst distinctively Norwegian gnarly pines and a seven p.m. arrival, all combined to make the dinner and hospitality at Kikut a standout. Again, we knew, we were a long way from home. This experience was different for us. Kikutstua is not a hut, it is a beautiful old world lodge (thinking like a Canadian here), not lavish, but simple and comfortable with hearty food aplenty. And, I for one, will always remember the knotted rope-ladder fire scarves (fire escape system) tied to the window ledges

Oddvin Lund headed off back to Oslo by ski that night. That was different too. We figured he would eventually arrive home after a 40-kilometre day with a pack on. We settled into a cozy bed dreaming of skiing some of what Oddvin had skied that night. I had a strong feeling that I would return to Kikutstua with Canadian ski friends again.

Next morning we headed southeast enjoying the lakes and sun and frosted landscape. We walked up icy tracks in places to reach the Sellanra Hyetta. We appreciated a sense of remoteness here as another flavour to Oslomarka.

On day four, we no longer felt like novice Oslomarka skiers. Trails were easy to follow. People were friendly and curious (three guys with packs and cameras – we must not have looked Norwegian). Our smiles were broad and our skis humming in the groomed tracks en route back to Sognsvann. We knew why we had come to Norway to ski and we were rewarded. But still we wonder why people, and I suppose I mean Oslo folks, are not more astonished by the ski-touring they have out their backdoors.

On return home, our friend, Nils Vikander, wrote me asking how the trip had gone. He had just returned from a typical Canadian snowshoe camping trip with portable wood stoves, canvas wall tents and hauling toboggans. He quoted the South African writer, Gerardus van der Leeuw: "The mystery of life is not a problem to be solved, but a reality to be experienced."

That's it. No problems in Norway, just an astonishing skiers' reality to be experienced.

Part II

Canadian

A Commentary on Clea Ainsworth's "Home"

Contribution by Holli Cederholm

There's time to turn
back. A raven
pin wheels above
the canyon, one eye
holding me, trackless.

Nothing can hold the dusk –
it slips, like the forgotten word
between mountains.
My lips, colder now,
pursed against the pale blue air.

Walking along the saw-tooth
tree line I know
home is irrelevant. This
last light, the residue
of a million years' journey,
has been creeping
towards me, always.

Clea Ainworth's "Home" embodies the very concept of friluftsliv – that nature is not to be worshipped from the outside, as it is innately part of the human being, as our existence within nature dictates our cultural identities. Yet, these words express friluftsliv for the modern age. It is a poem that denies finding home in the natural world as many of today's return-to-nature types or weekend adventurers seek for, rather it states that "home is irrelevant." The narrator realizes that the natural world, as is represented here by the waning dusk light, has always been a part of them, of humanity as whole, over a "million years' journey." Ainsworth's words grip the interconnectedness of it all in an era when the concept of place, of home is hard to come by.

CHAPTER 14

An Effort to Capture an Elusive Friluftsliv

Bob Henderson

I was a wide-eyed Canadian delegate invited to a January 2000 retreat and follow-up conference.[1] The experience remains pivotal in my maturation as a Canadian outdoor educator. The gathering considered friluftsliv and issues of how cultures dwell with, within and without nature. I was soon bewildered by the complexity of the word as an idea and a philosophy and a method of being and doing and as a cultural tradition, or rather cultural traditions, of conduct. Friluftsliv – a word "saturated in values" – is how conference delegate Nils Faarlund put it.[2] The Scandinavian notion of friluftsliv was elusive, but I sensed a retrievable and informing potential beyond its home borders. Friluftsliv was mysterious and enlightening if one chose to seek depth of meaning, but straight forward if one thought of it as outdoor recreation, no more. A fellow outsider looking in, Czech educator Petr Kubala, refers to the mysterious, ordinary and extraordinary friluftslivs.[3] I understood the ordinary: nature awareness, outdoors living and travel-skill development, and personal and social learning opportunities all gathered up together in everything from a pleasurable walk in the woods to a weekend outing to a seriously planned and seriously fun "expedition." But I wasn't then confident that I could explain the mysterious and extraordinary themes. Perhaps the mysterious was too culturally driven to transfer to Canadian ways.

As I write this now, five years, almost to the day, has passed since I was that Canadian student of friluftsliv in Norway. Another five years prior to that 2000 visit had seen me tentatively using the word/idea and the related literature of friluftsliv to describe a particular outdoor education I would advocate in theory and practice. I had discovered friluftsliv first in literature and found it would solve a central riddle within my Ph.D dissertation. I had come to shift my language from using the awkward phrase "the profound lived experience" to "friluftsliv," feeling all I hoped to say was captured in the term. For a Canadian thesis, I now had to explain the elegant term. After the many professional and informal talks, efforts in writing, work involving the translation of literature, and the three further visits to Norway that occurred over those many years, my own interpretation has been clarified considerably. I think I have arrived at a very Canadian view, more than an idiosyncratic view, of friluftsliv, all the while having the goal of serving as a Canadian ambassador for the word in all of its manifestations – philosophy/method/tradition – with hopes of informing a more enlightened outdoor education. In short, we Canadians can learn something from our fellow northern dwellers.

Now the time feels right to add my name to the mix of friluftsliv inter-preters and have a hand bringing together some collective understanding of the mysterious and extraordinary. Okay! If friluft-sliv is "saturated in values" and Scandinavian scholars and practitioners have that special cultural intuition for these values, how does one crack the code for an interpre-tation? What values? What ways? What expressions of "culture meets nature" can best inform those who are looking in from outside the Scandinavian culture? The kinship I have felt with fellow Scandinavian outdoor educators and the smooth fit of shared ideas have made the elusive friluftsliv seem an elegant and noble inquiry.

I will tell five Canadian outdoor education stories. Each story captures a disconnect for what friluftsliv is NOT as a means for providing a

Canadian interpretation for how friluftsliv might be understood in a North American context. These stories address a confusion or tension in North American outdoor education and recreation that are not so prevalent in Scandinavia.

Five Stories of Disconnect

1. "If you learn a skill without learning the way, you've learned nothing."[4]

Eric was one of my campers at a Canadian children's summer camp. He was ambitious and a fine canoeist. He had worked hard on his canoeing skills hoping to earn a canoeing award/badge of high standing years before most others are deemed eligible. I was his counsellor, not his canoeing instructor.

I was a regular evening and early morning solo paddler. I loved the lake's misty times and exploring back bays away from the camp with my own time. I never thought to take Eric. He had his canoeing instructor and was on a set path. He did win the canoeing award to a notable fanfare. During mid-summer of the next year, I noticed that Eric was pursuing horseback riding with the same zeal he had shown for paddling the summer before. I asked Eric one time, "How's the paddling going?" His replay shocked me, but I wasn't sure why. "Oh, I'm into riding now," he said. Years later, I realized why that singular moment had stayed with me. As a canoeist I knew *the way* of canoeing. Eric did not, and worse, I hadn't even considered showing him. Certainly Eric had learned the skill just as he had learned horseback riding; but the way had eluded him.

Eventually, I read *A Book of Five Rings* written in 1645 and concerning a Samurai guide to strategy. It contained the following important epigram: "If you learn a skill without learning the way, you've learned nothing." That's it! Friluftsliv is not about learning the skill; it is about learning the way. It is not about doing and having the act of an outdoor skill – let's say skiing – well-honed. Rather it is about being the act of skiing well. The way involves a relationship within nature – with others.

The same can be said for gardening, telling stories, making love… Friluftsliv is more about the way, than the skill. The disconnect here in this story involving Eric is between the skill and the way. In Canada, I worry that we teach the skill with less attention to sharing, as co-learners, in the way. In friluftsliv, we'd take our campers for those calm misty morning paddles. To borrow again from this other tradition, Eugene Herigel in *Zen and the Art of Archery* captures the way of these misty morning paddles:

> If one really wishes to be a master of an art one has to transcend technique so that the art becomes an artless art growing out of the unconscious.[5]

2, "Call it Recreation, but it involves far more than having fun."[6]

The canoe trips had been thirty-five days. Campers, ages 14 to 16, were arriving to the Toronto airport with virtually no transition time between a canoe tripper's nature/group reality and the urban family who-knows-what-else reality. I was in charge of the various trips and grew uneasy watching the campers acting as if they were still on the trail. While in fact, they were in an airport minutes from meeting parents and returning to various urban settings. Baggage was retrieved and children began the walk to the exit doors to meet awaiting parents.

It was all too much for Julia. She bolted, turned and ran the other direction. Immediately many friends likewise turned in pursuit to see "what's up." I was left to tell Julia's mother that "Julia had had a great time on her canoe trip." Slowly normalcy returned to this messy moment, but the obvious lesson gleaned from the experience was the need for some transition time between a long trip's ending and the sudden return home. Underlying this lesson is a more subtle one. The profoundly lived experience of joy with nature in a small supportive group who are involved with a most engaging technology of canoe, tent, fire and an entertainment based in song and storytelling, is too often left as just a fine recreational experience, for example, "Julia had had a great time on her canoe trip." But the recreational sense of well-being shifts towards a learning of some profoundness, perhaps where education may not have ever been perceived as having a mandate. But further, a shift towards therapy is also possible in the exuberant joy of the experience. So, call it recreation [if you must] but it involves far more than having fun. That's it! In North America, I fear, we tend to deny such experiences in nature their proper place as educational and therapeutic. John Livingston calls this particular notion of therapy, "being part of a greater enterprise." Thoreau spoke of "the tonic of the wild." Sigurd Olson keenly referred to a realigning with "ancient rhythms."7 Friluftsliv openly acknowledges nature's restorative therapeutic qualities. It is not just the mantra of the Scandinavian outdoor educator. It is a cultural understanding. This type of disconnect occurs when the "tonic" or realignment is denied. The parent, by the way, was justifiably not satisfied with my response – "she had a great trip." Neither was I. I think I'm doing a better job now as I write this. In friluftsliv, nature's presence on and within us is identified.

3. "That's Phys-Ed. That's fun."

An interdisciplinary field-based university course proposal was before the social sciences curriculum committee. The course was to be called, "Heritage and Environmental Issues of the Canadian Shield." I had proposed a week of guest lectures and seminars concerning an array of topics from place-based literature to resource management issues. The second week would entail a canoe trip from our northern base. We would now go on the land to help experientially make the lectures and discussions of the first week come alive. Sadly, I was cut short while describing the camping and travel experience where literature and topics from the first week would be peppered into the time living on the trail. "That's Phys-Ed. That's fun," was the galvanizing comment, which seemed to stifle my energy and put up the collective guard from the committee. I was sent away to reconsider the need for this second week. Obviously, credibility for academic merit and rigour was at stake. My emphasis on experiential relevance was undermined. I returned to the committee with the same proposal, but with a new language. Camping became "the primitive arts." Canoe travel became "traditional modes of travel." The proposal was reluctantly accepted.

There are many lessons here. One, do not emphasize the *fun* factor. For many educators, learning needs to be sombre in order to ensure standards.

Two, language is important. Speak to your audience. The first proposal was written as if meant for fellow outdoor educators. The second proposal was written for social scientists. Both these lessons have some relevance for promoting friluftsliv. However, the main lesson is the disconnect between experiential learning and the conventional teacher-directed transmission style of learning, which, largely by convention alone, is valorized over student-centred experiential learning. Friluftsliv in formal education must be experiential. It must be student-centred. In my twenty-five year career I have experienced many occasions where I have been required to defend the experiential components of outdoor education. Friluftsliv as experiential; this is understood in Scandinavia. A Canadian "indoor" outdoor education activity could not be called friluftsliv.

4. "And Bob's tripping partner, Zabe, who lived to tell the tale … "

Zabe MacEachren and I were freshly back from a rewarding two-week dog sledding trip in northern Manitoba. A journalist wished to conduct a telephone interview for a magazine article. I agreed and smartly (I thought) told her about our desire to capture the "old ways" of the North via the mostly gentle-moving and hard "good" work of sledding and camping. Ultimately, we wanted to belong within these old ways and be romanced into this winter land where dogsledding possessed a long tradition. When asked, annoyingly, about hardship and risks, I tried to deflect such questions for the more romantic qualities of heritage and traditions. These qualities were not, I was to discover, the story the interviewer/writer wanted. In the end, she wrote a death-defying high adventure story where we "lived to tell the tale."[8]

I felt a bit used, but was objective enough to be intrigued by the results. My interviewer wanted adventure, skill development, risk and the more hardship the better. She wanted, in outdoor education terms, adventure programming. I gave her friluftsliv. The adventure in our trip was the challenge of tapping into the past rendered as a felt experience and of developing a cultural awareness for the place and its patterns of living. In North America, I worry we make too much of a personal growth derived from physical hardship and perceived risk. Certainly there was a personal growth to be had on our trip. But friluftsliv is not adventure programming though it might look like it from a distance. In friluftsliv, the adventure and growth are likely more found as one of the spirit, of dwelling well on the land.

5. "I just want something practical."

The conference organizer wanted me on the Environmental Education program. She just didn't want my topic: "Friluftsliv: A Nordic Tradition We'd Be Wise to Consider." "I just want something practical," she insisted, "not ideas, vision, theory; but something teachers can do Monday morning with their students." I argued that friluftsliv was an idea, but one that you can do on a Monday morning. Indeed, it might just carry the kind of transformational energy that changes how Monday morning will look.

We remained at an impasse. The disconnect was between theory and practice, ideas and activity, reflection and doing. I had tried to link the binary in her mind; as friluftsliv is always understood as both concepts working together. Commonly in North American, I fear, one does not inform the other, as they should. I was adamant throughout our disconnect. Friluftsliv is idea AND activity, theory AND practice.

The Great Work

To sum up these five stories succinctly is to offer a Canadian insight into the elusive and mysterious friluftsliv "saturated in Norwegian values" as Nils Faarlund put it. Friluftsliv is a way, not a skill. Friluftsliv is acknowledged as a possible therapy for the human soul. Friluftsliv is always experiential. Friluftsliv is not adventure programming. The adventure in friluftsliv is more in keeping with an adventure of the spirit connecting with a place and a tradition. Friluftsliv is an idea and an activity. Behind all these stories is the simple joy of being in nature. This is the first principle of friluftsliv. So simple, it is elusive and mysterious for our modern ways. Nature is primary to friluftsliv – not a backdrop or "sparing partner" as Børge Dahle repeated often in our Hæverstolen retreat. There is belonging and a feeling of being home in friluftslivs.

I agree with Petr Kubala – the extraordinary friluftsliv exists. It was present in my original use of the phrase "the profound lived experience," which proved equally difficult to explain as friluftsliv. The extraordinary friluftsliv is a private understanding of the personal meaning friluftsliv brings to your life. It is profound, personal and rich in perspective.

The North American cultural historian, Thomas Berry, wrote in *The Great Work: Our Way into the Future*: "We might think of a viable future for the planet less as the result of some scientific insight or as dependent on some socio-economic arrangement as participation in a symphony as a renewed presence to some numinous presence manifested in the wonder world about us."[9] Friluftsliv is part of the "The Great Work" before us – toward reconciliation with nature, creating a wonder world about us. As Øysten Dahle said to me during the January 2000 gathering in Oslo, Norway, "Today, friluftsliv is both a counter culture and a tradition." The reconciliation with nature is the counter culture working against modern forces that would have us machine-like and image-driven, living the illusion that we have moved beyond a nature we can never leave. The tradition is the best of the ways human cultures have lived well within the natural sphere in recreation, education, lifestyle … and therapy (though few thought of it that way until recently).

Thomas Berry also says, in *The Great Work*: "Our world of human meaning, is no longer co-ordinated with the meaning of our surroundings."[10] The five stories presented above in a Canadian outdoor education setting with their disconnects from a friluftsliv setting suggest Berry is right; we are moving away from the understanding and meaning of our surroundings as the primary motive to outdoor education. Friluftsliv can help Canadians with this return to a *nature first* perspective

These five stories did not come to me out of nowhere. They emerged slowly as I have explored ways to explain friluftsliv in North American settings. The stories are easily supported by Scandinavian literature. I will stay true to that all-important first visit to Norway in 2000 and share favourite thoughts recorded dutifully in my travel notebook from friluftsliv educators. When Sigmund Kvaløy-Sætereng says, "Friluftsliv works to develop in people an inside relationship with nature," he is providing a similar understanding to the notion that; "if you learn a skill, without learning the way, you've learned nothing. The "way" in friluftsliv is this "inside relationship with nature."

When Nils Faarlund says, "First, there must be joy," he is, in my mind, linking to the third story where the experiential education component – the travel experience on the land – was devalued. Indeed, there must be joy in nature for the education to take on the quality of Thomas Berry's "Great Work," guiding us into a viable future, as the story shows, this time in nature. This is strangely more difficult (to achieve than it should be.

Again from Sigmund Kvaløy-Sætereng who said to our retreat group, "The worst thing you can do to people is to take away their opportunity for complexity." Here we have a link to the second story. "Call it recreation, but it involves far more than having fun." Indeed as one moves into an inside joyful relationship with a nature that is wise and is home, one moves into a realm of spirituality and complexity. Yes, there is obviously therapy in this. This understanding should be a cornerstone of outdoor education and well recognized culturally. In Canada it certainly is *not*. My answer to the parent of that bewildered run away teen at the airport could have followed something like this, "Julia's experiential ways within nature and our small group travel was rich in spirit and learning and connectedness with a new-ness that branches into the therapeutic. She may need some greater transition time for returning to the city than we have provided in this program." More importantly, I trust that in a more friluftsliv/nature-centred culture, the parent might have equally understood all of this as well. I remind myself, as educator, that I likewise wasn't fully present in the "friluftsliv understanding" of the situation then. I would be now.

When conference host Børge Dahle said, within his extensive dialogue, "nature is the true home of culture," he connects, for me, to the fourth story. That's it! Our dog-sledding trip was really about nature being the true home of culture. What the interviewer presented in the end was a misrepresentation where risk, uncertainty and hardship were the adventure of choice – nature not as home but as a challenge arena. She was, as they say, "giving the people what they want." Indeed, the phrase, "nature is the true *home* of culture," is both an expression of a set of traditions and a counterculture. And this dual understanding links to the fifth story; "I just want something practical."

Traditions of friluftsliv are simple, engaging, primal, interactions with nature: a morning paddle, a berry-picking excursion, a family trip, a walk with the dog, a well-planned extended outing. These are practical activities of simply living *first* in nature. We need to be 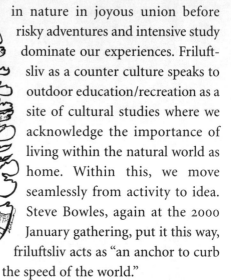 in nature in joyous union before risky adventures and intensive study dominate our experiences. Friluftsliv as a counter culture speaks to outdoor education/recreation as a site of cultural studies where we acknowledge the importance of living within the natural world as home. Within this, we move seamlessly from activity to idea. Steve Bowles, again at the 2000 January gathering, put it this way, friluftsliv acts as "an anchor to curb the speed of the world."

I have also learned to formulate these five stories from Norwegian literature bent on describing what friluftsliv is not. From Arne Naess, friluftsliv is a movement that requires a shift from a "vacationer's superficial sensibility":

> Conventional goal directed; to get there, to be skilled, and to be better than others to get things done, to describe in orders, to have and use new and fancy equipment – is discouraged. The ability to experience deep rich and varied interactions in and with nature is developed.[11]

Similarly Nils Faarlund has written of friluftsliv as, "not meant to shore up our modern way of life but to help us – as an individual and as a society – out of it." To this end, Faarlund's list of what friluftsliv is not is as follows:

Friluftsliv is not sport. It is not tourism. It is not a scientific excursion. It is not a "trade show." It is not outdoor activity." Rather friluftsliv is about identity (national/social and individual) related to "belonging to the land." Friluftsliv is a "living tradition for recreating nature – consonant lifestyles."[12]

I believe I have had some success in telling the five Outdoor Education practitioner stories above, as a means of capturing what friluftsliv is and is not as a personal and as a Canadian way to capture the friluftsliv I have been exposed to in print and through personal associations.

Friluftsliv, as an idea/philosophy and as a method and cultural traditions, is a complex set of meanings with far reaching implications for the individual spirit and for a culture's spirit. It is elusive and mysterious as I have tried to illuminate here, but it can also be staggeringly simple; as simple as walking the dog. As an outdoor educator here in Canada, I've learned that helping people meet the out-of-doors well should be life affirming, identity giving and values shaping. Much of this I've learned from Scandinavian educators who take the task of sharing friluftsliv seriously. Outdoor education/friluftsliv can involve all of the following: a way, a therapy, an experience, a seeking of home and belonging, an idea and practice to embrace.

The stories I have shared suggest that we Canadians have something to learn from friluftsliv. We must interpret the basic friluftsliv principles for our own context, but these same principles are among what we universally need as "The Great Work" forward.

CHAPTER 15

DWELLING WHERE I TEACH:
CONNECTIONS WITH FRILUFTSLIV

Michael Elrick

I was born in Guelph, Ontario, Canada, in 1963 and grew up digging forts and tobogganing in the backyard of my parents' home. Today, I still live in Guelph, reside in my old neighbourhood, and teach at my old high school. I continue to run the trails and paddle the rivers of my childhood. My children now know Guelph as their home and slide down the same hills (though with fancier sleds), climb the same trees and attend the same schools. And as far as I can see, when I die, my ashes will contribute to the organic layer somewhere nearby.

I have always wanted to start an article or speech with this proclamation because it declares "Who I am and Where I come from." The unique part is this: I am one of the few that teaches in their hometown. And this "uniqueness" has had a direct influence on, and has shaped much of my teaching. Life and work naturally intersect when, to use the words of Wendell Berry, "I eat my history day by day."[1] I might argue today, that "who I am is where I come from." Teaching and dwelling to me are tributaries of the same river. For many years, I have struggled to describe the kind of curriculum and teaching techniques I have been drawn to. Hence, when the idea of friluftsliv education was described to me, it lined up with much of what I believed in. It was as if someone had twisted my camera lens into focus after years of being slightly blurry.

For ten years I have taught what we call in Canada – An Integrated Curriculum Program.[2] Its name is CELP (Community Environmental Leadership Program) and it is best described as a package of regular high school courses grouped together and taught at an off-campus site. The students earn the following credits in their grade ten year: 1) English, 2) Careers, and Civics, 3) Outdoor Education and 4) Interdisciplinary Studies. The program, however, takes place outside of the sanctioned walls typical of most schools in our community. Daily, a bus transports us to and from a 55-acre summer camp that we rent in their off season. Several units take place in the city and one in a more remote wilderness setting several hours away. A second teacher is responsible for the English course, and I am responsible for the other three. The setting is one of intimacy with a strong focus on community. There are no "bells" and the same students learn together all day with the same teachers. We have a formal classroom with desks in one building, and we utilize another with a kitchen and living room. The camp property includes open fields, trails, a large forest and a small river. For five months, or one semester, this is school for twenty-four students and two teachers.

My outlook on life and my ways of teaching were born from a childhood of one house, one community and what I believe to be an inherited connection (to be discussed later). Specifically, its alchemy grew from my walks to school, trips to the swimming hole, excursions to the city dump, and, in particular, my connection to the local river. At age eleven, I became interested in the sport of slalom white-water kayaking, an activity I was introduced to from attending a typical Canadian summer camp. And when the water was open, I spent much of my time in it. With white water, it is necessary to learn how to roll, to turn the boat over and suspend oneself in the water. True immersion. And to know how to paddle and manoeuvre in rapids, from an athletic perspective, one has to intimately know the river and its ways. More than anything else, this daily river sojourn slowly flowed its way into my soul. A friluftsliv upbringing perhaps? Canadian style?

After high school, my kayaking pursuits and university education took me around the world for several years.[3] Returning to Guelph to live and work was not something I considered. It just … happened. But now, with some reflection time in my backpack, (a kind way of saying I have aged) I know that much of what I share on a daily basis with my students has a direct correlation with my own life's journey and personal connections to my home. I teach what I know. And what I know is that this land speaks to me on a daily basis. It speaks to me with stories and meaning and a sense of connection beyond what seems possible with textbooks and basic field trips. And I wonder, is an education taught with this perspective part of the missing link? Because, I might argue, today's environmental learning is failing us.

A typical day at CELP begins with a 20-minute bus ride. I enjoy referring to our school as "upstream" from town. Simply mixing the students from different high schools begins the community-building process. They have to meet the kids from "that school!" Upon arrival, we have a morning circle for announcements and one student provides a reflective reading for the day. English class follows for 70 minutes and the curriculum requirements are met with themes that meet the overall goals of the program – Community, Environment and Leadership. In the first week students are asked to write a paragraph about a memory for them in the natural world, a moment they felt a sense of connection to nature. The skills of reading and writing are used as tools to excavate and create relationships with themselves, their community and the world around. Integration occurs because much of the curriculum of the other three courses overlap and swirl together. For example, when students engage in debates, they are learning research and oral presentation skills from English and Interdisciplinary Studies. The topics concern local environmental and community issues, emanating from the Civics course. Research is done by bicycle, interviewing local citizens and visiting places

of issue – Outdoor Education. A journal is also kept, an all-encompassing mirror of reflection weaving throughout the four courses.

I visualize the program as a river's journey. We begin at a lake near the mouth of a river – our community. We then travel upstream, against the flow. This is a somewhat different approach to learning than most conventional education today, and sometimes hard to do. However, people used to always journey upstream, and there is much to be gained by traveling in this direction. We head to the source – where the real issues flow out of – past the band-aid environmental solutions we have produced to date. We ask the underlying questions of our problems and investigate truly eco-effective practices. And when we travel back downstream, we use the skills and knowledge to paddle with the flow – long term and sustainable ideas of how to live on this planet. We arrive back to our communities with a sense of responsibility, connection and purpose. We have engaged in practices towards deep ecology. In the process it is hoped students develop a personal life "ecosophy." Arne Naess would be pleased, I think.[4]

Our upstream journey begins with a five-night wilderness canoe or snowshoe trip, depending on the semester. We spend two weeks learning and practising the traditional travel skills of the region and reading stories of those who have travelled before. Though this unit takes place several hundred kilometres to the North, and goes against the "local" approach of friluftsliv, we have concluded that the remote wilderness setting has a power to "awaken" one's sense of connection with the natural world more quickly than our more urban setting. As well, there is something truly Canadian about going on a canoe or snowshoe trip. It is a window into Canadian culture and Canadian stories.[5] Upon return we make links and draw parallels by trying to live the lessons of our wilderness trip in our day-to-day lives. A recent student, Brent Goemans, captured this intended outcome in his journal:

> As I sat on the rocks and drank the tea, I looked around at the fog materializing off the water. I thought what a magnificent sight this was and how lucky I was to witness it. It was at this moment I realized that these sights are happening all the time. Nature is always here. It does

not just perform for people when they arrive. These
sights are happening all the time, some even more glori-
ous than I have ever seen .... I am now making an effort
to try to acknowledge nature even when I'm at home or
in the city.

After the trip, English class focuses on a reflective essay of the wilderness venture. It is a chance to write from direct and potent experience.
The careers course walks them through an investigation of their own skill
sets, future employment ideas and job application techniques. We
improve our communication and problem solving through activities
such as trust falls and group initiative tasks – learning to work together.
Every Friday is "community day" where, as a class, we share a meal and
clean up our site. A group of six students is empowered to design, shop
for, pre-cook and finally serve a meal for the entire class. We finish with
a full-camp clean up, including dishes, toilet scrubbing, mopping and
vacuuming. This covers healthy eating habits from the physical education course. And we investigate the interconnected nature of food from
different perspectives. Who grew this food? What chemicals were used or
not? How does the purchase of a banana directly impact the farmer who
grew it, both positively and/or negatively? We learn, through integrating
curriculum, that when it comes to probing the sustainability of our
planet, no learning happens in isolation. "All living things on the earth
are connected," as the Institute for Earth Education so eloquently states.[6]

One of my most important lessons of education to date arose from these
community days. When I started CELP, I thought that the most important
thing was getting outdoors, being on the land – the "E" (environment) part
of CELP. I designed lots of activities for that purpose. The Friday routine
was thrown in at the last minute from another program's model and from
the necessity for cleaning at the week's end. But something magical began
to happen on these days. I was struck by how the simple act of sharing of a
meal nurtured the growth of our class. Fridays became a big deal. At first I
didn't get it! It finally dawned on me that adventuring on the land wasn't
enough to truly build an environmental ethic. If my class couldn't get along
with each other and function as a community, we could never get anywhere

with the greater community around us. It took me a long time to realize that the skills of how we relate to each other are the same ones needed for how we relate to the earth.7 Perhaps there is much more to educating about food than I am presently aware? My students taught me why "C" (community) is the first letter of our acronym.

Nearing the source, my students teach a program called Earthkeepers™ to over 300 grade five students from our school board. For if a child can begin his/her life where the water is pure, perhaps this river may be clean in its journey downstream. Earthkeepers™ is a three-day program designed by the Institute for Earth Education.8 It is composed of a "head, heart and hands" section. For the head component the students learn ecological concepts. With the heart, the activities develop feelings for the natural world. Finally, in the hands, students commit to lessening their impact on the earth and sharing what they know with others. The program is full of creative learning activities and is woven together beautifully with the earning of four KEYS. These keys, in turn, give them privileged access to locked boxes with secret meanings about the earth. The true magic of the program, however, is in the relationship between the high school and elementary students. My students gain real, hands-on experience in teaching. The elementary students get an "awesome" education program and get to meet kids from high school! On Monday mornings in this unit, my students will often share that they ran into several of their little "Earthkeepers" in town on the weekend. Little do they know that the learning and role model effect continues, even after school hours. Over half of my high school students now have been participants' years earlier in Earthkeepers,™returning to the same place to share what they experienced. The students become teachers: returning again to the source.

Last June I had two former students simply "drop by" the CELP site. They wanted to "come back and see the place." They brought their girlfriends and boyfriends and told me, after their wanderings, that the campfire stones from their daylong solo spots were still there! Though words couldn't quite grasp the deeper meanings, their hearts were displaying a sense of place, sense of home and sense of comforting continuity. I run into my students about town all the time. I often feel my most important lessons happen here, not in official classroom time. When I ride my bicycle to work, buy local produce at the market or paddle with my children on the river, they witness me attempting to live a life with sustainable elements in it. They see my compassion, connection and concern for my "home." This is, I believe, the next layer in the foundation of an education system that teaches "sustained life" as former Chief Gary Potts of the Temagami Bear Island First Nation Anishinabe peoples once stated.[9] But because I grew up and live here, it all seems so normal to do.

As we spin around at the source, the downstream curriculum attempts to find ways we can live sustainably, ways that flow with our ecosystem or, as Bill Reese recently stated, "...ways when we see ourselves as a mere part of nature, and not separate from it."[10] In Civics, we explore political structure and discuss local, national and international issues. We learn how to participate in matters that have meaning to us right in our own community. I have always felt, though, that to make decisions about community, one must know community. So, for seven days, we take to the streets on our bicycles for just that purpose. On Day 1 we learn the rules of the road and feel, in our bones and muscles, that the bicycle is a viable form of transportation. Anchored by research for debates on local issues of sustainability, we bike to our water source, to the sewage treatment plant, and to City Hall. We bike to our waste-handling facility and to the old landfill. We bike to an organic vegetable farm and tour a local abattoir where they slaughter 2,000 head of cattle a day (perhaps the most powerful tour on the circuit). We visit an organic dairy farm and talk with people fighting to keep Wal-Mart in check. The community becomes the classroom. In between visits we picnic by the river, have ice cream at the historic Boathouse, and play "grounders" on park play structures. It is hard to capture in words, the joy I feel biking around my hometown with students, discovering and learning its complex inner workings and hidden places of beauty. The feelings of freedom, the welcome physical exertion and the visits with our local citizens all weave together for an incredible week. We meet our community on a level beyond what is typically possible. Sharon Butala once stated that, "To discover these truths (about the wonder and beauty of the world) we don't need to scale Mount Everest or white-water raft the Colorado or take up skydiving. We need only go for walks."[11] I might add "or for bikes rides."

Often our travels will take us by a small dam on the local Eramosa River where we stop for lunch. Boy scouts built it fifty years ago. It creates a pool to recharge the springs from which our city gets its water. Before departing, I gather my students around an outflow where a small rapid is created. Here I tell them a story. "This place," I explain, "is sacred to me. As a child, my friends and I took bike hikes here and spent hours skipping stones and swimming. In teenager days, we camped in the hills behind. As a young adult, I portaged my canoe traveling both up and downstream. And several years ago, when my wife and I had a stillborn baby boy, we spread his ashes here in ceremony." After an emotional pause, I tell them, "It gives me joy to see all of you enjoying this place – this sacred place." It is a moment, perhaps, that the previous four months have led up to. But it is a moment that is unique to my situation, and attempts to awaken questions in their minds of what being a true dweller is. The land must have elements of sacredness for us to love and care for it. It has that for me and I hope to instil the same with my students. I often wonder, when they return to this small dam, if they tell others this story. For now it is their story too. It is part of who they are, and where they come from.

In the final leg of the course we spend a day in our home community where the students plan, execute and evaluate an Active Citizenship Day. By consensus, they decide in small groups, how to "Better Their Community." On the actual day, the students take to the streets without direct teacher supervision and carry out their chosen tasks. It is a day of celebration as I bike from group to group and see them walking dogs at the Humane Society, flipping pancakes at a kid's breakfast program and performing self-written puppet shows about the environment. It is a culminating day of so much of what we have learned.

In English class the students read a book called *Halfway Man* by Wayland Drew. It is a wonderful story involving an upstream canoe trip to the source and back as well. And for six of my ten years I finished with a local canoe trip that literally lived out our river metaphor. We would portage out the back door of our high school in the city, down to the local Eramosa River, then paddle, pole, portage and drag our canoes upstream for a day, heading to a local park. Here we would camp for two nights, doing a solo and a year's end reflection – what we learned about the source – at the source. Then, we would paddle, in half the time, back home. The gentle current pulled us along. Next year we are initiating a grade 12 (age 17) integrated program called HEADWATERS that will complement the existing grade 10 CELP. We will be resurrecting this final canoe trip. The students will be milling wood from our off-site school property to carve out paddles for their trip.

CELP ends when we invite all the students and their families to a closing ceremony. Beginning with a potluck supper (the theme of food again), we move on to share slides and journal quotes of the semester, narrated by the students. Following this, the teachers award the students a certificate and honour each with a brief story. It is meant to be a transitional moment. The students will return to their home schools having completed half of their grade ten requirements. And, in tune with our overall philosophy, our program is never meant to exist in isolation. The skills and life lessons gained at CELP are meant to help them in their ongoing river's journey. This is simply school for five months.

Last summer I had the unique opportunity to travel to Norway to attend a family reunion held on a farm that has been in my lineage for over a thousand years. A journey to my source – way upstream! I ate roasted lamb with relatives, saw the house where my great-great-great-grandparents emigrated from in 1857 and shook my head at the resemblance of one elder to my own grandfather. But the most significant moment came when I travelled up to the family setter (a small cabin traditionally used in the summer pasture lands). The host of the reunion, Nils Rosholt, a large, gentle man of six foot-four, spoke of how every year he and all the men of the Rosholt farms (now a group of three divided farms) gather for a fall moose hunt. They have a fire pit which they circle around and "talk about things" as Nils stated, as if his English translation was not quite capturing his deeper meaning. He said they work at "getting along" as a family and that this is something they are "very proud of." And with those words, a tingle ran up my spine. My bloodline believes in community, works at nurturing this community, and is connected to their land – their home. And this has been "home" for quite a while. It was an affirming moment. This is where I come from. The words and aspirations of Nils run through me, like a river.

After being in Norway, I realized Canada is a young country. The mindset of "going west to find your fame and fortune" complemented more recently by the cheap fossil fuel era of constant mobility, perhaps have never allowed a percolation of stories to settle into place. But this may change as we move more into the next century. As a global community we are reaching the peak of oil consumption, and in an ironic way, it may return us to being a true dweller of one place. I think the type of education I am providing for young people lines up with this outlook, but I may never know in my lifetime. It has been a natural progression for me as a teacher and dweller, to share the stories, foundations and issues of my community with my students. Learning the term friluftsliv affirmed and clarified for me, this might be a way – a way of seeing the world from a long term, sustainable outlook. To date other ways don't seem to be working. As Aldo Leopold stated so many years ago, "Is it certain that only the volume of education needs stepping up? Is something lacking in the content as well?"[12]

CHAPTER 16

DUCT TAPE AND RABBIT WIRE: GETTING BY IN THE BIG LAND

Larry Innes

It's spring in the North. There is a perceptible difference in the warmth of the daytime sun, brilliant on the deep blanket of a winter's worth of snow, now retreating ever so slightly to the shadows between the spruce. This energy seems to infuse the land with new life. Everything seems to be in motion – from the flocks of snowbirds, recently returned, to the river rapids that are bursting from ice's embrace, to the caribou herds that after a long winter stasis have now resumed their timeless march.

The people are also on the move. Spring is a time for travel. Many of the Labrador communities lack road access, and are only reliably accessible by air. As soon as the ice sets in, travel by snowmobile becomes possible, but it is only in the spring when this mode of travel becomes truly enjoyable. There is something truly magical about being out on a bay, the world nearly perfectly white, almost perfectly flat, nearly floating over the snow towards a blue horizon under the warmth of the spring sun.

Today, I'm helping my wife pack for the month or so that she will spend with her family in "nutshimit." Among the Innu, the spring is the high season for traditional activities. Entire families decamp from the communities: children are pulled from school; houses are boarded up and left behind as people return to the land. They will live in canvas tents in the bush for as long as two months to hunt and gather, returning to ancient campsites and to a rhythm of life as old as the culture itself.

"Don't forget the duct tape. Or the rabbit wire," she reminds me as I head to the local hardware store with what I still after more than a decade among the Innu consider to be an impossibly short list of supplies – axe files, rope, a couple of tarpaulins. A new tea kettle – as big as I can find. An extra elbow for the sheet metal tent stove that her brother made yesterday. Fishing line, leaders and ammunition complete the list.

She's in the midst of sewing a new tent out of light canvas in the midst of our living-room floor. Our two children, young girls aged four and six, are doing their best to be helpful, although with limited success. Once complete, the tent will be about 12 metres square, and will be set using spruce poles cut on site, with a floor of carefully placed fir boughs. A stove – really nothing more than a sheet metal box – will be set near the door, the stove pipe run through a tin grommet in the roof. She often tells me that her mother could sew a tent in less time than it took her father to cut the poles, using the same type of old-fashioned hand-crank sewing machine that is now carefully packed and placed with the other supplies near the door, ready to go.

"Should I take the girls with me?" I ask, thinking that she would appreciate a chance to work unhindered.

"No, let them watch. That's the way we learn," she replies.

In this brief essay, I'm going to make some unlikely comparisons between the Innu concept of *nutshimit*, and the Norwegian practice of friluftsliv. Both concepts are grounded in particular cultures with very different relationships to nature, but share certain elements in common.

Attempting to draw parallels in a complex world – between the traditions and present situation of one culture with those of another – is both an impossible and increasingly necessary task. If we are to orient ourselves in an expanding universe, in a globalizing world where meaning itself has become a commodity, we must attempt such triangulation, or abandon ourselves to indeterminacy.

In such a world, the Innu are almost a fixed point of reference. They and their ancestors have inhabited the northeastern portions of what is now Quebec and Labrador since – and possibly before – the glaciers of the last ice age receded some 8000 years ago. Their territory, which they call *Nitassinan*, literally "our land," is an impossibly vast expanse of boreal forest and sub-arctic tundra, extending north from the Gulf of St. Lawrence to Ungava Bay, and eastward to the rocky coast of Labrador.

The camp is nestled within a cove, sheltering under a south-facing slope dotted with birch. Smoke curls from stovepipes, lingering over the tents in the cold morning air. Although it is now May, Nipissis, the lake, is still covered in ice, providing a landing surface for the ski-equipped bush plane, which circles slowly over the camp before descending. Snowmobiles race to meet the plane, pulling wooden *komatiks* laden with excited, sun-browned children, laughing as they launch over ice ridges. The few passengers disembark, and are warmly greeted. The plane is unloaded quickly. Sugar, flour and tea are packed into the *komatiks*, and the plane is quickly loaded with boxes of caribou meat, Canada geese, beavers, and porcupines, each addressed to a favourite auntie or other relative back in the community.

Back to the task of triangulation. Given that what has arguably been a critical tension between "tradition" and "modernity" within many cultures is now resolving into a shift towards an urbanized, globalized existence – the task of finding and maintaining authentic points of reference has become urgent. Finding such points of reference – where meaning is more than merely contingent – is imperative if we are to maintain and sustain connections to nature, place and culture.

Prior to the 1960s, the Innu were nomadic, their movements and their culture linked inextricably to the wide-ranging caribou herds of the vast Ungava – Labrador peninsula. However, over the last forty years, government policies and frontier developments have led to settlement, with significant and adverse social, political and personal consequences. For many Innu, life in the village is marked by idleness and a sense of loss and alienation, in strong contrast to being in *nutshimit*, which roughly translated means "back in the country," where life is active, rich and meaningful.[1]

Near the camp, a small stream flows into the lake; an *ashkui* (open water in the ice) has formed. Two young men sit attentively in a goose blind made of alder branches and spruce boughs. The afternoon sun is waning, and soon the geese will begin to fly. They will try to call them down to the water, within reach of their shotguns. Until then, they will tell each other stories – some old, some true, and others simply scandalous – and make plans for walking to the burned woods to look for signs of caribou, if the weather holds for a few more days. Tonight, they will search their dreams for them.

Time to draw those parallels.

For many Western societies, the shift (or dislocation) away from living in a deep relationship with nature, nestled in the rhythms of a culture adapted to a particular place has occurred gradually, gathering momentum over centuries.

In contrast, for the Innu and for many indigenous peoples, the shift from the traditional to the modern has occurred all at once, and largely without their consent. The result is nothing less than a crisis. Indigenous youth in particular are quite literally caught between worlds, unable to find a clear path between them. Among the Innu, this is manifest in social dysfunction, drugs and solvent abuse and some of the highest youth suicide rates on the planet.[2]

Back in the village, a cold northeast wind is blowing. Potholes line the narrow dirt streets, filled with rainwater, snowmelt and garbage. A lean dog peers cautiously from under the porch of a small house. A truck with a broken windshield drives by, slows down, and then moves on. Despite the weather, the door to the house is open, and from inside, rap music booms from the large TV. Teenagers in jeans and baseball caps share a dilapidated couch, a case of beer balanced between them, eyes glazed, attention flickering over the booty and bling on display in the latest music video. Nothing else to do.

Friluftsliv, as a movement, emerged as part of a broad cultural response to the challenges of modernity in Norway, beginning in the 18th century. It is about the recovery of meaning through personal engagement with "Free Nature."[3] It recognizes that our practical understanding of the world – as human beings, physically present in the world, and capable of action – is an essential part of the broader set of experiences, concepts and relationships that define our cultures and give our lives meaning.

As a practice, friluftsliv gently seeks to reconnect us with our pre-understanding of the world – that is, to an authentic awareness of what it is to be in the world and to experience nature on her terms, while simultaneously situating and interpreting these experiences within the horizons of a culture that has also embraced modernity.

Nutshimit is not practice, but a place – a place where traditional Innu culture can be lived, and where the impositions of the dominant culture are less intrusive. It is a place of healing, where families are able to reconnect, away from the pressures of village life. And more fundamentally, it is a place rich with meaning, where the Innu language comes alive, where the stories that connect the people to the places can be told in their full context, and where even dreams are part of the reality.

And in these differences, the comparison ends. But in the differences between friluftsliv as a practice and *nutshimit* as a place, there is a suggestion of a potential synthesis.

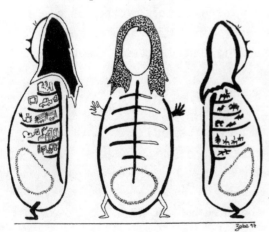

The conwayor in the friluftsliv tradition is a guide or a pathfinder, assisting in transition from the detachment of modernity to identification with free nature. Among the Innu, it is only recently that the need for similar guidance has emerged. Over the past few years, however, there has been an increasing emphasis on the development of programs for youth that are grounded in the experience of *nutshimit.* These programs are being advanced not only as a means of looking back to the nomadic traditions of their grandparents, but as a means of gathering strength to address the present and future challenges of village life.[4]

Back in the camp, a woman is repairing snowshoes with babiche lacing cut from raw caribou hide. Her hands move quickly in complex patterns, quickly filling in the tears and gaps. Her oldest daughter is kneading bannock, which will be baked on top of the sheet metal stove, while simultaneously tending to a small child, suspended in a hammock tied between the poles in a warm corner of the tent. Johnny Cash growls softly from a radio tuned to a classic country station, transmitting by satellite. Her younger daughter sits nearby, a French lesson book on her lap, watching attentively. Making connections.

CHAPTER 17

EMBRACING FRILUFTSLIV'S JOYS: TEACHING THE CANADIAN NORTH THROUGH THE CANADIAN WILDERNESS TRAVEL EXPERIENCE

Glen Hvenegaard and Morten Asfeldt

In late July 1990, we were hiking in the Coppermine Mountains along the Coppermine River, north of the Arctic Circle in the Northwest Territories of Canada. After more than six months of planning, our group of eight was nearing the end of a 25-day canoe trip. It struck us on that day how powerful this experience had been for our group in so many ways; we were only just beginning to find our rhythm with each other, with the land, and with the travel experience. We were all very satisfied about the experience, having learned many lessons and gained many new insights about the Canadian North and wilderness travel. We can remember distinctly that day, walking back to the river wondering how we might provide a similar experience for students in the future. At that time we were both on an energetic quest to make careers of teaching at a university in outdoor education and geography. Little did we know that after 15 years and hundreds of days as tent, hiking and paddling partners, we would become teaching partners in a course that we believe is an extension of our collective childhood experiences exploring the natural world. (Glen's experiences were based in southern Alberta and Morten's experiences were based in northern Newfoundland and the

Yukon.) Through these experiences
we knew the landscape around
us as both playground and
home.

We now co-teach two
courses at the University of
Alberta's Augustana Faculty:
Physical Education 388 (Arctic
Canoe Expedition) and Geography
341 (Geography of the Canadian North).
Central to these courses is a 21-day canoe expedition in the Canadian
North. An overarching objective of these courses is to facilitate a wilderness travel experience for students that will allow them to begin to know
and feel that wild place. In some ways, it is an attempt to provide for students what we both experienced as children, the sense that nature is
home rather than wilderness. We hope that after spending 21 days living
in nature that students begin to feel a sense of belonging and knowingness rather than those associated with being in a strange place. We
believe, as do others, that the best method of increasing environmental
concern and action is through direction personal interaction with the
natural environment.[1] For example, Alan Ewert suggests that experiential
education can promote pro-environmental behaviours through aware-
ness-building, attitude-formation and empowerment.[2]

Course Descriptions:
These optional courses were first offered in 1993, and have been taught
every second year since. Senior students accepted into the courses begin
meeting in the winter semester. The specific goals of the courses are for
students to:

- engage in an interdisciplinary learning expedition,
- discover and explore a very special, yet largely unknown part of
  Canada including its people, landscape, flora and fauna and to
  provide an organizational framework for that discovery and
  exploration,

- have substantial input into the creation and shaping of their own experience and the challenge to investigate and share topics of personal interest,
- develop wilderness expedition planning and leadership skills,
- gain an appreciation and awareness of the Canadian North, and wilderness generally, so that they might develop a sense of knowingness, a sense of place and a desire to spend time in nature and work to protect it.

In the winter term, students first develop an ideal river profile based on the skills, interests and desires of the class. Then, armed with this profile, students conduct research on potential routes, considering the following characteristics: trip length, river difficulty, cost, historical and cultural significance, geographical features, flora and fauna and any other unique features. Finally, based on options presented in class, the group selects the route to be travelled. In addition, the practical matters of expedition planning are undertaken by the students: food planning and packaging (including dehydrating large amounts of food), equipment selection and preparation, and safety and logistical planning. Time is also devoted to developing a mission statement and accompanying group norms and expectations in order to guide and focus the journey.

On the geography side, time is devoted to examining the biophysical environment and how that has influenced the human geography of the north. The north's historical background, settlement patterns, religion, language, politics, resource development and the importance of First Nations groups are also explored. Each year, special time is devoted to specific topics unique to the region or current issues (e.g. the formation of Nunavut in 1999 and diamond mining).

During the expedition, we have used specific activities to successfully to meet our objectives. First, journal writing and reflection time are central. Each student keeps a personal journal where they are meant to reflect on both the practical (e.g.: where we went, what we did, how far we travelled, what we saw) and philosophical (e.g.: what did I think and feel? what does this mean? so what?) aspects of the day. In addition, a group journal is also kept in which one member of the group, including instructors, takes a turn making a daily entry that is shared aloud with the group the following morning. This journal plays an important role in group formation and bonding as well as requiring students to make public, and hence assume ownership for, their experience and reflections.[3] These group journal readings have become a highlight of our journeys and have taken on many forms (e.g. prose, poetry, song, art and humour), and at times become very emotional. Journals are a traditional outcome of expeditions and are recognized as important learning tools to increase student learning.[4]

Second, in partners, students take turns co-facilitating, or leading, the group. They assume this role for two 48-hour periods, and in consultation with the course instructors, are responsible for facilitating the planning and decision making for that time. This includes: paddling in the lead canoe, map reading, route finding, campsite selection, providing a thought for the day and facilitating other decisions and discussions as necessary.

Third, we have a series of activities associated with the natural environment. Each student is responsible for providing two ten-minute interpretative presentations, conducting a daily research project, and completing two nature identification field tests.

Fourth, the expedition also has considerable unstructured time, or learning room, where Aage Jensen's form of "fumbling and tumbling"[5] is the dominant activity. This includes meal-time conversations, exchanges with paddling partners, evening hikes, and layover days every third or fourth day. These are times of spontaneous discovery where students can freely engage the land and each other and pursue their curiosities. We believe this is an essential element of the wilderness travel experience.

Finally, we have intentionally chosen three weeks as the duration for these expeditions. From our experience, in this amount of time students lose their "normal" patterns of living and develop new ones that are in harmony with nature. Our world encourages us to think in specific time blocks such as hours, days, and weeks. During a three-week expedition, we find the middle week is often pivotal because during the first week, student patterns of living, thinking, and exploring are disrupted; in the second week, new patterns are established; during the third week, those patterns are solidified and students begin to think about how they can maintain those patterns in their home environments. In a two-week expedition, that important second week of establishing new patterns is missed and students beginning thinking about home without really having to embrace and contemplate the disruption of their everyday lives.

We believe these courses offer students a unique introduction to the Canadian North and to wilderness travel. Our methods are consistent with many aspects of Norwegian concept of friluftsliv. The purpose of this paper is to explore how the relevant concepts of friluftsliv are exemplified in our arctic course program.

Friluftsliv on the Program

We will not spend much time in this paper defining the characteristics of friluftsliv because there is much material on this topic elsewhere in this volume. Instead, we have chosen to focus on the "joys" that friluftsliv might produce. Nils Faarlund considers joy to be the driving force of friluftsliv according to the Norwegian tradition. In this context, joy is "an all embracing experience, absorbing, deeply moving." Faarlund also suggests that joy requires "free nature, confidence and awareness."[6] We break down the joy portion of friluftsliv into stages, or components, that are relevant to our trips to the arctic: the joy of discovering the place, the joy of knowing a place, the joy of feeling at home, and the joy of living simply. In each case, we explain the relevance of that particular type of joy and how we embrace that joy on our trips.

Joy of Discovering the Place

The joy of discovering a place involves gaining knowledge of, and appreciation for, its unique features. Just as one gets to know another person, getting to know a place requires both systematic and spontaneous processes of investigation, a commitment to deepen and continue the relationship, a genuine interest and a sharing of insights. All of these require a substantial investment of time. Students in our program are encouraged to address all of these aspects as they discover the Arctic. We encourage our students to become "nature connoisseurs," as described by D. Pepi, in which "thinking, feeling, and acting are integrated deliberately in order to obtain the richest experiences possible from natural objects and events."[7]

First, we urge our students to systematically explore all aspects of the Arctic environment. In the classroom, we provide an overview of the natural features we are likely to encounter, including, for example, landforms, flowers, birds and archaeological sites. As Michael Weilbacher suggests, "the road to environmental literacy begins with nature study."[8] Our students research a topic of special interest with a paper requirement to develop a deeper knowledge. At the start of the canoeing trip, we focus on the identification of the more readily accessible and reliable natural features, such as flowers and glacial features. We provide time to practise these skills, encourage the use of reference books, model the process of identification, and encourage competency with field tests. As the trip progresses, we model the process of discovery, inviting students to come join us on that voyage.[9] As well, we encourage students to reflect on their observations, with the hope that they discover or reinforce generalizations and relationships. We try to provide large blocks of time to take advantage of spontaneous discoveries without feeling the pressure to move on.

Second, students develop confidence in their skills of discovery. We provide immediate positive feedback to students about their progress, regularly discuss new and anticipated discoveries, and ask questions along with students, rather than simply providing answers. One task that gives students the opportunity to become the group's "expert" is an individual research project. Students systematically gather and record data about a particular topic (e.g. wildflower blooming times, weather trends, campsite impacts), summarize information, draw conclusions, and suggest applications. Students have found that a detailed exploration into some aspect of the north provides greater satisfaction and deeper learning. As they discover new features, they encounter excitement, fear, and uncertainty but, it is hoped, they will have the confidence to continue to expand or broaden their searches.

Finally, the joy of discovery creates a desire to share new insights with others. Learners become teachers, and teachers become learners.[10] It is a natural urge to enthusiastically pass on new information, enhancing the experience for both giver and receiver. In the classroom, each student writes a research paper about a feature likely to be encountered on the canoe trip. The students need to be prepared to give a spontaneous presentation to the rest of the group whenever that feature is actually encountered. Thus, the joy of discovery melds the results of fascination, appreciation, sharing, and understanding, all in the group experience. The daily routine of canoe tripping brings many other opportunities of this nature.

Joy of Knowing the Place

The act of knowing a place involves discovery, but it also involves reflection and understanding about the components of that place, the interactions among those components and the significance of those features. First, experiencing a place can be superficial, in terms of time spent, knowledge gained, appreciation developed. However, that experience can be deepened substantially with a basic overview and framework of the essential components. In the classroom, we spend time highlighting the basic physical and human features that characterize the north. Key elements that drive northern processes are emphasized, including the latitude, permafrost, seasonal patterns, weather patterns, prevailing winds, landforms, water and wildlife. Students need to know what to expect, and how to name and describe those essential features. Without this step, it is like having a room full of friends, without knowing any of their names. Without names and a way to describe those features around us, it is difficult to gain any further insight. However, naming natural features should not be an end in itself; this should lead to deeper understanding and a lifelong friendship.[11]

Second, further insight occurs when students begin to recognize patterns and relationships. Flowers growing on the south-facing slopes, peregrine falcons nesting on riverside cliffs, wolves denning in sandy eskers and good fishing in calm eddies are all examples of insights that result from daily personal experiences. However, without the basic framework for understanding and specific expectations, much would be missed. More systematic study results in even more insights. Adding the layers of human history, from ancient, historical, and current time periods, creates numerous possibilities for new insights. The unique combination and interaction of components make the Arctic a truly unique system. Where possible, we, as instructors, provide modelling and frameworks to which these insights can be added.

Third, it is exciting to begin to appreciate the significance of these observations and interactions. How will you know if a bird sighting is unique? How will you know if an archaeological site is significant? Research prior to the trip, reading during the trip and knowledgeable instructors are all needed to answer these types of questions. It is important to know if a species, site or interaction is significant so that the group can know if it is worthwhile spending extra time to identify, explore or reflect about those features. Furthermore, engaging in the moment, when appropriate, allows us to heighten our sense of appreciation (e.g. accidentally coming across archaeological sites or gyrfalcon nests).

Finally, appreciating the significance of our unique northern ecosystem should develop in present-day travellers a profound respect and caring for the land.[12] We need to know the significance of the features encountered so that we can understand the potential for negative impacts, and the options to avoid or minimize those impacts. Past research suggests that experiential understanding of a place naturally develops concern about the welfare of that place. (See Notes 1 and 2.) Our group prepares group norms and expectations of our experience, including the goal of "Leave No Trace" travel.[13] In this respect, we do not want to learn about environmental impacts through trial and error, but ensure minimal impacts with adequate preparation, common expectations, suitable equipment and modelling by the instructors.

Joy of Feeling at Home

Spending time and having unique experiences in a place gives meaning to that place[14] and has the potential to create a lasting bond with that place. That bond develops when one begins to understand the essence of the place and feeling at home in that place.[15] An analogy is how the physical

structure of a "house" becomes a "home" after experiences in that house make that place meaningful. In the same way, a region takes on deeper meaning when one experiences that place and learns about the members, interactions and significance of that community. We encourage students to move beyond the simple naming of flowers and birds (although that is an important stepping stone) to begin feeling kinship with fellow members of the Arctic ecosystem. In doing so, we encourage students to consider questions about human relationships with nature, the role and impacts of nature travel, and what the future holds for the Canadian North.

Often during the second and third week of our canoeing trip, we begin to feel a sense of belonging in this place. Instructors and students have taught each other how to feel comfortable and enjoy being in nature. This level of comfort opens us up to all of the opportunities that nature may offer. We have gained confidence in our identification skills, have learned many insights about interactions among natural features, and have developed an appreciation for the significance of the place. We have felt the rhythm of the landscape and sensed the sacredness of the place. Students develop a desire to learn much more, but realizing that time is now short, and state a desire to return again. In a sense, they want to feel a deeper sense of connection, wherever and whenever they are in contact with nature.

At the same time, students have often stated a yearning for a similar feeling at their regular "home" place. We often hear how farmers, ranchers and hunters have developed a deep sense of connection with the land, but this process requires considerable time and effort. It also depends on active learning, a positive attitude and time for reflection. However, many people in their busy lives of work, family and recreation, don't develop that sense of connectedness. But, having experienced it in one place (the North), that feeling can be replicated in other environments. It is a shame that one has to feel it first somewhere other than one's "home" place.[16]

Joy of Living Simply

Essential to extended wilderness canoe tripping is the need to travel lightly simply due to space limitations. There simply isn't room for all of our modern conveniences. This is also an intentional element of our journey: to strip ourselves of the gadgetry of our modern world so that we are unencumbered in our exploration and discovery of the place.[17] We want all our senses to be focused and engaged. We hope that by living simply we reduce the number of obstacles barring our quest for developing relationships with nature and each other. We seek a genuine human moment rather than a "virtual moment." We have been asked why we don't make daily reports back to schools or news providers as is common on many adventures today. We respond that it would take us away from the place and tempt us to focus on what "others" want and expect from our experience rather than simply letting the experience be what it is. To engage in this daily high tech communication would force us to continue living a pattern of life governed by the 24-hour clock, prime time TV and radio broadcasts. These are the very patterns of life that we are trying to escape as they have become barriers to discovering, knowing and feeling at home in nature.

By travelling with simple food, simple clothing and simple equipment we must be aware of, and work in harmony with, nature as opposed to seeing ourselves as conquerors of nature. In essence, we are governed by the rhythms of nature. When the wind blows too hard, we hike instead of paddle; when the bugs are bad, we paddle; when wildlife is plentiful, we stop and observe; when we are hungry, we eat; and when we are cold, we put on more clothes.

Having said this, some may be critical of us for not travelling even simpler, but we must be aware of our responsibility to students and our institutions to provide a safe experience that meets the current standards for wilderness travel with groups. Therefore, we do carry a satellite phone, but it is understood that it is only to be used in emergencies and only then after a group decision to do so. We also carry appropriate first-aid kits and wear modern life jackets and high-tech rain gear. However, in a relative sense, we travel very simply with limited clothes, one-pot meals, and simple writing tools. The only entertainment is that which we can generate ourselves. We believe the critical element is time spent in nature and not the not the place of one's equipment the continuum between high and low technology.[18.] This simplicity allows us to become much more aware of our surroundings, to feel the cool breeze, hear the bird songs, observe with heightened sensitivity, think more clearly and act with greater intentionality.

Conclusion

Living out the concept of friluftsliv is both a process and a state of mind. The joys offered by friluftsliv on an extended wilderness expedition, as described for these courses offered at the University of Alberta's Augustana Faculty, include the joy of discovering the place, joy of knowing the place, joy of feeling at home and the joy of living simply. These courses are our attempt to replicate self-motivated time in nature that we both knew as children and young adults. Our goal is for students and instructors to become natural in the natural world. This can be achieved by getting back to the basics, as exemplified by the Norwegian concept of friluftsliv. In addition, such extended wilderness trips allow for an opening up of the mind, body, and spirit to deeper physical, sensory, emotional and spiritual experiences of nature. With this state of mind, we begin to feel at home in nature, rather than just visitors.

CHAPTER 18

THE ROLE OF CRAFT-MAKING IN FRILUFTSLIV

Zabe MacEachren

If friluftsliv means "a way home to the open air," then craft-making plays a critical role in this journey home into a culture immersed in nature. Craft-making is the hands-on experience of making items from material obtained from the land that allows us to live in nature. If people take with them into nature, items or tools they have purchased and have little understanding of their means of production, then they are simply tourist-like visitors travelling superficially in the culture and on the land. How can we consider ourselves intimate with nature if we feel lost about where to look for suitable craft material in the locale in which we live, and if we lack the know-how to harvest material sustainably? Can we consider ourselves part of a place when our hands are unfamiliar with shaping its materials into the durable and useful stuff of life – the very stuff that allows us to live simply and well in a place? When we can make our own outdoor living equipment, then we will better understand friluftsliv and the role craft-making plays in creating a deeper connection to being in the natural world.

Contact with nature was always part of my life, something I never could get enough of. Somewhere on my journey from camper and summer canoe tripper to outdoor recreation graduate and teacher, I asked myself an important question. What were the most meaningful times in my life, times when I felt most a part of the natural world around me? The answer arose in a patchwork of reflections of experiences based in trying to make something with my hands from material I myself had gathered. In order to satisfy my desire to learn about nature, I had set myself the goal of trying to learn how to make all the things I would need to travel in the Ontario Northwoods – canoe, snowshoes, mukluks, eating utensils and so on. This desire resulted in many experiences, both successful and frustrating of learning to work with materials such as wood, birchbark, leather and clay. Usually I was alone in my struggle to teach myself things and to learn from "how-to" books, but occasionally I was fortunate to witness and benefit from the wisdom of First Nation Anishinabe elders with whom I lived and worked. Eventually I noticed that most elders choose to pass on their culture to youth not through lecturing but through the activity of making a craft, and sharing some lore about this activity that gave their own travels on the land a greater purpose. I realized that many teachings and perceptions of the land were embedded in not only the experience of using a craft in one's travels but also in making the indigenous crafts associated with a particular place. These realizations led me to pursue graduate work in this area.

My dissertation, "Craftmaking: A Pedagogy for Environmental Awareness," can be seen as an exploration of the role crafts and craft-making plays in understanding friluftsliv.[1] In the modern Western industrial world, the term craft is currently devalued. Crafts are considered "lesser" arts because of the earthier qualities of their materials: clay versus gold, wood instead of marble. As well, the utility component associated with a craft also means that the made item is bonded to a function that serves to tie the maker or user to the land; in comparison, the conceptual qualities of fine art, as evident in abstract modern paintings, allows the viewer to reason that human thought can rise above any tie with the land. Studying the history of terms such as art, craft and technology and how they increasingly became differentiated, is really a story of how people became separated from the earth through their development of social hierarchies.

My interest in finding a way back home to the open air or into nature kept me bound to the term "craft." If anything, I felt it was important to attempt to reclaim the term's earthy association with the land and insist upon functionality. Without utility, many created items deemed beautiful are simply toxic landfill problems. I recognize crafts as a mediator between nature and culture. Crafts connect people to the land through their utility; items to fulfill our daily needs that require the shaping of earthy substances provide a recognizable and genuine dependency on the material of the land. Craft-making encourages people to identify themselves as a part of nature because our need for tools and crafts in order to live, provides us with a reason to create items and use our unique human gift – our opposable thumbs. To make something of utility is to conserve and honour the gift of material received from the earth; to make something of beauty is to demonstrate respect for the beauty and unique qualities embedded in the material received from the earth. The word "craft" can be both a noun and a verb so it represents both the process and the product of friluftsliv.

The socialization to outdoor life that friluftsliv entails is represented in the role craft-making plays in education. Many programs that are considered environmental or nature-based education make reference to the importance of craft-making. Unfortunately, many of these programs lack a critical examination or detailed explanation as to why craft-making activities are emphasized and in what ways they serve to connect people to the land.

An early educational movement that emphasized craft-making was the Boy Scouts, today called Scouts. This organization arose from many separate attempts to address the growing restlessness in youth observed after the industrial revolution (and perceived to be a result of the reduction in opportunities to play and wander in nature). The writing of one of Scout's early founders, Ernest Thompson Seton,[2] provided some of the most comprehensive guidebooks ever written for youth. Seton's work was heavily based in acquiring craft-making skill. The dedication in his first book directed at a youth audience, *Two Little Savages* states: "To WOODCRAFT by one who owes it many lasting PLEASURES" and his preface refers to the lack of resources for youth who desire guidance in quenching their thirst for nature.[3] Although Seton would not have been familiar with the term friluftsliv, his writing provides documentation of the first attempts to develop a curriculum that supports aims similar to friluftsliv in North America and provides some justification for the value of obtaining wood-craft skills. Seton's widely published work influenced a span of youth that included the final years of frontier life in North America to the back-to-the-land movement associated with the hippies of the seventies.

Others who, like Seton, have not used the term friluftsliv but have written about the role craft-making plays in creating a cultural connection to the land should be mentioned. Mahatma Gandhi describes how the central pivot of all education should be learning a local craft that can be expanded upon to other material production processes, thereby integrating and exploring culture's ties to economics.[4] Kurt Hahn, the British/German founder of Outward Bound and many other experiential-education ideas, considered learning craftsmanship one of the basic pillars of a sound education; developing craftsmanship was considered the foundation of a good work ethic that led to the creation of the cultural artifacts that could be considered to represent the genius of civilizations.[5] Rudolph Steiner, the Austrian who founded Waldorf Education, developed a well-thought-out sequence of handwork activities involving only natural materials. His handwork program aims to address the development of the whole child and not just the relation to the child's mind.[6] Shortly after the Industrial Revolution, a very gallant effort was begun in Britain by William Morris and others to revive and continue the skills of fine craftsmanship. This effort became known as the Craft Movement or Craft Revival and was spurred on by both an awareness of the reduction of natural spaces due to growing industries and the fear of what long-term shoddy workmanship in culture would result in. Traces of this movement spread to many part of the world.[7] It is suggested that the craft revival was the largest effort that ever attempted to address the problems of modernity.[8] All these educational ideas, although never referring specifically to friluftsliv, serve to highlight the ways that craft-making fosters connection with life in the open air.

As a professor who works with teacher candidates with a special interest in outdoor education, I am often amazed at what little skill these teachers hold in the area of craft-making. They may be able to play all kinds of nature-based games and even identify many species of trees, but they have little experience in putting their knowledge and body together in order to make a craft. Most of these young educators have been immersed in a world of computers, outdoor equipment catalogues and gimmicks proclaiming to connect a person to nature. Few know how to select wood to carve a spoon or build a fire, let alone know where to find material to make snowshoes. Their hands are not calloused from or familiar with holding a tool, such as a carving knife. Craft-making experiences develop skills such as using one's body to carefully handle and shape material nature and using one's mind to design items that will carefully interact with the land.

It will take time to introduce such teacher candidates to a curriculum that would promote friluftsliv through craft-making. Each region needs to look at its local environment and the cultural crafts that have sprung forth from it. Curriculum designers' efforts to do this will be motivated by witnessing the empowerment and sense of satisfaction expressed by students after they gain confidence in such challenges as using an axe for the first time in order to make something needed for an outing. In order to develop worthy programs in craft-making for friluftsliv educators, we might refer to the curriculum at Sámi University College in Norway. Here the Sámi teacher candidates must spend additional months at school learning *duodji*, which is their native term for handicrafts. This university has recognized the role craft-making should play in passing on a culture and ensures their future teachers are well versed in it. In order to graduate, teacher candidates must be able to demonstrate proficiency in a variety of techniques associated with making traditional crafts, such as birchbark containers and knives.[9]

The craft-making component of a friluftsliv education should require the people of each region to learn, maintain and revive (if necessary) its own unique cultural craft traditions. This means many eyes must become attuned to the subtleties of the materials a place offers (for example knowing which hillside provides larger tree rings for a basket maker to use). Late-night discussions around a campfire must ponder ideas concerning why this region is known for a particular design or form of a craft (for example, which stories share an account of discovering a new way to weave snowshoes or attach a boot to a ski). Such detailed craft knowledge linking us to a place is being rapidly lost in today's world.

In North America, one can usually find a book or map that links various snowshoe and canoe designs with different regions of the continent. Questioning and exploring why so many regional variations arose in craft-making traditions, like canoe, skis, shelter and snowshoe making, would encourage learning about unique niches of tradition rooted in friluftsliv. What are the advantages of a flat or upturned curve on a snowshoe, or the size of its weaving? What general weather or landscape features exist in a region that would benefit the traveller using a traditional craft design? How would being very attuned to the specifics of a region allow a craft maker to fine tune a canoe to regional water conditions or a ski shape to local snow features? How can a craft be made to suit an individual's body size and needs? What does it take to encourage a person to feel as if using the craft just extends their relationship into the land as when wearing footwear made of local animal leather feels simply like one's own skin? Attending to the unique features of a region and learning what materials are offered by this region to be shaped into various crafts requires a lifetime of learning and sharing. Caring enough to learn these bioregional crafts and their history serves to continue the tradition of locals traveling frequently in a place and demonstrating a love and intimacy of both being in and of a place. To me this is the aim of friluftsliv.

The right of public access to countryside, or *allemansrätt*, plays a role in craft-making. Various countries' traditions have each established norms which have led to policies concerning access in various regions and pertaining to various activities, such as collecting food, flowers and craft material like birch bark and wood. On many canoe trips, I have paddled along Ontario shorelines knowing that two hundred years previous the voyageurs would have paddled this same shoreline with a different sense than my own of human ownership over land and trees. If voyageurs needed bark or spruce roots to make repairs to a canoe they simply had to walk inland until they found a suitable source. Today, most people would be restricted from collecting material on private property without permission, even on Canadian Crown land, land held in trust by the Crown for the use of all Canadian citizens. I envy the voyageurs for the perceptions they held, which would have encouraged them to freely wander upon the land accessing craft material with little sense of private possession.

As an educator in today's time, I have various ways of dealing with the concept of access and ownership as it arises in craft-making contexts. Overall, I aim to provide my students with an opportunity to begin to view the land and the more-than-human world from which material is obtained, in a new manner that includes a sense of animism, communal property and greater access for those in need. Through discussions, stories and comments I raise awareness about what is meant by harvesting material appropriately and address the ways this understanding has changed throughout history. I may raise such questions as: "Who was the first person to own land?" and "How did the concept of land ownership come to be?" When working with teacher candidates, I encourage them to begin to perceive the school ground as a place in which to reclaim a sense of access and as a common ground from which to collect craft material. I envision schools where primary children plant trees and then in later grades harvest trees in order to make woodcrafts. I like to think that someday art cupboards and supply rooms full of paper will not exist, but instead each school will have its own school ground with well-established parcels that can be used for harvesting craft materials and planted crops that can be used for making the "stuff of life."

Some educators refer to hiking as a friluftsliv guide's main tool to encourage people to feel comfortable and enjoy nature. I would refine this concept by suggesting that to have a purpose that accompanies the hike allows a person to find greater meaning in why they should continually wander on the land. Noticing tree notches and large galls that can be used for carving bowls, even if not harvested on the hike, encourages an interaction with the land based upon dependency – the land provides us with the material we need to live. In this way, we therefore are not just tourists visiting the land but rather more like wildlife participating in its natural cycles by foraging. The utility aspect of a craft encourages a sense of immersion in the world because it provides an honest reason for being on the land. When we walk upon the land and pass by places where we have collected bark, spotted deer, sat and whittled a spoon, then these areas serve as landmarks to our memory of past interactions. The land begins to talk to us as we walk by. The more past interactions, the more the land will seem to speaking to us. When a person hikes with some awareness of possibly finding material to make a walking stick, basket, spoon or knife handle, a reason for being on the land is provided that encourages a deeper sense of immersion in a place. This deeper sense of being part of the land results because we have a reason to interact with the land that the mere social enjoyment of being outdoors does not provide. The tool or crafts made by out-of-door hikers becomes a link from their city life back to the open-air life. The reason for the hike recalls in us our dependency on nature; we remember that nature provides us with the material for life – a fact far too often forgotten in a cluttered urban world of bought equipment, gadgetry and trivial paraphernalia. Understanding resulting from many experiences craft-making creates awareness of the downstream effects of leading a material life, whether in an urban or rural landscape. A craft made from material obtained on a hike and through the process of quietly shaping it, allows the craft to remind us of our connectivity and the serenity of being in nature. Even if the craft resides on a desk in a cluttered, noisy office it can be glanced at and remind of us of another way of being in the world. The craft can also be picked up and used as a tool to more consciously immerse us in the natural processes of living.

Craft-making is a metaphor, whether we are making a crooked knife or a ski, snowshoe or a mukluk for travelling on the land. To make a craft we must slow ourselves down and learn from the material we handle. The grain of the wood informs our moves; the terrain we expect to travel guides our design forms. This craft-making interaction with nature is serene and enjoyable, and it provides meaning to our work of travelling the land. Making a craft serves as a microcosm for peacefully living in nature; craft-making is about exploring friluftsliv.

CHAPTER 19

FRILUFTSLIV TRANSPLANTED: THE NORWEGIAN IMMIGRANT EXPERIENCE IN ALBERTA

Ingrid K. Urberg

"If you had a choice, Mom, wouldn't you rather be out in the forest, in the woods, than stuck in the office?" Then I thought, well he's a true Norwegian. Whether he got that from going to Norway or from us; we've had a very outdoor life. We've done a lot of skiing, a lot of outdoor activities with them (our children when they were growing up in Canada). Taking them out hiking and things, so maybe that has influenced him… Solveig Ardiel (Norwegian Immigrant, Edmonton, AB).

During the past three years I have had the pleasure of interviewing several dozen Norwegian immigrants who currently reside in Alberta, in conjunction with an oral history project – *The Norwegian Immigrant Experience in Alberta*.[1] I am particularly interested in issues of identity and place, and one of the standard questions I ask participants is, "What does it mean for you to be Norwegian?" The responses I have received to this question are varied and complex, but a striking commonality (despite differences in generations, age at time of migration, educational and work backgrounds and geographical origin in Norway), is mention of a passion for the outdoors and nature. Some examples include: "I think of the mountains and the trees" (Kari Brittner); "All the passion

that is in a Norwegian for the land, the language and for the nature"
(Solveig Ardiel); "cross-country skiing" (Verner Steinbru); and "going
out with the *spark* with my grandchildren" (Inga Schneider). Positive
memories of walking, biking and skiing to school, playing outside and
spending time in the mountains and by the water all play a central role in
my subjects' recollections of their formative years. The interviews also
reveal that most immigrants brought this love for the outdoors and outdoor activities with them to Canada, and adapted it to their new surroundings. Though each immigrant experience is unique, some clear
trends emerge in terms of their friluftsliv mentality.

Though these Norwegians came to a country known for its nature and
outdoor opportunities, they soon discovered that their attitudes about
the outdoors often differed from those of their new neighbours. They
were surprised, even shocked, by the flatness and vastness of their new
land, and by the dependence on cars for transportation. Karen Fimrite
was ten years old when she moved to the Grand Prairie region of Alberta
from a small island in northern Norway, and she recalls how she and her
family were viewed as curiosities because of their walking habits:

> We walked the distance (to our neighbours) and walked
> to church. Thought nothing of it, because in Norway
> you walk anyways. We were accustomed to walking. Peo-
> ple here thought we were odd, because we would just
> walk to visit someone. They thought that was very, very
> different. But, of course in Norway, we would walk the
> eleven kilometres to my grandparents on my mother's
> side. Thought nothing of that.

Despite the harsh Alberta climate, vast distances and greater availability
of cars, Karen, who is now in her sixties and still a resident of the Grand
Prairie region, has remained an avid walker, "I walk and walk. That's a
given. I've always been a walker, and I thoroughly enjoy it."

These differences in attitudes were also evident in the ways in which
Norwegian immigrant families allocated their resources. Inga Schneider
recalls how she was more used to skiing, skating and using a *spark* (a

Scandinavian kick sled) than the other kids when she moved to Athabasca at the age of eleven. Her father sent for skis and skates for her from Calgary, and she was one of the few country kids with this type of equipment. Though they were not any better off financially than their neighbours, her father clearly viewed these activities as intrinsic to a proper upbringing. Inga has, in turn and like many other participants in my project, prioritized spending time with her children and grandchildren outdoors. She has a Norwegian kick sled, which she had shipped from Norway to Winnipeg, and she still takes her grandchildren out on this *spark* when they visit her in Bentley, AB.

Contacts with other Norwegians – family, friends and church communities – initially provided the immigrants with a supportive friluftsliv environment. Reidun and Thorleif Berg, for example, lived in Winnipeg as a young couple before moving to the Edmonton area, and they were part of a group of fourteen Norwegians that regularly went to a cabin and fished together. Others were part of Scandinavian church groups that arranged picnics and outdoor excursions. Those who came as youngsters, as is evident from Inga Schneider's account, had parental support and role models. Sometimes this parental influence was far reaching. Kaare Hellum, who came to Canada as a university student, received a pair of skis from his parents in Norway, and this gift allowed him to ski in the mountains. He recounts with some humour, "So I got the good old Norwegian Becksom skis. I had my knickerbockers from Norway, so I skied like I belonged to the last century. I didn't care." Verner Steinbru, who immigrated to the Grand Prairie region as a boy with his family, found a supportive and fostering environment among these more recently arrived Norwegian immigrants while working in Vancouver as a young man. Verner rented a home with several Norwegian students, and not only did

his language skills improve, but he honed his cross-country skills while skiing with his housemates.

Skiing and ski jumping were, likely due to their Nordic origins, the two activities that seemed to inspire the greatest degree of comradeship among the Norwegian immigrants. Indeed, the most visible signs of a Norwegian friluftsliv legacy in Alberta today are Nordic ski clubs. Kristian Nyhus, who emigrated in the 1950s, told me of how he worked together with other Scandinavian immigrants in the 1970s to form the Edmonton Nordic Ski Club. Today, the web site of the Edmonton Nordic Ski Club states that "membership is open to all who enjoy cross-country skiing."[2] This group is one of the sponsors of the high profile Canadian Birkebeiner, a cross-country ski festival, which is held each February. Inspired by the Norwegian Birkebeiner, which commemorates the rescue of the Norwegian Prince Haakon Haakonsson in 1206 by warriors on skis, the Canadian event celebrated its twentieth anniversary in 2006. Though the 55-kilometre race with a pack is the premier event, there are a variety of distances available for participants, including the 2.5-kilometre "Ole's Two-Bit Tour" for children and people learning how to ski. Camrose, the community in which I live and work, also has an active Nordic ski club, the Camrose Ski Club, founded in 1911 by early Scandinavian settlers to the area. Though the founders were first and second generation Norwegian immigrants who were primarily competitive skiers and ski jumpers, the ski jump is still serving as a local landmark. The club today is open to competitive athletes and recreational skiers, young and old.[3] Enjoyment, healthy lifestyle and inclusivity are the focal points of the club's mission and events.

Yet another example of this friluftsliv legacy is found at the Augustana Faculty of the University of Alberta. Located in Camrose, Augustana is the only university campus in Canada with Norwegian roots. It has a strong cross-country ski team and the only university biathlon team in Canada, and students who are new to cross-country skiing can take lessons through the physical education program.

In an attempt to convey the meaning of friluftsliv to an English language audience, (the Norwegian educator) Nils Faarlund emphasizes the joy associated with engagement with free nature.[4] This joy and feeling of well-being are not contingent on or primarily associated with sporting events, and indeed, a focus on enjoyment and inclusivity, rather than competitiveness, is the most striking trend in my discussions of friluftsliv and outdoor life with Norwegian immigrants. Though a few of my subjects were competitive skiers and ski jumpers in their day and are rightly proud of those accomplishments, most stress that competition is not the primary focus of their outdoor life and activities. In fact, a number who are still highly active people adamantly state that they are not particularly athletic or sporty. Following are some of the responses I received when I asked the immigrants to define friluftsliv and to discuss its role in their lives:

> "To get out in the fresh air and do whatever activity you love best." (Verner Steinbru)
> "To enjoy being outside in fresh air." (Anne Marie Hazanoff)
> "The attitude that whatever you can do, you do outside. To appreciate the outdoors. The great enjoyment from being outdoors." (Olga Terning)

Knut Haga mentions his children when asked to define friluftsliv. Knut came to Canada at the age of fifteen to join his brother, and he later married a Canadian woman of Russian descent and started a family. Knut bought skis for all of his children, and they found a hill and regularly went cross-country skiing together in Calgary. In typical Norwegian style, they packed lunches and the focus of their trips was not distance or speed, but rather pleasure. Knut adamantly stresses that the purpose of these trips, as well as outdoor summer activities such as swimming at the lake, was to cultivate his children's' enjoyment of the outdoors, and he defines friluftsliv as "to get fresh air and enjoy nature…one of the healthiest things there is."

This final example, as well as the quote that heads this article, brings us to the issue of transmission. My interviews reveal that the passing down of a friluftsliv philosophy was seldom a conscious and never a controversial decision. Friluftsliv held and still holds positive connotations for these immigrants, and it was taken for granted that this should be passed down to children and grandchildren. Immigrants thought more about controversial issues such as language transmission – i.e. Should Norwegian or English be the home language? – than they did about friluftsliv. However, as immigrants reflect back on their lives, most realize they have prioritized this lifestyle and have tried to pass friluftsliv values down to their children. Those who see evidence of this enjoyment of the outdoors in the lives of their adult children, feel a sense of satisfaction. Olga Terning, for example, is proud of the fact that her four children all continue to enjoy the outdoors, and three of them still ski. Numerous other immigrants speak with pride of their children's' love of the outdoors, and cross-country skiing is often given special status and mention in these descriptions. Those who have noticed that their children have moved away from this lifestyle, on the other hand, view this as a loss, and at times as a failure on their part as parents or grandparents.

While the majority of immigrants are satisfied with the ways in which they have maintained their friluftsliv activities, not all were successful in doing so. These immigrants express feelings of loss and at times regret due to their inability to maintain the type of relationship to the outdoors in Canada that they had experienced in Norway. Kari Brittner, for example, could not maintain the walking, skiing and mountain trips that were part of her youth in Norway once she came to Canada. This was due to changes in her familial and work situation, as well as to changes in the physical landscape. She misses this and remembers her outdoor days in Norway with fondness. However, she has maintained the friluftsliv mentality for without this attitude she would not view this as a loss.

It is also interesting that a number of Norwegian immigrants who came to Canada as children and returned to Norway as adults became conscious of the friluftsliv philosophy that their parents had passed down to them only after these visits to their homeland. This awareness gave and continues to give them a sense of belonging in Norway, and they use it as a means of reconnecting with relatives and with the physical landscape. Solveig Ardiel, who emigrated from Norway at the age of six, returned for the first time to visit when she was twenty-one. This was a pivotal experience in her life, and she became aware that the connections she had with the outdoors were part of her Norwegian heritage. Recognition of this connection instilled in her a desire to consciously cultivate this in her

own life in Canada, and later to pass it down to her children. As the opening quote indicates, this is a story of a successful transplantation of the
friluftsliv philosophy. This example, as well as the others provided here,
demonstrates that not only did the Norwegian immigrants' attitudes
about the outdoors – their friluftsliv mentality – shape their new lives
and identities in Canada, but these attitudes also impacted and continue
to have a marked impact on the lives and identities of their families and
communities. The stories of these immigrants reveal the (lasting) power
of friluftsliv in their (everyday) lives.5

PART III

International

A Commentary on Wendell Berry's "A Walk Down Camp Branch"

Contribution by Tayler Knopf

Wendell Berry is a farmer near Port Royal, Kentucky and writer of many novels, poems, essays, and short stories. Mr. Berry's work stems from his belief that a person's work should be rooted in relationship with "place." As a person sensitive to the land on which he lives, his works have centered in the themes of healthy rural communities, appropriate technologies, sustainable agriculture, reverence, peacemaking, the interconnectedness of life, and good work. His writings aim to slow violence against others and the natural world, environmental destruction, ignorance, hubris, greed, and the industrialization of life. Mr. Berry was born in August of 1935. He is quoted as saying: "What I stand for is what I stand on."

The simple eloquence of Berry's words combined with his passionate belief in connection with place and landscape join almost seamlessly with this understanding of friluftsliv. In this particular selection, Berry speaks simply of how a particular path has become a part of him.

The dog runs ahead, prancing and looking back, knowing the way we are about to go. This is a walk well established with us – a route in our minds as well as on the ground. There is a sort of mystery in the establishment of these ways. Any time one crosses a given stretch of country with some frequency, no matter how wonderingly one begins, the tendency is always toward habit. By the third or fourth trip, without realizing it, one is following a fixed path, going the way one went before. After that, one may still wander, but only by deliberation, and when there is reason to hurry, or when the mind wanders rather that the feet, one returns to the old route. Familiarity has begun. One has made a relationship with the landscape, and the form and the symbol and the enactment of the relationship is the path. These paths of mine are seldom worn on the ground. They are habits of mind, directions and turns. They are as personal as old shoes. My feet are comfortable in them.

Wendell Berry

CHAPTER 20

The Czech Outdoor Experience: Turistika and Connections to Friluftsliv

Andrew Martin, Ivana Turčová & Jan Neuman

The purpose of this chapter is to offer an overview of the Czech outdoor experience providing details of the indigenous Czech approach involving the concept of "turistika" activities. The turistika approach of Czech origin has some parallels and connections with Scandinavian friluftsliv. One example is the influence of Norwegian adventurer, Fridtjof Nansen (1861–1930) on the Czech skiing movement.[1] Included are descriptions of outdoor education development involving the Sokol (physical education movement) and Turistický organizations from the middle of the 19th century, and then more formal stays in nature and informal tramping and outdoor life. As well, the 20th century origins of the Junák (Scouting) and Foglar movements and of schools in nature are traced.

Developments in experiential education programs since the Second World War, and more recently, are then described. These programs have been led by the Faculty of Physical Education and Sport at Charles University and by the Vacation School's methods of dramaturgy and experimenting in nature. Finally, more recent outdoor changes, since the Velvet Revolution of 1989, are identifed.

Czech Outdoor History and the Development of Turistika Activities

Komenský (Comenius)

The Czech educator Komenský (Comenius,[2] 1592–1670) regarded in Europe as the "Teacher of Nations" wrote about outdoor experiences and games 400 years ago. He is revered in the Czech Republic and his work can be understood as a basis for the roots of establishing education through experience and prior knowledge – experiential education, and education in nature – outdoor education. Comenius was convinced that teaching and learning must be interconnected with experiences in nature and must be a preparation for life itself. He believed in educating the whole person, involving educating the mind, body and soul through experiences, using all the senses. Comenius also supported the use of games and play in achieving educational outcomes and believed in travelling as a means of completing youth education.

The following sections discuss the historical development, cultural differences, and context of outdoor terms within the Czech Republic, particularly the indigenous nature of turistika activities and its links to friluftsliv. When studying all these connections, it is important to consider that Czech outdoor history has been externally influenced by the country's geographical position in the centre of Europe.

The Sokol Movement and Turistický Club

The rapid development of the biggest physical education movement Sokol (founded in 1862) and the Turistický club (Klub českých turistů, KČT – the official title of the Club of Czech Tourists, founded in 1888) internally influenced outdoor education in Země koruny české (Czech lands[3]). Sokol organized trips to significant places in Czech history, which linked to an increasing nationalist movement, and a return to Czech culture and national self-conscience and identity during Austrian Habsburg rule (1740–1914) and German influence.[4] For example, the first day trip was organized in April 1862 to the top of the mountain Říp (an important mountain in Czech legends and history). Other trips outdoors were motivated by patriotism and the desire to learn about nature and its beauty. Gradually, different types of outdoor games and exercises were included into the trip programs along with walking and social pastimes.

At the beginning of the last century, British influence, linked to the scouting movement of Baden-Powell, spread across Western Europe and influenced Czech pioneers of outdoor activities. The majority of these activities were developed in physical education movements, sport corporations, the Turistický club and scouting organizations. An important turning point in forming Czech turistika was the year 1917, when J.S. Guth-Jarkovský (1861–1943) – founder of the Czech Olympic Committee, editor of the Turistický magazine *Časopis Turistů*, and head of the Turistický klub – published the book *Turistika-turistický katechismus*,[5] which due to its range of information about turistika has not yet been superseded in Czech literature.

Guth-Jarkovský made the first attempt to define the term turistika – travelling for fun with the aim of learning about nature and its beauty. Turistika has the basics of sport, but it differs in that it is mainly about aesthetic and educational experiences. The original form of turistika was on foot (walking, hiking). More recent forms of turistika use movement for learning about nature, for example airplanes, trains, cars but predominantly bicycles, canoes, boats and skies. According to Guth-Jarkovský, scouting, focusing on movement and stays within nature connected with camping, can also be included as turistika, along with the combining of activities that use different means of transport. Mountaineering and easy forms of climbing also belong to turistika. However, travelling is a part of turistika only in the case when its primary goal is learning and the experience involves an aesthetic perception of nature.

Stays in Nature

Stays in nature in the Czech context are historically related to the Sokol movement, to camping and also to outdoor activities. Going outdoors and undertaking physical activities was a framework for bringing a group of fellow nationalists together effectively. Initially, the Turistický club was instrumental in developing a range of previously traditional turistika activities, which included active movement (travelling on foot or by bike, skis, and canoe), outdoor and cultural activities (learning about nature, local history and sights, theatre, and life of local people). By the end of the 19th century, due to British and German influence, there was also a rapid development of outdoor sports, especially rowing, water sports, skiing and cycling, which further influenced the separation of sports from turistika activities, and newer types started to be formed – on bikes, canoes, skies and winter turistika.

Interestingly, until recently many authors have translated turistika as "tourism" despite its specific Czech context.[6] While tourism definitions do involve travelling and movement away from local environments, turistika activities can be divided into several types, according to what means of active transport is used – on foot, by bike, skis or canoe. The difficulty in translating turistika is that it begins the process of diluting something that is particularly culturally unique and specific to the Czech context and environment.[7]

Tramping

A particular Czech historical and cultural phenomenon, inspired by the German romantic youth movement Wandervogel, British scouting, American Woodcraft and the American culture of the Wild West, also involved many young people informally going tramping (camping or hiking) on weekends. Tramping as a movement fulfilled the demands of young people for a life of freedom in natural surroundings. It was also a protest of young people against the middle-class way of life in towns and against political hypocrisy. Tramping can be, in this respect, considered as a spontaneous way of coping with new society rules and restrictions. Tramps (those who go tramping) developed their own culture, their

own slang, songs, clothes, flag, anthem, rituals, magazines, literature, sports (especially canoeing, kayaking) and small settlements (cottage colonies). These special settlements with wooden cabins and simple places for camping with a campfire were built in beautiful natural environments especially near rivers around Prague and other bigger towns.

Activities were adapted to the specific conditions of the country. It developed further the creation of an indigenous Czech culture of turistika activities that combine outdoor sports and activities such as camping with music and artistic creativity with social entertainment. Successful companies, such as the Bat'a shoe factory, also organized these activities with groups of young workers to improve teambuilding. Emil Zátopek started and developed his athletic career to Olympic gold, as one of Bat'a's young men. Tramping traditions are still alive today; particularly unique is the popularity of the many tramping songs.

Junák (Scouting) and Foglar Movements

The founder of the Czech-scouting organization, Junák, was the secondary schoolteacher, A.B. Svojsík, who visited England in 1911 to learn about a new type of youth education outdoors – scouting. He subsequently visited Norway, Sweden and Denmark. He decided to accept these new educational methods and adapt their publication and organizational rules to Czech conditions. From the beginning, Svojsík tried to connect scouting with Sokol's stays in nature, but he did not succeed and as a result founded Junák in 1912, as an independent organization. In Czech literature the term *výchova v přírodě* (outdoor education) is found in Czech translations of E.T. Seton's adventure books[8] (about the American Woodcraft movement) and was adopted in the 1920s by A.B. Svojsík.[9] Scouting summer camps involved children and young adults spending usually two to three weeks living in nature, playing games and learning outdoor skills.

In 1925 Jaroslav Foglar (1907–1999), experienced scouting leader, journalist, educator and writer, lead his first scouting camp by the river Sázava and another many other camps followed. Foglar helped create many special features of Czech scouting. He started to cooperate with the magazine *Mladý Hlasatel* (The *Young Herald* magazine for Scouts) in

1930, and in 1937 he founded reading clubs, which later became quite numerous. Foglar communicated through the magazine with 13,000 members. His stories were based upon his long-term work with children on summer camps. His reading club movement was very important for Czech scouting as it helped to spread these ideas even in the most rural areas of the country. In the same year, his famous book *Hoši od Bobří řeky*[10] (*Boys from the Beavers' River*) was published. The book was about boys forming friendships whilst exploring and having adventures in nature. It influenced a whole generation of young men, concerning their relationship to nature, camping, and overcoming barriers leading to their self-education. In 1938, Foglar also started his most famous cartoon serial "Rychlé šípy" ("Swift Arrows") in the *Mladý Hlasatel* magazine, which every child and adult in the Czech Republic knows. His educational methods were very progressive, but did not always correspond with traditional scouting, so Foglar often found himself in trouble with other scout leaders.

In the 1930s, Sokol focused on the development of stays in nature, which involved physical exercises in natural environments, such as walking trips, and camping and camps on the move – summer camps involving turistika activities usually moving from one campsite to another. A specific part of Sokol's stays in nature was also the use of the environment for developing basic movements (walking, running, jumping, climbing, carrying loads, overcoming barriers). These activities led to the building of artificial obstacles (leading to today's sport playgrounds and ropes courses) placed in the natural environment with groups overcoming these challenges in different ways, which served to improve the fitness and courage of young men and women. This trend was developed even under the increasing influence of German Fascism. Exercises and stays in nature in Sokol were methodically worked upon to a high standard even before the Second World War and criteria for awarding qualifications were established. Exams consisted of theory, professional knowledge (giving signals, orientation, knots, archery, grenade and boomerang throwing, camp works and constructions), learning about nature, camping, swimming, camping games, field physical education and first aid. Other requirements were doing public service and practising leadership skills in the camps.

Friluftsliv and Turistika

There is little first-hand evidence about the close connection of the Scandinavian friluftsliv philosophy and turistika activities in Czech literature; however, there is a variety of indirect evidence. Guth-Jarkovský admits in his book that Fridtjof Nansen should be included among those personalities whose ideas helped to create the basics of Czech turistika. This close connection is possible to find throughout the whole of Guth-Jarkovský's text. On many pages he emphasizes the importance turistika has devoted to learning, observing and protecting nature. He puts at the forefront aesthetic experiences and the possibilities of educational influence through nature. These are all features, which are also found as characteristics of friluftsliv and noted by Guth-Jarkovský as providing evidence of learning about the Norwegian way of outdoor life and practising turistika.

Friluftsliv and the Czech Skiing Movement

The Czech lands have a long tradition in skiing, which was influenced by Norway and the all-round Czech sportsman and enthusiast Josef Rössler-Ořovský. He first learnt about skiing in Norway from foreign journals and then tried to order ice-skates from Kristianie (today Oslo). The Norwegian company, Heyde & Gustafsson, sent him the prices of ice-skates and also skies, which the enthusiastic young sportsman ordered and received on January 5, 1887. He tried them in the following days on Wenceslav's Square in Prague and went on to found the first skiing club in Europe outside Scandinavia in 1887, the Czech Ski Club Prague. Josef Rössler Ořovský was also the founder of other modern outdoor sports, for example, Czech yacht and canoe clubs. In 1891 the translation of Nansen's book,[11] *The First Crossing of Greenland*, arrived in the Czech lands. This book had historical importance for the development of skiing not only in Czech lands but also throughout the whole of Europe.

Norwegian skiing also inspired the Czech aristocrat Earl Harrach, as he ordered several ski pairs for his woodsmen in Norway in 1892. Czech craftsmen adjusted the skies and then began to produce them according to the Norwegian pattern. By the end of the 19th century the rapid development of skiing began. Among the first foreign instructors to come to live in the Czech lands were Norwegians – for example, Hagbarth Steffens who improved the teaching of skiing and contributed to the increased interest in winter turistika. At the beginning of the 20th century skiing and much of sporting life were also influenced by the famous Norwegian sportsman Sigmund Ruud, who lived in Prague from 1928 to 1931, and led courses in ski jumping.

From the information above it is clear that the example of Nansen, Norwegian outdoor life (friluftsliv) and their skiing instructors influenced the rapid development of skiing in the Czech lands and helped to found the tradition of skiing popularity, which remains today.

Outdoor Development Since the Second World War

The development of outdoor sports and outdoor recreation was interrupted by both world wars, but quickly restored upon their conclusion. During the Second World War physical education, sport and scout organizations were dictated to by German occupation, resulting in many members of these organizations working for the resistance towards anti-fascist revolt. In 1945 many organizations, which existed before the war, started again, including the Turistický club, Sokol, Junák (scouting) and other physical education organizations; but that was not for long. The Czechoslovak communist regime took over power in 1948 and virtually kept all communication channels with the outside world closed for the next 40 years. Organizations such as the scout movement were banned. The Soviet influence began to spread throughout all spheres of life. At this point a forcible unification of sport and youth organizations took place and, in spite of the totalitarian approach, the democratic development of traditions, including tramping and scouts, was never completely restrained.[12] The very character of these activities opened the chance to resist the system and achieve "forbidden" goals – 'Walls have ears, but trees, rivers and mountains do not!' This unifying aspect has contributed throughout Czech history to the development of a unique involvement with the outdoors that is both active and passive, as a way of building self-esteem and attachment to the Czech nation and language, while often functioning under the influence of oppressive out-side regimes.

After the Second World War turistika and outdoor activities were incorporated into the school curriculum. Schools in nature provided opportunities for children living in big cities and polluted areas to live in nature for a week or two, studying normal lessons alongside outdoor activities and involving education about nature. Many schools also incor-porated ski trips, ski courses, hiking, summer courses and outdoor sports into their school related activities and curriculum. The intention was to change the school as a teaching institute into an institute of education.

It can be argued that physical education in schools has lost its holistic goal and focuses on physical fitness and skills.[13] However, outdoor edu-cation continues to follow the ideals of the Greek holistic philosophy of education, *kalokagathia,* which concentrates on activities involving mind, body and soul.

The Faculty of Physical Education and Sport at Charles University

A department of outdoor sports and outdoor education was started in 1953 at the first Physical Education Institute of Higher Education – the Faculty of Physical Education and Sport (FPES) at Charles University Prague.[14] The program was in many ways original, as it associated sport and turistika activities with group experiences, activities in natural envi-ronments and learning about the landscape. One of the main features of the program was the integrated approach to education. From the begin-ning it included sports, games, creative activities, and learning about nature. Development of these concepts was slowed down by the political normalization, as opinions (those which did not correspond with the socialistic views) were suppressed. However, within the Socialist Youth Union organization new experimental forms of outdoor education emerged, despite the tensions of the Communist regime.

It is of interest to note that the basic compulsory course "turistika and outdoor sports" at the FPES had activities called *cvičení v přírodě* (out-door exercises) for over 30 years, without the staff knowing that some of these activities were called "ropes courses" abroad. Besides ropes courses, the course includes various exercises done outdoors using just the resources of nature – activities like throwing stones, climbing trees, jumping across streams or crossing a stream on a tree.

For lecturers and students of FPES, Norway was an example of a country with a positive relationship with the natural environment, as well as an example of an excellent natural environment for sport. However, the first contacts with the Physical Education Faculty in Oslo happened during the political freedom of 1968 – 69. At the beginning of the 1970s many exchange opportunities between the Norway and Czechoslovakia faculties happened. Czech university specialists had the chance to become familiar with Norway's friluftsliv.

However, a more thorough understanding of friluftsliv happened after the Velvet Revolution of 1989 (the peaceful overthrow of the Czech Communist regime). Members of the outdoor sport department of FPES met with lecturers from the friluftsliv department of the PE (physical education) faculty in Oslo, and experts from both universities then organized an international seminar in Prague in 1994.[15] Two diploma theses covering the friluftsliv topic were also completed at FPES.[16] The environment for deeper exchange of experiences and knowledge was established and this has helped develop a better understanding of the turistika and friluftsliv philosophies.

Vacation School Lipnice

In 1977, with considerable support of educators and volunteers, Vacation School Lipnice (VSL) was founded (which then linked to Outward Bound in 1993). Both VSL and the FPES have their philosophical roots linked to *kalokagathia* and, through the combination of sport, turistika and creative activities, have been foremost in the development of outdoor education programs over the past 30 years. Their method of course design involves dramaturgy (from the sphere of theatre, film and TV) , a method used to plan, select and then order individual activities and other events with the goal of maximizing the final course effects. The key thing for all dramaturgy considerations is to determine and realize the pedagogical, educational, recreational and other aims that the course wants to reach.[17] Personal growth, connection to nature and cultural heritage may all to varying degrees have a central place in a dramaturgy course.

The Outdoors Since 1989

The Velvet Revolution in November 1989 changed the face of the whole Czech society. Since the fall of Communism, organizations have tried to reconnect their activities with Czech traditions that had flourished until 1948, and have also tried to pre-serve those positive elements that had appeared in the follow-ing 40 years. Tramping and cycling are still very popular, and many small informal groups spend weekends at campsites often working with forest admin-istration on various environ-mental projects. Groups of adults and families continue to maintain basic traditions at log-cabin sites with many people leaving the main cities at weekends and during holiday periods to spend time in forest cottages, experiencing traditions that are also still common in Canada and Norway. Many people also continue the traditions of mushroom and berry picking, along with playing games whilst walking in the many forests of the Czech Republic. Walking and cycling in the countryside is made easier by an extensive network of well-maintained and signed paths, which link forests, villages and towns. There are also a number of other institutions developing more formal outdoor education programs – schools, specialized ministry workplaces, civic youth organizations, environmental and commercial organizations.

Conclusion

Similarities between turistika and friluftsliv have been illustrated. The basic concept of Czech turistika outlined by Guth-Jarkovský, was influenced by Norway's Fridtjof Nansen. Due to friluftsliv influences, turistika stresses building connections through aesthetic experiences and nature's beauty. Norway's influence helped to develop sport and nature in the Czech lands especially skiing and ski turistika, which are favourite pastimes and have strong tradition even today amongst the citizens of the Czech Republic. Both concepts, turistika and friluftsliv, can also provide inspiration for other countries. We hope that this book, as well as our chapter, will encourage the interest of others for a deeper study of turistika and friluftsliv and the way they have evolved from the natural environments and cultures of both countries.

CHAPTER 21

FRILUFTSLIV AND AMERICA

David S. Gilligan

Jotunheimen, Norway, mid-June: The rumoured mountain landscape is mantled in thick, marbled clouds fresh off the seething North Sea, the ground blanketed by hard spring snow. But fresh, soft flakes precipitated out of the brooding clouds and stellar crystals crusted with rime from their passage float through the grey sky. We posthole up, wishing for skis, our minds set on the top of the Skagastolsdalen, trying to make little of the days-old avalanche wreckage at the bases of slopes on either side, and the snow falling with increased insistence. We should turn back and retreat to the lodge at Turtagro, a day's slog below. But I have an idea in my head that the dangers at hand seemed unable to obscure: to experience Norway from its top to its bottom, from the mountains to the sea, in less than a week's time. We continue upward.

There is something here in this elemental landscape that is hauntingly familiar to me, like a lost song on the wind from ages, dark and dim and mostly forgotten, yet deeply imprinted on my consciousness. Something that the landscape has yielded to its inhabitants, that its inhabitants have passed on down through time, and that somehow, hundreds of years later and thousands of miles distant, made its way into my childhood through books and stories and imaginings. The myths, the sagas, the folktales of the Norse somehow made it through countless land wars, the Christianization of Europe, the migrations and dispersals of peoples, the humanism of the Renaissance, the Industrial Revolution, even the confusion of the post-modern era. Some grain of truth these tales bear about the nature of the human plight still has relevance for us today, perhaps more now than ever. Some thread of knowing of the relationship between humankind and nature has woven its way through the years and continents that finds its source in the ancient worldview of the Norse. I am seeking the origins of that thread – the grain of such truth – in the landscape that bore such people, for it is often through understanding land, or nature, that one comes to understand culture.

Ice. Burning ice. Biting flame. According to Norse mythology that is how life began. From out of the unfathomable void of Ginnungagap, where the extremes of cold and heat met and mingled, the first life was born in the form of Ymir, the Giant, who in turn was followed by Audumla, the great-mother cow. In time, successive generations of Audumla's offspring birthed the three brothers, Odin, Vili, and Ve, who overthrew Ymir and made the world from his flesh, bones, and blood. But the gods withdrew from the circles of the world, and dwelt afar in Asgard, and left those of the earth to fend for themselves, to be rewarded if virtuous and courageous by a chance to fight in the Last Battle. Though the gods departed and only rarely walked the earth, their realm, and all realms, were linked by the central world-tree, Yggdrasill, whose health and vitality was reflective of that of the world.[1]

All this seems far-off and fantastic to the average person navigating the complexities of the modern world, but there are important truths to distill from these early tales that are essential elements of Norwegian nature philosophy. One of these truths is that wild, elemental nature is the birthplace of all things, even the creative forces (i.e. gods) of the world. The Norwegian landscape, with its glaciated mountains, deep-cut fjords, frothing waterfalls, barren tundra expanses and long, dark winters are constant reminders that nature is still, today, not something to conquer or subdue, but something to meet on its own terms with respect and even reverence. A second truth is that the world is free to evolve on its own, and we are free within its spheres, to make a life as we may. A third truth is that the fates of the world, the people in the world, and even the powers outside the world, are inextricably linked, and the health of each is dependant on and reflective of the others, as symbolized by the world-tree, Yggdrasil.

These central truths of nature as the home of culture, free citizenship and participation in nature, and the interconnectedness of all aspects of nature all comprise the philosophical foundation of Norwegian friluft-sliv, literally translated into English as "free-air life," or "free-air living." Friluftsliv was first used as a word by Norwegian icon Heinrik Ibsen, and was quickly adopted during the post-industrial romantic period of Norwegian nationalism as an essential part of Norwegian national identity.[2] National heroes such as Fridtjof Nansen insured that friluftsliv, as both a philosophy and practice, made it into the Norwegian mainstream by promoting it in the form of outdoor sporting life.[3] Decades after Norwegian independence, friluftsliv experienced a resurgence when Norway, long a frontier nation, made concerted efforts as a nation to industrialize. Largely in response to the industrialization efforts of the 1960s and 1970s, several prominent figures, Peter W. Zappfe, Arne Naess, Sigmund Kvaløy, Nils Faarlund, Børge Dahle, emerged as sort-of spokespeople for friluft-sliv, further defining the philosophies (sometimes in disagreement) of the notoriously indefinable concept of "free-air living."[4]

While the philosophical foundation of friluftsliv seems decipherable, its meaning and everyday usage are continually evolving.[5] Today, when I ask Norwegians how they define friluftsliv, the answers seem all over the place. When I consult my own friends in Norway, the answers are elusive, philosophically charged, and at times mystical. Friluftsliv is living in nature, with nature. Friluftsliv is going home. Friluftsliv is being one with the wind while plying the briny waters of the North Sea in a traditional wooden sailboat, drawing sustenance from the ocean and singing and laughing and being glad. These are my interpretations of the thoughts of Roar Moe, a long-time friluftsliv instructor for *Voss Folkehøgskole* (folk school), who now lives on the remote island of Little Faeroy, where he runs coastal friluftsliv programs, and Richard Lennox, British ex-patriot and former friluftsliv instructor for *Olavskulen Folkehøgskole*, who has sailed and kayaked the length of Norway even to Svalbard. Only one friend, Ivar Nordmo of Bergen, confronts what may be the reality of friluftsliv in our times. He tells me, convincingly, that friluftsliv means different things to different people. To some it means going for a walk in the Nordmark on a weekend. To others it happens on a snowmobile. Everyone seems to load it up with what definition serves them best. In one intense conversation with Ivar, Richard and my colleague Doug Hulmes (over beer and whisky at the Coastal Cultural Center harbour in Bergen), Rich held up his four-fingered hand (one finger lost in a mysterious sailing accident), looked at us with utmost intensity and said "Do not try to tell people what is and isn't friluftsliv!" To a shopkeeper in Bergen, friluftsliv is simply skiing. The newsstand sells a glitzy magazine – the equivalent of America's *Outside* magazine, called *Friluftsliv*. There are those who would consider the magazine blasphemy.

So what does friluftsliv, with its roots in nature, as the home of culture, free-citizenship and participation in nature, and the interconnectedness of things have to offer the world? In particular, what does it mean in a place like the USA, where modernity is the norm, where culture is almost wholly imported from other places, where wild land is set aside as museum pieces, where most people's sense of cultural identity extends no further than superstores and superbowls, or is stretched so far back to some distant place and past that it is difficult to make sense of?

If you look at a map and draw a line from Norway to the northeastern USA., then across the girth of North America to the west coast, you will take in Maine, the Midwest, the Intermountain West, and finally end up somewhere on the Pacific coast of California, Oregon or Washington. If you were to travel that line, you would leave a Europe where most of the inhabitants have co-evolved with the landscape over a period of thousands of years. In places such as western Norway or Scotland, culture and landscape have become so inseparable that the common North American concepts of what is natural and what is wild become blurry, until eventually the idea of a separation between nature and culture seems almost absurd. Landing in Maine, you would encounter a place where indigenous Americans lived for many thousands of years in a similar relationship with landscape, with noticeably less "impact" on the land, largely due to lower populations and more primal technologies.[6] But to think that the first Euro-Americans encountered wilderness on the far side of the North Atlantic is a fallacy. North America at the time of European contact was a cultural landscape, with forests burned and cleared for better hunting, rivers diverted for irrigation, cities, and a whole laundry list of extinctions since the first nomadic hunter-gatherers arrived some 10–15,000 years ago.[7] Today the landscape in Maine, particularly the rural landscape, may still be a cultural one. Euro-Americans arrived there well before the industrial revolution, after which it became increasingly possibly for people to live in a place and derive no sustenance from it. Nearly four hundred years of occupation has allowed for a certain degree of co-evolution between culture and landscape, especially prior to the mid-19th century. Farmhouses made of local timber are a common sight. Lobster and other seafood are still the food of choice on the coasts. There are folk legends with their origins in the same place they are told. People have accents and are generally proud of where they are from. The urge to buy into mainstream American modernism is not felt so acutely as in other regions of the USA. The distinction between nature and culture, wilderness and civilization, is still a bit blurry.

Travel west. Take in the industrial centres of the Midwest, the steel towns, then the orderly farms of the heartland, the great vale of the Mississippi. Here is the centre of the most developed nation of the world, and aside from a few woodlots and state parks here and there, the landscape is almost wholly given over to the plough or bulldozer. Yet still aspects of tradition survive. The Midwest too has been settled by Euro-Americans for a few hundred years, barely long enough for cultural traditions to begin to reflect the landscape from which they were born, barely long enough for a people to become native to land.

Keep going west, up and over the relief of the Rocky Mountains, and the scene seems to shift. The arid lands here remained relatively uninhabited by Euro-Americans (with the notable exception of trappers and explorers, first, and military outposts, second) until after the industrial revolution. When people came in great numbers, the railroad insured them resources from afar, thus the culture that emerged was estranged from the land it was built upon, and to this day we are but a veneer pasted onto the landscape of the American West, with little cultural roots in the thin soil. The trend continues west to the coast, where the veneer is in many ways the thinnest and most recent, the most foreign to the land it covers up. There in California, at the edge of the western world, you might find prominent Buddhist, ecologist, poet, and essayist Gary Snyder who, from his Japanese-style farmhouse in the foothills of the Sierra Nevada, would tell you that it takes a minimum of three-hundred years of habitation for a people to become native to a landscape.[8] There seems to be deep wisdom in this statement, though I would emphasize participatory habitation. If a culture derives its resources from elsewhere it may never develop a co-evolutionary relationship with the land it is built upon.

There is hope. Along the way west you would also pick up the philosophical messages of such individuals as Henry David Thoreau, John Muir and Aldo Leopold. Among these three figures a uniquely American philosophy of nature emerged, which though widely misunderstood by mainstream American culture, still contributes to the shaping of the American worldview. How do these philosophies agree with or disagree with the philosophical underpinnings of friluftsliv? Does friluftsliv have anything to offer us here in the USA?

Not surprisingly, the first of our three American nature philosophers, Henry David Thoreau, emerged as a voice during the romantic period, around the time when Ibsen was first coining friluftsliv. Thoreau's philosophies, like friluftsliv, may be viewed largely as a response to industrialization and increasing modernity in the world. It is not surprising, then, that the thoughts of Thoreau are in essence the same as those of friluftsliv philosophy. Thoreau, who eventually found genius all his own, was first a prodigy of Ralph Waldo Emerson. Thoreau grew up in Concord, Massachusetts, and spent the majority of his life there, with the notable exception of several sojourns to the north woods of Maine, which at the time was relatively wild and inhabited only by small numbers of the Penobscot and Mi'kmaw First Nations. Thoreau's philosophies, though widely ranging, can perhaps best be summarized in two of his most famous quotes. The first, written in explanation of Thoreau's Walden living experiment, reads as follows: "I went to the woods because I wished to live deliberately, to front only the essential facts of life, and see if I could not learn what it had to teach, and not, when I came to die, discover that I had not lived."[9] Here, Thoreau, like Ibsen and Nansen after him, looks to nature to find the essence and meaning of life. He goes there because he wishes to live deliberately, which is to say intentionally, or on purpose, rather than be swept away by the mediocrity and unintentionality of the modern world. Thoreau seemed to say that mindfulness is best attained in less-developed settings, and best maintained by a simple, participatory life in such settings.

Thoreau's second big message to the world came some years later, in a public speech he made in Concord, which was later published as the essay "Walking." Here, Thoreau says, first, "I wish to speak a word for nature, for absolute freedom and wildness, as contrasted with a freedom and culture merely civil, – to regard man as an inhabitant, or a part in parcel of nature, rather than society."[10] Shortly after, Thoreau refers to wilderness as "the raw material of life,"[11] and in a lyrical exposition on the qualities and necessity of wildness, concludes, "in wildness is the preservation of the world."[12] While it may seem that the idea of a dichotomy between "wild" land and "civilized" land flies in the face of the friluftsliv idea that nature is the home of culture, a closer look into Thoreau's words reveals that his ideas were not at all inconsistent with those of friluftsliv. Thoreau writes of wildness as a quality that all things may have, and wilderness as the place where wildness resides. Wilderness, as the "raw material of life" is essential for life, and further, wildness is essential for wilderness. In wildness, then, is the preservation of the world. Similarly, in friluftsliv philosophy, nature is essential for culture, and without nature culture cannot exist, or will wander homelessly (as perhaps aspects of modern culture are doing today). In both cases, life and culture precipitates from elemental nature ("wilderness" according to Thoreau; "nature" according to friluftsliv philosophy). Thoreau further explains that it is not just elemental nature ("wilderness"), but the quality within elemental nature that is essential for the well-being or preservation, of the world.

Following in the footsteps of Thoreau, and making many of his own as well, was the romantic, mystical nature philosopher, intrepid explorer and political activist, Scottish-born John Muir. While perhaps not as far ranging in his philosophies as Thoreau (who also pioneered philosophies of racial equality and civil disobedience that later influenced individuals such as Gandhi and Dr. Martin Luther King), Muir was certainly more single-minded. In his famous quote, "Climb the mountains and get their good tidings. Nature's peace will flow into you as sunshine flows into trees. The winds will blow their own freshness into you, and the storms their energy, while cares will drop off like autumn leaves,"[13] Muir clearly echoes the romantic thoughts of Ibsen and Nansen. After over a decade of exploration in the then remote California Sierra Nevada, Muir turned his attention towards advocating for the establishment of National Parks. Like Thoreau before him, Muir saw what sudden industrialization could mean for relatively undeveloped North America, and he saw preservation of land as a solution to the imminent problem. But Muir also argued eloquently for the inherent value of nature for its own sake, not just for utilitarian use by humankind.[14] This aspect of Muir's philosophy seems contradictory to the idea that nature is the home of culture, and may represent an important contribution to a uniquely American philosophy of nature. If nature has inherent value and should be preserved for its own sake, what role do humans have in nature? Are we still "a part in parcel" as Thoreau argued, or are we separate? If, as later congressional legislation passed in the Wilderness Act of 1964, "man is a visitor who does not remain," then nature seems to cease to be the home of culture, and culture is rendered homeless by being severed from its roots. Muir, however, did advocate for regular visits and interactions with reserved land, and later went on to form the Sierra Club, who's chief goals were advocacy for preservation and organizing trips into the mountains in hopes of maintaining a relationship between culture and nature.

Aldo Leopold, the third and last American nature philosopher I will discuss, grew up in a different era than did Thoreau and Muir. By the time Leopold had reached adulthood, America had seen the effects of the industrial revolution, and most of the landscape had been developed to some degree. Leopold lamented the "world of wounds" he came to know throughout his life, and as the last wolves and grizzlies of the lower 48 were backed into narrow corners and the blank spaces on the map were all filled in, Leopold wrote with blunt clarity of the need for a land ethic where the role of humankind was changed "from conqueror of the land community to plain member and citizen of it."[15] America had emerged from the First World War as one of the most powerful nations in the world, and this was widely felt on the landscape as economic interests overshadowed any semblance of ecological interests. Leopold called it as he saw it when he said, "a system of conservation based solely on economic self-interest is hopelessly lopsided. It tends to ignore, thus eventually eliminate, many elements in the land community that lack commercial value, but that are (as far as we know) essential to its healthy functioning."[16] In short, in an effort to industrialize and gain prominence in the global economy (which we succeeded in doing by the time of Leopold's death, despite his efforts), we were cutting the life from under us. Nature, the home of culture, was wounded and dying. Wilderness, which Leopold regarded as "the raw material out of which man has hammered the artefact of civilization,"[17] was going extinct. Even then, in the 1940s, Leopold regarded civilization as an "artefact," as if its continual renewal (based on the availability of nature, or wilderness, as a raw material) had been a thing of the past for many, many years. In another passage, Leopold lamented the increasing gap between culture and nature when he said, "Your true modern is separated from the land by many middlemen, and by innumerable physical gadgets … if crops could be raised by hydroponics instead of farming, it would suit him quite well. Synthetic substitutes for wood, leather, wool, and other natural materials suit him better than the originals. In short, the land is something he has 'outgrown.'"[18] Interestingly, while Leopold lamented the seeming separation of nature and culture, he, like Muir before him, advocated for a new non-utilitarian concept of conservation and the preservation of what was left of America's undeveloped land.

Perhaps both Leopold and Muir foresaw what was to come. Today the United States is home to some 300 million people, not counting the hundreds of thousands of migrant workers that don't make the census. That said, each American also has twice the environmental impact as someone from Sweden, three times that of someone from Italy, thirteen times that of someone from Brazil, thirty-five times that of someone from India, 140 times that of someone from Bangladesh or Kenya, and 280 times that of someone from Chad, Haiti, Nepal or Rwanda.[19] With such an appetite for resources, if not for the efforts of such individuals as Muir and Leopold, what little is left of our undeveloped nature would have long since been subdued, ploughed, built up or paved over. The dominant American cultural identity has been in place for some two, maybe three hundred years, and centres around economic status, a high standard of living, and, as ever, being the land of opportunity. What does a country like ours have to learn from a small, semi-arctic strip of mountains and dissected coastline on the fringe of Europe?

Norway, in contrast to the United States, has a population of four million. Its population density is one third that of the USA.[20] Norwegians claim the highest standard of living on the planet, due in part to their rich oil reserves in the North Sea. The landscape is partially subdued but largely undeveloped, and undeniably rugged. The dominant Norwegian cultural identity has been in place for many hundreds of years (if not thousands), and centres around political and economic independence, cultural heritage, and notably, friluftsliv.

Does the apparent disparity between these two countries render the philosophies of friluftsliv irrelevant for the American culture? Certainly not! Friluftsliv rather offers a glimmer of hope for modern America.

First, it encourages us to explore our own cultural roots, far back in time and miles as they may be, and seek to understand how we did in fact co-evolve with the landscapes from which we came. For Euro-Americans, this means the landscapes of Scandinavia, Ireland, the British Isles and the Continent – all-rich with myth and history that is essential to our understanding of culture, place and displaced culture. For African Americans, Latin Americans, Asian Americans and Native Americans it means the same: an intentional look into our roots and our ancestral indigenous relationship with landscape. Second, friluftsliv encourages us to recognize and explore the indigenous cultures that lived and still live in the lands that we may occupy. This is very different for Americans than it is for Norwegians, who themselves, along with the Saami, are indigenous to their own land. For Americans, this means the Native American cultures specific to our bioregion: in Maine the Mi'kmaw, Passamaquadi and Penobscot; in California the Piute, Shoshone, Maidu, and Miwok. Third, friluftsliv encourages us to develop a sense of home in our own place, to live in a participatory relationship with the land, to recognize nature as the home of culture and to actively pursue and indigenous connection. What is an indigenous connection? To be indigenous means to have a mythology that is rooted in the place where you live.

Snow falls on the mountains of Jotunheimen for the next two days, urging us to shelter in the DNT hut at the head of the Skagastolsdalen. After innumerable card games and the last drops of single malt, we clean and organize the entire hut several times over while the snow falls. We shovel out the windows to let the light in. We split kindling and stack it perfectly to dry on the stovetop. We dig a snow pit outside and find an obvious weak layer in the snow, meaning avalanche danger is potentially high and our best bet is to wait it out and let the snow settle. Even after just two days I can start to see why every wood surface on the inside of older Norwegian houses is carved with intricate designs, why the sweaters are so perfectly knit, where the time comes from that allows for the obvious emphasis on detail and quality. I can start to see under what conditions a creation story like that of the Old Norse came about. I can start to understand the long winters that allowed for the appearance of trolls and giants, and folk heroes such as Askeladden (Ash-Lad). With

Askeladden in mind, we decide that when the weather clears we will continue our journey into the interior. The Fates of old seem to have woven
our threads that way, for better or for worse.

According to the Norse tradition, at the end of all things, when the
world tree Yggdrasil withers and approaches death, the gods and men
join together to do battle with the evil giants in the Last Battle of Rag-
narok. In this battle all things that were pass away. All who enter into the
fray do so with the foreknowledge of doom, but fight with courage
nonetheless in the face of death and change. When the ashes settle and all
the gods and giants have left the circles of the world, when all seems
utterly hopeless and in ruin, a man and a woman, long hidden in the
heart of the world tree, emerge from within Yggdrasil, and through them
the world is renewed.

The philosophical tenets of friluftsliv include nature as the home of
culture, free citizenship and participation in nature, the interconnectedness of all aspects of nature, and I would add the courage to persevere in
the face of uncertainty. These tenets both compliment and revitalize
American nature philosophy, and may guide us towards a participatory,
rooted relationship between nature and culture. The myths of old may be
more relevant to us than ever before. Like the Norse gods Odin and Thor,
Frigg and Freya, we live according to our philosophical dictates in spite
of the fact that there may be no promise of return, with the hope that
when the ashes settle, the world again will be renewed.

CHAPTER 22

FROM TOMTE WISDOM TO FRILUFTSLIV: SCANDINAVIAN PERSPECTIVES OF NATURE

Douglas Hulmes

My mother would carefully place the "tomte" on the shelves of our living room bookcase every December about a week before Christmas, along with miniature goats made of straw, and sheaths of grain that she said were for the birds who were in search of food during the snowy months of winter. The tomte were the little people or elves of my Swedish ancestors' culture, and they brought a sense of humour and delight to the darkening days of winter, as well as a reminder of how we must treat each other and nature with respect. If we didn't care for nature's creatures, the tomte might play nasty tricks on us.[1]

From these early childhood memories of my Scandinavian heritage, I developed an interest for learning more about the folklore and mythology of the Nordic people and their relationship to nature. As an environmental educator, I have come to appreciate the values of stories to teach lessons and draw analogies. This form of cultural wisdom, shared through stories, fables and myths, forms the basis of awareness toward the good as well as the bad or dangerous aspects of nature. Academia refers to our "mythopoetic" connections to nature; the sources of wisdom that form a sense of moral and ethical relationship to the natural world as well as our relationships to one another.² Much of this wisdom is rapidly being lost by the homogenizing process of modern American culture.

For a variety of reasons, many of our grandparents and great-grandparents who came to this country as immigrants felt an obligation to refrain from speaking their mother tongues, and were also led to believe that folk beliefs and traditions had no relevance in their newly adopted homeland. Others left their homelands due to unfortunate circumstances and rejected these traditions as reminders of a dark past. Probably an even greater factor was the influence of religion and science that relegated these beliefs and traditions to the level of antiquated fairy tales. They were also found to be somehow contrary to the teachings of Christianity and the objectification of nature through science.

My initial introduction to the Swedish tomte eventually fuelled a lifelong fascination with my Scandinavian heritage, including the history, mythology, folklore, and traditions that I felt was entirely missing from my formal education. The journey I have taken in recovering my cultural heritage eventually led me to a Norwegian word, friluftsliv, a concept that bridges the mythopoetic folklore of Scandinavia with a way of being with nature that invokes a sense of wonder, respect and joy in being present and at home in nature. The direct translation of friluftsliv means, "free-air life." My perspectives of friluftsliv are still developing, and my hope is that this essay will trigger an understanding and desire to explore its application to the American relationship to, and use of, nature.

The Search Begins

My academic journey first led me to major in environmental sciences. After completing a rigorous undergraduate degree based in geology and ecology, I found myself searching for a deeper philosophical and spiritual connection with nature that was not fully satisfied by scientific understanding.

I continued to be drawn back to my childhood connection with nature that also included an emotional and mystical connection through, in part, the myths and folklore that I was fortunate to have been given as a child. I wanted to personally experience my cultural heritage, the landscape through which it was formed, and possibly gain more of the wisdom that I felt must be still available.

I looked for an opportunity to work and teach in a Scandinavian country. A student of mine, who had attended the *Voss Folkehøgskole* (folk high school) in Voss, Norway, suggested that I might find a suitable position in this unique Scandinavian educational system. In 1991, I took a six-month sabbatical from my job as a Professor of Environmental Studies at Prescott College in Arizona, and taught in a Friluftsliv program at *Olavskulen Folkehøgskole* (folk school) on the island of Bømlo off the west coast of Norway.

While my formal academic training is in the environmental sciences and environmental education, working at Prescott College has also encouraged me to incorporate elements of Experiential and Adventure Education into my teaching. Teaching at the Friluftsliv program in Norway allowed me to introduce elements of environmental education, ecology, natural history, and environmental ethics as my contribution to the Folkehøgskole's program in sea kayaking in traditional Greenland Eskimo boats, sailing traditional Norwegian wooden boats, climbing and mountaineering.

Since this experience, I have returned to Norway several times, with classes of Prescott College students. The first course, that I taught in the summer of 1994 entitled, "Explorations of Norway from Sea to Icecap," resulted in a series of newspaper articles written by local reporters that traced our ten-day segment of sailing a replica of a Viking ship up the Hardangerfjord. We became known as "the American Vikings in Norway."

After the class was completed, I visited Telemark College where I had heard about a new program called, "Norwegian Nature and Culture." This year-long program was designed to teach international students about the Norwegian culture and its historical relationship to nature. It was a perfect match! I met the director of the program, and she had already heard about my class (Norway has only 4.5 million people, so news travels fast!) I was invited to teach in the program, and in 1996–97, I returned to Norway as a guest professor at Telemark College, with Norway's first interdisciplinary environmental studies program.

The Telemark District, in the mountainous countryside, is one of the traditional cultural gems of Norway. I spent a wonderful year there teaching and studying Norwegian roots of culture and the landscape that has dramatically influenced the people's character, mythology, folklore, language and perspectives towards nature.

Through these experiences I have come to embrace the Norwegian concept of friluftsliv as a means of communicating many intangible ideas that form my deep love and connectedness to nature. The term bridges the mythopoetic folklore of my ancestors with the natural sciences and environmental education theory that I have pursued in my professional life along with the joy I experience in nature. It is a term that I feel has tremendous value for Americans who are searching for a deeper relationship with the natural world than that provided by conventional opportunities and programs in Outdoor Recreation, Outdoor Education, and Adventure Education. My perspectives of friluftsliv are still developing, but my hope is they will trigger further explorations and evaluations of our relationship to and use of nature. This concept beckons to Americans at a critical time in our history, to re-evaluate our relationship with nature from the Norwegian perspective.

A Comparison of Cultural Views toward Nature

The term friluftsliv is an idea that was created by the Norwegian author, Henrik Ibsen in his poem, "Paa Vidderne," (directly translated "On the Heights"), at the end of the 19th century:

> Well, then come!
> in wind and rainstorm,
> 'Cross the highland's rolling heather!
> He who wants may take the church road:
> I will not, for I am free!
> In the lonely seter-corner,

My abundant catch I take
There's a hearth, and a table,
And friluftsliv for my thoughts.[3]

With the introduction of this term, Norwegians adopted an expression that has been used to describe a cultural relationship to nature that has evolved with a people and the landscape that has formed their character. The Norwegian concept of frilufsliv is beautifully expressed in *Wisdom of the Open Air: The Norwegian Roots of Deep Ecology*, by Peter Reed and David Rothernberg. This book also explores related work by other Norwegian philosophers including Arne Naess, Nils Faarlund and Sigmand Kvaløy.

While it can be argued that friluftsliv is a romantic Nationalist creation, it also offers us a different cultural perspective that is needed at a time when the fundamental assumptions of Western culture are that nature is a commodity to be exploited. Outdoor recreation has often become one more way for humans to exploit nature. As one of the fastest growing industries in America, outdoor recreation and all the gear that equip us to enjoy out door pursuits, has for most Americans become a form of reward for our industrious, stress filled lives.

The English language and the culturally biased ways we have been taught to use nature has resulted in a dominant view that it is a commodity to be exploited and used primarily for consumptive purposes that benefit humans. We take for granted phrases like "natural resources," "real-estate," "vacant land," "resource management," "land use," "public lands," "private lands," and "no trespassing" without questioning the origins of the ideas they express. These cultural perspectives can be traced back to the roots of Western civilization. Plato argued that nature is transitory, where as the idea or concept of nature is truth, and Aristotle proposed that everything in nature has a purpose, and that purpose ultimately is for humans, the highest form of life. This anthropocentric and hierarchical form of thinking has profoundly influenced interpretation of Judeo/Christian thought, Western philosophy and science during the Age of Enlightenment, with the influence of Descartes, Newton, Bacon and others, a Cartesian, mechanistic reductionist view of the world was promoted. Man was seen as the only being with a soul and who was ordained by God to control nature through rational logic and science. Through the influence of this ideology, Adam Smith and John Locke, the shapers of Western economic thought, further determined that land and private property supported individual freedom and potential for obtaining wealth. Through the capitalist system, nature was relegated to the position of a commodity to be exploited for personal gain. As Max Oelschleager states, in *The Idea of Wilderness*, "Capitalism and democracy coalesced with machine technology to effect the conversion of nature into a standing reserve possessing market value only Modernism thus completes the intellectual divorce of humankind from nature."[4]

While some of the ideologies that promoted an ordained control of nature were disputed by artists, philosophers and writers during the Romantic and Transcendental Period, the Industrial Revolution overshadowed cultural perspectives that questioned these assumptions. Henry David Thoreau, argued throughout his book, *Walden,* of the importance of living a life of simplicity with nature, and questioned our culture's obsession for material wealth. He stated, with respect to nature, "a man is rich in proportion to the number of things which he can afford to let alone."[5] John Muir, who wrote, "the Universe would be incomplete without man, it would also be incomplete without the smallest transmicroscopic creature that dwells beyond our conceitful eyes and knowledge,"[6] promoted in contrast to the anthropocentric assumptions of Western civilization, a view of the intrinsic values of nature to exist for its own sake.

More recently, Aldo Leopold called for a "Land Ethic" in his book, *A Sand County Almanac*, "There is as yet no ethic dealing with man's relationship to land and to the animals and plants which grow upon it The land-relation is still strictly economic, entailing privileges but not obligations."[7] Rachel Carson, in her book, *Silent Spring,* called to question man's ability to control nature, arguing that "The 'control of nature' is a phrase conceived in arrogance, born of the Neanderthal age of biology and philosophy, when it was supposed that nature exists for the convenience of man."[8] Naturalist writer, Barry Lopez speaks to the mystery, wonder, and sacredness of connecting with nature in a way that I feel is represented in the essence of friluftsliv:

Whatever evaluation we finally make of a stretch of land, no matter how profound or accurate, we will find it inadequate. The land retains an identity of its own, and still deeper and more subtle than we can know. Our obligation toward it then becomes simple: to approach with an uncalculating mind, with an attitude of regard. To try to sense the range and variety of its expression – its weather and colours and animals. To intend from the beginning to preserve some of the mystery within it as a kind of wisdom to be experienced, not questioned. And to be alert for its openings, for that moment when something sacred reveals itself within the mundane, and you know the land knows you are there.[9]

Despite the wisdom of some of America's greatest philosophers, naturalists, and scientists, America has remained focused on an anthropocentric view of nature that is a commodity for exploitation, and that should be controlled exclusively for the benefit of humans.

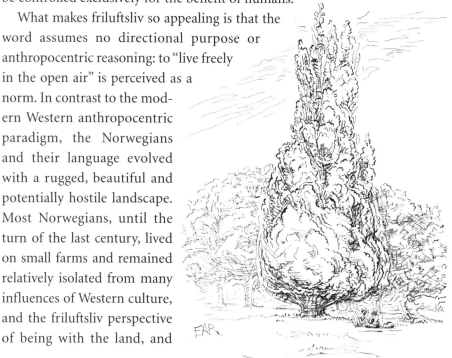

What makes friluftsliv so appealing is that the word assumes no directional purpose or anthropocentric reasoning: to "live freely in the open air" is perceived as a norm. In contrast to the modern Western anthropocentric paradigm, the Norwegians and their language evolved with a rugged, beautiful and potentially hostile landscape. Most Norwegians, until the turn of the last century, lived on small farms and remained relatively isolated from many influences of Western culture, and the friluftsliv perspective of being with the land, and being home in nature reflects many Norwegian qualities of independence, self-reliance, confidence and humility.

Norwegian culture is a product of nature and landscape; Norwegian people are largely independent and pragmatic towards the use of nature even as they are humbled by their lack of control over it. They know that, while one could alter nature, ultimately, one also needs to respect nature and through wisdom and *fornuft* (common sense), one was always at home in nature. In contrast, American ideas of outdoor recreation have tended to reflect more of an imperialistic and capitalistic view of nature with a goal to overcome or conquer it.

Friluftsliv from an American Perspective

I find it challenging and enjoyable to investigate the idea of friluftsliv from an American perspective. I have had an opportunity to explore this concept from a different culture and language and have given myself the freedom of interpretation that is not as possible within the confines of my native English language and predominantly American way of thinking.

I have seen and experienced, through my Norwegian friends, varied examples of friluftsliv. One friend lives on a traditional farm in a forest setting in the mountains near Tynset, where the farm has been handed down within the same family for generations. Another friend lives on an island off the west coast and has built his own log house with a sod roof in the traditional manner, using materials from the land. Yet another friend lives in Bergen next to preserved natural open space, and enjoys opportunities to experience what I would call urban friluftsliv. He has also kayaked the entire Norwegian coastline over a period of 17 years, and has definitely experienced friluftsliv from a grand and more traditionally understood interpretation. My final example is of a friend, who was a student of Nils Faarlund in the early 1990s. Nils Faarlund is a prominent Norwegian friluftsliv *vegleder* (leader of the way) and proponent of living a simple life close to nature. As a result, my friend changed his academic direction from physical education to friluftsliv, and has chosen to live out his philosophy at a traditional *husmannsplass* (tenant farm) situated on a small island on the west coast near the mouth of Sognafjord. He utilizes traditional wooden boats, keeps a flock of sheep descended from the Viking period, and has created a centre for people to come, learn and experience coastal friluftsliv.

Each of these Norwegians know their land intimately and to varying degrees live, recreate and feed both their souls and bodies from the land and the sea. Even in the urban setting, there are wild blueberries to be picked while exploring the nearby forest, and *pinnsviner* (hedgehogs) to be accountable to while on evening saunters. With many of my Norwegian friends, I have felt a sense of belonging to a place that is too frequently missing in the American culture. One friend explained, that for her, friluftsliv could be skiing in the mountains that ring her home near Mulde, or it could be a simple walk to the coast with her mother to light a fire and talk.

I have come to feel the presence of the *nisse* (Norwegian equivalent of the Swedish tomte) and trolls that live by my Norwegian friend's home in Bergen. Mystery and wonder still exists in a small-protected woodland, not only for the children, but also admittedly for the adults who live there, and still find magic in an evening saunter through the woods and bogs. I felt my friend's magical sense of belonging to a place and knowing it well enough to be neighbours with the forest and creatures who dwell there. To be at home in nature, where you live, and to know that you belong is an essence of friluftsliv that I have come to discover to be a common quality with my friends in Norway. As the Norwegian poet describes in his poem, "Snow and Fir Forests":

> Talk of what home is – snow and fir forests are home.
> From the first moment they are ours,
> Before anyone has told us, that it is snow and fir forests that have
> a place in us – and since then it is there always, always.
>
> Come home, go in there bending branches
> – go on til you know what it means to belong.[10]

I realize that I and many of my American friends have similar feelings and experiences where we live, but the English language does not have a concept like friluftsliv that encapsulates these notions in a single beautiful word.

It takes time to know a place, just as it takes time to know a friend. To let the land share its stories and also know the stories that the people who have lived with a place, often for generations, is an ingredient of friluftsliv that is too often missing in the American culture. The stories of the Scandinavian nature spirits; like the nisse, huldra, noeken, trolls and Swedish tomte have been handed down through the generations and can be read in children's books like those by Salma Lagerlof, *The Wonderful Travels of Nils*,[11] or *Puttes' Adventure in the Blueberry Forest*, by Elsa Beskow.[12] These stories have attempted to capture the essence of magic and wonder that a people, who have lived with the land, feel with the places where they live, and through these stories, they keep the mystery of a place alive and real.

A special tradition that is shared by many Scandinavians is the planting or the knowing of a special *tuntre,* a sacred tree planted in the centre of the yard on a family farm that reflects an intimacy with a place.[13] The importance of caring for the tree is a moral reminder of caring for the farm or place where one lives. One Norwegian told me that the *tuntre* provided a direct connection with the nature spirits that lived underground at his farm.

The cultural traditions of connecting to the land in a mythopoetic way, provided people with a way to explain their feelings of connection with nature, and sense of mystery, wonder, and fear that they experienced living with the land. The stories also gave children moral and ethical guidance to their relationship with the land. Unfortunately, these have been largely lost to the descendants of Scandinavians living in America. I fear, with many of my Norwegian friends, that these perspective of being with nature and the place where they live are also in danger of being lost in Norway, as the younger generations of Norwegians are being seduced by the American culture, new technologies and urban attractions within their own modernized culture.

Friluftsliv is living simply and simply living. It is taking the time to appreciate where one is in the moment with nature. It is the journey, not the destination that is the goal friluftsliv offers a contrast to the typical American form of outdoor recreation, which has too often become an extension of the fast pace adrenaline driven culture, where the outdoor pursuit satisfies a need for excitement, escape or even therapy for treating the ills of our society. Outdoor recreation has become an extension of American consumerism with the perceived need for the latest fad in gear and gadgetry to enhance the thrill of the outdoor experience. It has become a reward for working in an industrialized technological society, and is one more commodity to be purchased.

Current land management practices and the U.S. Congress endorse this form of recreation as another commodity to be consumed from a resource that requires management, and the move to require fees for an outdoor experience and access on to public lands is a striking contrast to the Norwegian concept of *allemannsretten* (every man's right), which complements the notion of friluftsliv in assuming that like the air that sustains all life, being with nature is a right that in most cases should not require a fee.

The opportunity of comparing and contrasting ideas of friluftsliv with English and American ideas of Outdoor Education, Outdoor Recreation, Adventure Education and Environmental Education intrigues me from an academic perspective. I have come to appreciate the spectrum of definitions and attempts of establishing clear limits to these definitions. I also find it interesting to dissect the words and consider their Anglo/Saxon and Nordic roots. The English breakdown of outdoor education creates the understanding that it is learning that occurs beyond the door, or place where you live, while in contrast, friluftsliv, free air life, conjures the notion that there is not a separation from where you live and being in nature – you are at home in nature.

Aside from the distant and sterile aspects of the English language that describes our options of being in or with nature, there seems to be a rather anthropocentric bias to many of the English options. Within the spectrum of definitions used to describe Outdoor Education is the idea that it involves the learning of any subject in an outdoor setting ranging from the arts and sciences to outdoor recreational sports. The British-influenced Outward Bound perspective of Outdoor Education involves the learning of skills that are needed for outdoor pursuits such as rock climbing, skiing or kayaking.

Outdoor Recreation includes a spectrum of pursuits that ranges from organized team or individual sports to more leisure activities such as hiking. Adventure Education assumes that an unknown outcome is part of the plan. And finally, Environmental Education involves a combination of goals and objectives that teaches students ecological concepts and ethical relationships to and responsibility for living sustainably with nature. Recently, "Place-based" Education has been used in lieu of Environmental Education, and emphasizes the importance of knowing specific geographical areas from ecological and cultural perspectives.

Is the Idea of Friluftsliv Unique to Norwegians?

The nuances and feelings I have experienced and described while being in Norway are not unique to friluftsliv or certainly experienced only by Norwegians I have experienced many of these feelings long before I knew of the Norwegian expression, and I am certainly a "product" of the American culture. I, like many of my American naturalist heroes and heroines including Henry David Thoreau, John Muir, Aldo Leopold, Rachel Carson and Barry Lopez, have a deep connection to the land and nature. From my perspective, these writers are some of the most eloquent and passionate spokespersons for that connection.

What I find to be challenging and offensive of the American culture is the language and obsession with the consumer mindset that dominates media and language to the point where I unconsciously refer to myself s a "consumer" or "product" of the American culture. The use of these words seems to be a form of cultural brainwashing that can be clearly observed in everything ranging from our way of viewing land and the commodification of nature, to the way we view outdoor recreation.

The recent publication of *National Geographic's* "Explore" provides a good example of our culture's acceptance of the selling of nature. Our attraction to being in nature is coloured by a mindset that has influenced the language we use to describe our experiences We use words like "extreme," "sport," "adventure," "thrill," "adrenaline rush," and "shred" to describe the ultimate outdoor experience. These experiences often require purchasing the latest equipment that are the "cutting edge."

I find myself resistant to keeping up with the latest fads and technologies. I guess that is where I have found a sense of closer identity with my friends in Norway, the Norwegian language and word friluftsliv, which supports my need to experience nature, landscape and life in a more basic way: to simply enjoy being in a place, getting to know the people and culture in a more genuine way. I feel a need to take the time and patience to discover the profound truths of being that cannot be rushed, should not be simply purchased, and allow for the mystery and wonder to appear, often when doing the simple tasks of living and being in a place where I can be absorbed in and with nature.

To comprehend the magnitude of our cultural attitudes towards nature, landscape, and in context, friluftsliv, we must trace our cultural roots as they relate to Western civilization. We must also consider what has been lost or is in danger of being lost from our cultural heritage that gives us a source of hope and potential for discovering or rediscovering our cultural roots with nature and the wisdom still available to us In response to these needs, I have designed a series of classes that traces history by considering evolving attitudes towards nature from Palaeolithic cultures to the present as related to mythical, philosophical, religious, scientific and literary perspectives. The anthropocentric attitudes we have developed towards nature have evolved through these disciplines and have influenced one another in ways that are not generally considered in our fragmented educational framework. It is critical to see and understand the assumptions our culture has made towards nature, and the implications this new understanding has for the fields of Environmental Education, Outdoor Education, Experiential Education and Adventure Education.

Concluding Thoughts

Sitting around a simple wooden table in a room lit with candles, the wind howling off the North Sea and buffeting the island of Litle Fearøy, four kindred spirits, one Norwegian, one Brit, and two Americans, talked softly into the night, sipping Scottish whisky. Our discussion drifted to the idea of friluftsliv and the value of living the simple life. Roar Moe's commitment runs deep in his Norwegian blood. He has been living in this cottage on Litle Faerøy; living the simple life of coastal friluftsliv for twelve years, and while tested by nature and loneliness, one can tell from the depths of his blue eyes that he has found his way home.

As my life unfolds, I reflect on my family, and friends who have become my family, and my need to feel at home in the place where I live. I have come to realize that home is in nature, with friends who share a vision of life that brings a return to simplicity, closeness to nature, the sharing of stories, the feeling of belonging and the knowing that we are part of a continuing cycle that is profound, beautiful, and at the same time frightening and perplexing. We do not and can not travel this journey alone, and finding kindred spirits who share a common understanding of the need for friluftsliv has been a remarkable gift that began with my mother placing the tomte on the book shelves of my home so many years ago.

CHAPTER 23

EXPERIENCE OF PLACE: LESSONS ON TEACHING CULTURAL ATTACHMENT TO PLACE

Brian Wattchow

For many outdoor and adventure educators in countries such as Canada, the U.S., the U.K., Australia and New Zealand, natural areas are often presented as ideal learning sites where participants can be challenged physically, mentally and emotionally. These learning places have become idealized educational terrains where, according to John Miles, "physical, mental, emotional, and spiritual faculties are all engaged" and "[a]ttention to one part of our being waxes and wanes, but there is connectedness, a continuum throughout the experience."[1] Miles went on to argue that the rare gift of teaching in these places carries an ethical responsibility:

> [the educator] must teach responsibly for nature and wild land values ... must help their clients learn the special lessons about nature and human nature which may be revealed in wild places, lessons which may help them back home to do their part to assure sustainability of nature and civilization.[2]

236   NATURE FIRST

However, educators often use universal terms such as "wilderness" and "nature" uncritically, taking for granted the heritage of ideas and values attached to these concepts. Why should some lessons only be available in the "wild." and how should that learning be "brought home"? Andrew Brookes has argued that such universalistic tendencies may be damaging to the prospects of an education that is more responsive to local places, traditions and practices, where what is taught is an outcome of a careful negotiation between people and place.[3] An education like the one outlined above by Miles, that continues to be unaware of the local complexities and particulars of place experiences, may even pose a threat to local places. The American ecological philosopher, Aldo Leopold, was warning over half a century ago that most outdoor experiences had become, "a self-destructive process of seeking but never quite finding, a major frustration of mechanized society."[4] He believed that the key to a more intimate relationship with nature lay in the development of genuine perception. Yet the most serious obstacle set in our path, according to Leopold, "is the fact that our educational and economic system is headed away from, rather than toward, and intense consciousness of the land."[5]

What then is "place," and how might it provide educational possibilities that move towards, rather than away from, an experience of cultural attachment to local places? According to Edward Relph, "[t]he word 'place' is best applied to those fragments of human environments where meanings, activities, and a specific landscape are all implicated and enfolded by each other."[6] Thus, it is precisely our experiences of a place, which exists in the tension between our sensing bodies and the cultural constructions that govern our interpretations of what a place might mean to us that stands to provide important lessons for education. In other words, we must apprentice ourselves to an experience of place, if place is to become our teacher.

The real challenge here is to consider what an education that is personally and

Ravbua

culturally responsive to a local place might look like in practice. My encounters with traditional Norwegian friluftsliv provide some thought provoking possibilities. Of course, considerable effort is required to reconsider what may be drawn from these encounters for our own contexts, and I will attempt to make some concluding statements later in this chapter that address this task. But first it is necessary to re-tell the stories of these experiences and draw the reader into those encounters with Norwegian people and places.

Traditional Friluftsliv: A Norwegian Education in Place

A few years ago I travelled and worked for a time in Norway and encountered friluftsliv in several forms. Norway has a wide range of natural environment, many of which remain ecologically healthy. It is a wealthy nation, though not heavily urbanized, that has maintained a strong sense of rural life. According to Arne Naess, "Norwegians walk, run, creep into nature to get rid of whatever represses them and contaminates the air … They don't talk about going out, but in and into nature."[7] Nils Faarlund has described several of the distinctive features of friluftsliv as a reliance upon the rhythms of nature, with roots in the in the European Deep Romantic Movement of the 19th century, and where nature becomes the site of human fulfillment.[8]

Modern outdoor recreation and tourism, as already described by Leopold, is considered a threat to traditional friluftsliv.[9] Indeed, much of what we might call outdoor recreation is considered profoundly different to friluftsliv. Børge Dahle outlines the key differences as follows:

> Outdoor activities are often motivated by pleasure in activities and social fellowship. Most forms of outdoor activities do not have a long tradition in Norwegian society. Often they are play and sports activities that are practiced in nature-orientated surroundings on the participant's premises. The activities are of a positive character for the individual and can be positive in a societal connection, but can be problematic from an ecological perspective.[10]

The international visitor to Norway might easily miss the rich meanings of friluftsliv as a form of cultural practice and education that is indeed a negotiation with local places, if their experience is confined to taking in the picturesque scenery and touring the many folk culture museums. Friluftsliv, as an active socialization to nature, must be lived intensely if the encounter is going to lead to meaningful comparisons with the visitor's home.

Encounter 1: Walking in the "Barnas Naturverden"

The *saelehuset* sits on a rib of ancient rock that runs as a shallow shelf across the flank of the hill. As I approach along an undulating yet gently rising trail, it merges and disappears into the countryside, then suddenly reappears, surprisingly close as I crest a little ridge. Its earth-covered roof, with grasses and flowers pulsing in the breeze, creates the impression that it is an extension of the hillside. It is a dwelling completely in and of its place. For some time the massive pine-log construction, six by twelve long paces around the perimeter, overwhelms my sense of the detail. Then I get up close, run my hands across its structure, and begin really looking at the building.

Despite the size of the logs I cannot find a single gap where a winter wind might penetrate. The door reaches only to my biceps and I have to stoop as I step across the foundation log that forms the base of the door frame. The door jam is lined with a layer of sheep's wool to keep out even the slightest flurry of winter snowflakes. After exploring the two rooms I sit on a low bench, leaning my back against the pine logs, and brew some tea. A shaft of sunlight enters through a small window. I hear the wind rush down the flank of the hillside, and curl around building. I feel the building resist its pressure. I hear the grasses growing on the sod roof lie down in the breeze. The *saelehuset* speaks: "I've been here forever. This is where I belong."

But am I deceived? For I already know that the dwelling is only a few years old and that it was constructed as part of a unique project to design an outdoor experience specifically for the children and people of Rennebu county that would embody the local landscape and culture. Yet there are no construction marks on the ground outside as the heavy logs were cut only a few kilometres away, lower on the mountain, and then dragged up here above the treeline over the winter snows, and left here for the actual building to begin in the summer. The design was extensively researched to reproduce a Viking dwelling of around 1,000 AD. The *saelehuset* is one of three such buildings that encircle a small mountain region and make up the legs of a walk that can easily be undertaken by young children.

I was introduced to the *saelehuset* and the area on a day walk some weeks earlier by Børge Dahle, the founder of the *Barnas Naturverden* (Children's Nature World) project. We had sat for a while, taking in the mountain sun, on the hillside above the house in a rough circle of stones. After a while Børge pointed out the stones, which I had hardly noticed other than their angular pressing against my back, and told me that we were sitting inside the circle of a 2,000 year old hunting hide (blind). Reindeer would have been herded up the valley until they galloped over a subtle fold in the hillside just beside the hide, from where they could readily be speared. Flint arrow and spearheads could still be found in the grasses nearby. The flintheads were made from an exposed seam of rock within view further up the hillside: "I've been here forever."

I returned on my own to complete a three-day walk, experiencing the different dwellings and the pathways that connected them through the mountains and forests. The Children's Nature World project took several years to research, plan and complete and involved negotiation on multiple levels from national government through to local communities. Diverse groups informed the project, ranging from anthropologists to keepers of local legend and lore, and farmers and community members undertook the construction. But the dwellings are only one of several integrated features that make the project "work" as an education in friluftsliv, and one that models a responsiveness to local place.

The trail into *saelhurst* climbs up gently from the road head and can easily be walked by a young child in half a day. This simple approach walk is an extraordinary experience in itself. A "retired" local farmer took it largely upon himself to design and build this section of the trail. In places where it makes sense to pause you will find a large flat rock or rough-hewn wooden bench waiting. This is especially the case if the place is one that would be attractive to children, such as beside a small running stream. Sections of the trail are stepped with flat pieces of slate, which were sledded from a nearby range in winter. But the most stunning feature is the sign-stones.

Where the track breaks out above the treeline a rough row of angled rocks (like small cairns) stand in place and mark the way. An adult can see between them from one to the next. But when you bend down to a child's perspective, the way forward is not so clear. It takes a small adventurous journey to leave one sign-stone behind to find the next, just beyond the little slope, and then the next just out of sight around the gentle spur, and then the next … The sign-stones seem to have been adopted by their place. They are covered in moss and lichen and some have weathered during the freeze and thaw of a few cold winters. As I walked the little track small alpine birds would flit ahead of me from one to the next, using them as vantage points. I have never encountered a pathway so recently conceived and constructed; yet so evolved into its landscape. This small walk is, in its own right, a profound lesson in friluftsliv philosophy and practice.

The final feature of the Children's Nature World project involved the publication of a children's picture storybook, written by Børge and beautifully illustrated by Signy Ramsem. It also includes an excellent map of the area. The book, *Smajutulan: I Barnas Naturverden*,[11] tells the story of a small group of young children who go on an adventurous journey through this same country. They have to learn to live in the dwellings, to fish the streams and to "read" the mountain weather and terrain. Along the way, they encounter many of the mythological characters and stories of the region. It would be quite possible for children to read the story, or have it read to them, as the young adventurers make their own journey of many small footsteps through the *naturverden*. A copy of the book can be found in each of the huts.

All of these features, the path through the land, the dwellings and the book, make up a remarkable encounter between people and place, and the sensitivity given to the child's experience points to a finely tuned pedagogy-of-place. In planning the project, Børge told me, it took many years for him to learn to "see" again as a child, and I suspect that this is the genius of the project and a lesson for us all. There have been several worthwhile attempts to describe an education that is responsive to local places,[12] but rarely do they escape an adult conception of place. In the *Barnas Naturverden*, it is place that is the teacher.

Encounter 2: Friluftsliv as Coast-Life

Later in my visit to Norway I worked with Børge and students from The Norwegian University of Sports and Physical Education who were completing a friluftsliv leaders program. As part of their final examination students were required to develop a program that teaches the friluftsliv of a particular region. I participated as an international "censor" (examiner) for the ten-day long "exam." Students had already completed extensive inquiry into the local culture, and had collected stories and histories of the places we ventured into. For example, students had discovered from locals that an old pathway crossing a mountain range had several different names for different sections, each depicting a storied aspect of local history. A large boulder might be the home of a troll-spirit, for example, that should be spoken to in order to request safe passage. There seemed to me to be both an aboriginal sense of the land and a commitment on the part of the students to gather these local stories, carefully interpret them, and build them into a friluftsliv education experience.

A feature of this particular program was an experience in "coast life" in the Hardanger Fjord region. We were given access to two traditional boats of the region. One was a reconstruction of a Baron's boat from the previous century, completed by the local community. The other was an authentic Hardanger Attring (eight oars) in-shore fishing boat, which was over 100 years old. Boats such as these were not uncommon, and they were not stored away in dusty museums. Instead they were in use on the waterways to maintain access to an experiential local heritage. We sat side-by-side in the boats and rowed around parts of the fjord for several days, often singing as we rowed, with the students conducting "lessons" in local fishing techniques, storytelling aspects of local history and lore, and painting and writing.

Later, I was also fortunate to spend some time with Børge Dahle and his family at their coast house in an archipelago of granite islands at the outer limits of the Trondheim Fjord. Børge had several "old boats," 90 to 120 years old, all in use. The students from the friluftsliv program would visit this place for several weeks and physically, emotionally and intellectually learn to live a "coast life." They would row and sail the old boats, camp out on the islands, fish and collect seafood, paint, draw, write and work on the boats.

We took out Børge's *AFjordbat*, the traditional small fishing boat of the Trondheim Fjord region, and tied it up alongside a small jetty. Seawater immediately began to fill the boat through numerous small splits in the timber planking and this continued until the water level inside the boat matched that outside. The boat was then left in the water overnight to allow the timber to pick up the water and swell until it became watertight. The following day the water was bailed out with a small-carved wooden scoop. One or two small splits, or leaks, were still evident and Børge pulled some woollen thread from his jumper and used a sharp knife to push it into the leaks until the water coming in slowed to a trickle.

As it is with many wooden boats, the apparent connection with the "tree-ness" of various sections of the boat's construction is striking. The "knees" that provide rigidity as the internal framing of the hull, can easily be recognized as sections of tree where the trunk runs into the more horizontal root system. The rowlocks were small cross-sections of narrow trunks with short sections of branches left attached. A flat was cut or planed onto the split trunk and it was pegged to the gunwale. A leather or rope "keeper" loop was then tied through a hole drilled through the branch "stump" and the oar handle passed through the loop. When pressure was applied on the oar it would snug neatly into the "V" formed by the old branch and trunk. Even the lapped planking that made up the clinker construction of the hull was sectioned and deliberately chosen for specific parts of the hull. As the planks rose higher away from the keel of the boat, a twist was needed to create the distinctive "Viking" shape of the bow and stern.

Boat builders use no plans to construct these craft. In the same way that the traditional builders of Greenland sea kayaks measured them off of their own body dimensions, the small boat builders of Norway developed a system of measures based on arm spans, forearm lengths, hand spans and so on. Virtually all of the materials were sourced locally. Timber would be sourced from nearby forests, as would various tars and sealants that would be distilled from the trees. The sheets (ropes) and sailcloth would be soaked in a boiling tannin brew made from spruce bark to proof them against rot in salt water. Each boat was a symphony of human/organic knowledge and practice centred in its local place: "I belong here."

When we had finished bailing out the *Afjordbat* we stepped the mast and rigged the sails. Prior to sailing we made several trips to a nearby small cove and carried back a few dozen roundish granite stones, each one weighing perhaps five to seven kilograms. With this ballast we made two neat stacks, one in a box around the base of the mast and the other at the back of the boat close to the rudder. Børge explained that the roundness of the stones was a "good feature" as they would roll out of the boat more easily if we capsized and leave the wooden boat to float. Angular stones might stick in the boat and sink the hull. In the North Sea, where water temperatures may be less than seven degrees Celsius, and survival times if immersed would be measured in minutes, I was motivated to find the roundest stones possible!

There is that magical moment, in any sailboat, when you leave the land, the sail sheets are pulled in, the wind fills the sail, the hull heels over and boat is pushed forward before the breeze. In this case we were in a tight, granite-bound channel created by several islands and we sailed away on a broad reach before the fjord opened in front of us. The fjord was several kilometres wide and we sailed a straight course all of the way across. A stiff breeze had the boat leaning well over, and the granite boulders jostled each other into position. Several leaks sprung from sections of the hull that had been above the waterline and had not yet "taken up" any water, and the hull flexed markedly as it shouldered its way over the small swell. The sail hummed in the breeze and the timbers and sheets creaked as they took up the strain. The *Afordbat* was speaking.

When we reached shelter in a small cove the sail was lowered, an oar placed in one of the rowlocks on the leeward side of the boat, and the boat rowed through the turn. Then the sail was raised, sheeted in and we sailed away on the next tack (a course set at an angle into the wind) of several kilometres. Børge explained that fishermen using these boats had been very conservative sailors. Few could swim and a capsize was more likely during turning manoeuvres. A capsize at sea could cost the lives of most of the male members of an extended family. Sailing the boat, out to the fishing grounds could accurately be described as a complete "applied local ecology." The technology of the boat, the sailing knowledge, sea lore and the skilled body of the sailor, all were extensions of a close relationship between the person, local culture and place.

Lessons on Teaching a Cultural Attachment to Place

Why have I gone in to so much detail re-telling these stories of my experiences of Norwegian friluftsliv? There are two answers to this question. First, the stories and places are inextricably linked. The telling and reading of stories such as these can stand alone as a lesson in cultural attachment to place. Each of us becomes compelled to interpret the story and consider our own teaching and life contexts, and the places where we live and work. In essence, the stories remind us to ask the questions so eloquently framed by Wendell Berry in his book *Home Economics*: "What is here? What will nature permit us to do here? What will nature help us do here?"[13] Even more than asking such questions, friluftsliv "lives" them as a daily practice.

Second, it seems to me that we stand in danger of forgetting or erasing the fundamental role that these types of place experiences play in our lives, particularly as we continue to further "industrialize" our teaching practices. I refer here to the application of technocratic practices in education such as the rationalization of the curriculum, the quest for uniformity of educational goals and practices regardless of local conditions, and the belief that learning experiences must be fully investigated, predicted, rendered into factual accounts, and thus controlled. Outdoor and adventure educators are no less immune to the impact of these so-called "developments" than other educators. They would seem to deny what is most needed in education; an ongoing personal and cultural negotiation built upon a carefully listening to our local places. This is precisely what a lived experience in friluftsliv offers.

Lucy Lippard provides an important insight when she reminds us that children, as well as adolescents and adults I might add, will learn about places quite simply be being allowed to be-in-place.[14] Yet, even more than this, friluftsliv provides an important opportunity for educators to extend this understanding into a meaningful pedagogy that responds to place. If we present learners to outdoor places where we, as educators, have already forgotten or erased the "local," and replaced it with our preferred visions of outdoor spaces (such as wilderness), we diminish the experience in a profound way.

Friluftsliv in Norway is, of course, itself one type of privileged encounter with place. Certainly it has many culturally specific values and practices that would not easily translate to other cultures and places. Encounters with a friluftsliv that include versions of recreation that Leopold would call "endless frustrations," or even an "extreme" friluftsliv of hyper-individualized risk takers are also possible. Yet the friluftsliv I encountered seemed largely to have embraced experiences where possibilities were expanded and open, and where potentials were not curtailed, and where elements of the personal, the cultural and the natural were "free" to roam and connect. All that it seemed was required of me to experience such a friluftsliv was to step into these stories, suspend some of my taken for granted beliefs for the outdoor experience, and turn an ear to the speaking land: "I have been here forever. This is where I belong."

CHAPTER 24

Landfullness in Adventure-Based Programming: Promoting Reconnection to the Land

Molly Ames Baker

Let us venture back to the early 20th century, to the glory days of nature study in America when naturalists, such as Anna Botsford Comstock and Enos Mills, were promoting an "essential nature literacy" that necessitated direct contact with plants and animals in their natural surroundings. It was a time when botany walks were common and "a lively, experimental curiosity in plants and animals was nothing unusual; it was simply one component of the engaged citizen's life."[1] Move forward to the mid-1900s, however, and we find Aldo Leopold lamenting the fact that field studies had been succeeded by laboratory biology as the pure form of science, and that memorizing the names of the bumps on the bones of a cat now took precedence over gaining an understanding of the native countryside. Leopold observed that our collective relationship to the land had been compromised to the point where we were fast approaching a state of "landlessness." He noted in his Round River essays:

> The problem, then, is how to bring about a striving for harmony with land among a people many of whom have forgotten there is any such thing as land, among whom

education and culture have become almost synonymous with landlessness.[2]

Landlessness, according to Leopold, was manifesting itself in two distinct but related ways: the literal loss of places wild and free; and the figurative loss of our collective awareness of, and admiration for, the land.

Before the turn of the 21st century, Barry Lopez spoke to this concept of landlessness, noting that almost four decades later it had reached an unprecedented level. In his book *Rediscovery of North America*, Lopez stated: "We have a way of life that ostracizes the land."[3] As the suburbanization of America evolves at an ever-increasing rate, landscapes are becoming more homogenized and we often find ourselves in "Anywhere, USA."[4] During the past century, our collective environmental literacy has declined dramatically. As noted by Paul Hawken; "That an average adult can recognize one thousand brand names and logos but fewer than ten local plants is not a good sign."[5]

These combined realities – irreversible loss of undeveloped land, plus changes in our national relationship to land – have created the need for reconnection, both on a personal level and national scale. The day has passed when participants can leave adventure-based programs with a sense of accomplishment, but without a sense of their relationship to the land. It seems, then, that as experiential educators it is incumbent upon us to assess whether our students are becoming actively engaged in the landscape or merely passing through it. Simply put, are we promoting landless or landfull experiences?

Landlessness in Adventure Education

It may be assumed that the environment plays an integral role in adventure-based programming simply because it is there. Oftentimes, however, the land becomes a backdrop surrounding the adventure experience.[6] The myriad of modern-day forces distracting our awareness from the land can be both overwhelming and insidious; it is all too easy to divert our attention toward the activity, the group, the gear, the gadgets – to be pulled away by the map, the altimeter, the GPS, by everything but the very landscape that can inspire our travels. The most notable of the many factors that conspire to create a landless trip are traditional programming objectives centred on inter/interpersonal skill development, coupled with students' tendency to focus first and foremost on the technical and social aspects. The likelihood of a landless trip increases when instructors demonstrate a higher baseline competence in technical and people skills rather than in land skills; or when they are teaching in new areas where they have limited knowledge of the landscape. Frequently, the extent to which the land is emphasized is dependent more upon the interests and expertise of the individual staff, rather than the mission statement, training or curriculum of the organization.

Granted, an increasing number of adventure-based programs are placing a higher priority on the inclusion of environmental objectives in their curricula. However, the implementation frequently centres on Leave No Trace philosophy (LNT), with a handful of natural history classes added whenever possible. Although commendable as a starting point, this approach tends to frame LNT practices as technical skills with natural history curricula becoming disjointed or lacking in context.

The bottom line is that even on a month-long course in a wilderness setting, students' awareness of the land can be limited to its direct impact on their immediate experience (i.e., the weather, a pretty sunset or a breathtaking view). Likewise, they may relate to the landscape solely in terms of negotiating it, whether through route finding, river crossings or campsite selection. When interactions with the land are viewed in this way, students may not consciously relate with the land, and may, instead, become passers-by travelling through "Any Woods, USA." The upshot is that landscapes may become interchangeable and the unique aspects of a particular place, along with any potential connections to it, may be lost.

Promoting "Landfull" Experiences

In face of the realities of landless programming, experiential educators can take a tangible step to address disconnection with the land by promoting "landfull" experiences. If an experience is to be landfull, it necessitates rethinking adventure, as we know it today. A landfull adventure is not a journey away, guided by the pull of modern technology and distractions, but rather a journey home, to discover a sense of belonging to the land. As Meyers so aptly describes it in his book, *Lime Creek Odyssey*:

> We cannot come to know a place by rushing in and rushing out. I often wonder just what it is that people see in the wilderness when they come for a week or two each year. I imagine their spirits are refreshed and their time here is quite pleasant. I know they learn a great deal. But what do they see? I believe there are some things that can only be seen if you stay awhile. Others become visible only to those who gaze at a landscape and think, this is my home.[7]

This notion of discovering home may challenge or even run counter to mission statements and curricula in adventure-based programming. Yet, it is vitally important that we provide students with opportunities to develop "land" skills (in the same way we promote leadership and technical skills), if we are to address the need for "essential nature literacy." As in the glory days of nature study in the early 1900s, the key is for students to discover an engagement with the land that extends beyond simply knowing the names of trees, to include a personal approach of relating to the land. This discovery is not only a site-specific sense of place, but also an ongoing relationship with land that transcends time and place. The essence of landfullness is when the personal process becomes less intentional and more a part of our identity – in other words, relating to the land is a part of who we are.

The question then becomes how to go about promoting landfull experiences. We must recognize that as a society we are not in the habit of relating to land in a direct and intentional way. Accordingly, landfullness necessitates that we move beyond an inevitable awareness or a convenient consciousness of the land. It requires experiencing the land in its entirety through all of the senses including the emotional/affective – not only as it is today, but also as it was in the past and will be in the future. Most importantly, it requires an intentional exploration of our own interactions with, and relationship to, the land. This act of striving to be intentional is what enables the land to become more than a scenic backdrop; as we actively engage with the land it becomes more integral to our experience. It is through purposeful consideration of our relationship to the land that we develop our own ever-evolving personal process of coming to know a place. Rather than travelling through the land, we begin to travel with and in the land.

The Landfull Framework: Levels of Landfullness

The intent is not to replace traditional goals of personal growth and group development, or to override the curriculum with an environmental agenda, but rather to introduce a landfull approach. The "Landfull Framework" is proposed as a holistic approach to integrating environmental education into adventure-based programming that allows for flexibility based on differences in program type, instructor background and student groups. By using the framework as an ongoing theme, instructors can easily repackage existing environmental studies activities and natural history curricula so that what students may have perceived as isolated classes will be seen as part of a cohesive whole. More specifically, the Landfull Framework:

- Recognizes that people come to know a place in different ways;
- Challenges students to develop an intentional, not merely a convenient, consciousness of the land and to actively consider their relationship to it;
- Enables students to discover and develop their own definition of landfull that is personally significant, and to become self-directed in moving through the levels of landfullness.

The Landfull Framework consists of four levels: (a) Being Deeply Aware, (b) Interpreting Land History, (c) Sensing Place in the Present, and (d) Connecting to Home. Although the framework can be used in a linear progression, it is more effective to mix activities and classes that focus on all four levels consistently throughout the course/trip. When the framework is clearly laid out to students at the outset, they have a shared vocabulary and a mental schematic to support the integration of activities. Moreover, when all levels are integrated, students are able to discover the ways in which they connect to the land sooner. Each level has a specific focus and corresponding questions, as described below.

Being Deeply Aware

When a group arrives at the trailhead, participants find themselves at a place on the map that may mean nothing to them personally. In this stage, the focus often is simply on the activity and the group. Using a topographic map analogy, a student's thinking is based on a "summit mentality" and the land is seen as a backdrop, or merely a route to the summit, but little more.

- Focus: Increase awareness of one's surroundings
- Questions: Where am I? What's around me? Who is around me?
- Activities: Students ground themselves by becoming conscious of the lay of the land on both a micro and macro scale through different activities, such as:
  (a) Sensory Awareness games (e.g., Meet Your Neighbours – each student goes off to get acquainted with something that interests them, then have a "party" where everybody introduces his/her "new neighbour" and tells its story);
  (b) Mapping Initiatives – students use ropes on the ground to outline where they are including the state, park/forest boundaries, mountain ranges, rivers;
  (c) Location Celebrations – take time out to observe surroundings in an engaging way (e.g., have a birthday party for a tree to celebrate its age including balloons and singing);
  (d) Art Gallery – students take turns being the "docent" (Tour Guide) along the trail by sharing with others the "masterpieces" of artwork that they find most intriguing.

Interpreting Land History (Natural and Cultural History)

Reaching this stage, students are somewhat aware of their surroundings, but only through direct observation. At this point, depth can be added to the students' experiences by increasing their knowledge of the area through both natural and cultural history. Instructors may tend to focus more on natural history than on cultural history, perhaps due to lack of knowledge or concerns about perpetuating stereotypes or historical inaccuracies. However, cultural history often creates a more tangible connection to the land than does natural history in students' minds. By highlighting both the natural and cultural history of a place, the likelihood of making the land come alive may be increased. Rather than relaying historical facts and figures, instructors can reveal the story of land and people over time to spark curiosity using the following examples:

- Focus: Increase knowledge of the uniqueness of a particular landscape
- Questions: How has this land changed over time? What and who have lived here in the past? How did they relate to the land?
- Activities:
  (a) Site Specific Interpretation – take time to contemplate points of interest such as cliffs, signs, names on a map, or found objects that may be overlooked as "junk;"
  (b) Journaling – students write their personal land histories (e.g., their story with the land over time); "A Day In the Life Of … "
  – students write from the perspective of something/somebody that used to live on the land and then guess each others' perspectives;
  (c) Role Plays – identify people/land use groups from the past and take on roles for a day, for a dinner party, or for a debate at a town meeting;
  (d) Skits – dress up as an historical figure and appear on the trail or in camp with a story to tell (a few leaves and duct tape make a great beard!);
  (e) Melodrama – as a group, act out the story of the land and people over time, and if no information is available have different

groups interpret signs in the landscape and act out their version of what could have been the story);

(f) Time Travel – connect to people from the past through food, gear, and/or stories (e.g., If we were here 100 years ago, what would we be wearing? Eating? What would the land look like?).

Sensing Place in the Present

If land history is the story of land and people over time, sensing place is feeling a part of the stories. Sense of place is a dynamic and personal construct that addresses how we assign value to a place and was first applied to landscapes in 1974 by the geographical philosopher Yi-Fu Tuan.[8] Sensing place is the continuous development of a personal connection to a particular place that evolves from, not only spending time there, but also from learning about its land history. In addition, one understands how the place is unique and is able to articulate one's connection with, relationship to, and feelings about, the place. Using a topographic map analogy, students in this stage have gained appreciation of the entire mountain; they are as aware of the marshes at the base as the peak itself. The following illustrates this:

- Focus: Facilitate connections to a place that are personalized and ever-evolving
- Questions: How is this place unique? Who lives/passes through this land now and what is their relationship to it? What does this place mean to me?
- Activities:
    (a) Mapping – students draw a map of the route and then add overlays to it including personal highlights, group benchmarks, and sense of place landmarks – aspects of the land that were personally significant;
    (b) Topo Naming – rename terrain features on the map based on your personal experiences and/or impressions of the land;
    (c) Solos – students are given solo time both at the beginning and end of the trip/course to contemplate how their relationship to the land has changed over time;

(d) Art Gallery – students are given ample time to find a spot and create a masterpiece that represents their interactions/relationship with the place, and then students explain their creations to the group.

Connecting to Home

The objective of this stage is to enable students to bridge the gap between backcountry and front country. It is this transference of landfullness to everyday life that creates relevance for the land skills developed during the trip/experience. Connecting to Home is not a single closure activity to be conducted on the last night in the field, but rather an ongoing effort to develop a conscious awareness of how we relate to the land around us and the role it plays in our everyday lives.

- Focus: Promote the linking of landscapes – the transference from the backcountry to the front country (home)
- Questions: How can this place link to other landscapes and experiences with the land? When does the land become home? When does home become the land?
- Activities:
  (a) Water Talk – discuss the water supply at camp and then have students share where their water comes from at home;
  (b) Daily Walk – link the skill of being an active navigator in the woods to increasing awareness of one's surroundings at home. Have the students draw or map out the route they take to work/school at home, everyday, including significant landmarks along the way;
  (c) Time Warp – students envision what a particular piece of land looked like 50/100 years ago and then consider what their home-town looked like at the same time;
  (d) Constellation Myths – locate a constellation in the night sky during the trip and then discuss where the constellation would be located at home; then create a myth of how it came to be;
  (e) Back Home Discoveries – parallels of discoveries made on the

trip/course are made to home (e.g., a tree on the trail is linked to a tree in the neighbourhood; vista on the trails can spur discussion of what is my "vista" from home/office).

The Sense of Wonder – actively contemplating the land – serves as a catalyst for moving between the levels of the Landfull Framework. For example, when participants spend time in a place and learn about its land history, their sense of wonder, at some point, will be engaged. By learning more about land history, and further wondering about the place, they will begin to contemplate what the place means to them personally, and thus be propelled into the Sensing Place stage. Sense of Wonder refers to the concept introduced by Rachel Carson (1956) in her book *Sense of Wonder*.[9] It is a state in which one is actively interacting with another entity, whether it be tangible (e.g., a tree), or intangible (e.g. time); this interaction engages the person mentally through the processes of inquiry (e.g., posing questions as in a state of curiosity), and/or physically through the senses (e.g., seeing, hearing, smelling, tasting, and/or touching), and/or emotionally through feelings (e.g., affective sentiments of awe, appreciation, etc.). Sense of Wonder represents the reflection/processing step that is integral to the experiential learning process.[10]

The benefits of teaching from a landfull perspective are numerous. At a minimum it adds a new, and often unexpected, dimension to the expedition. Students may gain an increased knowledge of the landscape, develop an appreciation for the uniqueness of a particular place and/or discover a personal connection to the land. Ultimately, students may be able to transcend a site-specific sense of place by developing an ongoing relationship with the land that is integral to their everyday lives. As a reinterpretation of the "essential nature literacy" that Anna Botsford Comstock, Enos Mills and Aldo Leopold all strove for in their time, this landfull approach is aligned with experiential philosophy. The pull of modernity has existed for centuries, and will continue to disconnect us from the land with greater force and diligence in the future. Striving to actively engage students with places is a sure step towards creating a collective connection to landscapes and a more sustainable future.

CHAPTER 25

WHY OUTDOOR LEARNING SHOULD GET REAL

Chris Loynes

I have previously likened trends in outdoor learning to the "McDonaldization of Society,"[1] a title used by George Ritzer[2] in the title of his book on globalization. My point is that, like Ritzer, I see trends that seek to make everything the same wherever it is experienced. Ritzer used the burger to make his point. I think the ropes course – skiing, rafting, bungee jumping, mountain biking and many more activities lend themselves to this globalized treatment, "adventure in a bun." I view this as something that is counterproductive to effective outdoor learning wherever it is practised. My concerns are that an "off the shelf," commoditised approach to providing adventure experiences is counter to the organic and emergent nature of experiential learning outdoors as people respond to the rich mix of environments, individuals, groups, cultures and activities involved. I also think this approach develops values that are counter to those educators should be developing in our students in a world of social and environmental injustice.

Charlene Spretnak[3] argued for a "resurgence of the real" and in doing so drew on the English romantic tradition to make her case. In looking for a more hopeful and positive response to what I saw as a widely negative practice, it was heartening to consider that one author thought the seeds of what I was looking for were also embedded in the roots of U.K. outdoor-learning practice. This chapter explores my journey of reconstruction as I seek a form of practice that is based on values that will help outdoor learning contribute to the educational needs of today.

I am writing this from the perspective of a white, English man who has been exploring the professional and cultural diversity in our work. This will inevitably give my remarks some ethnic, gender and cultural bias. I have become curious about the way an idea becomes an institution and, as such, is applied as a political tool both within and between countries and professions. I am also interested in what lies behind the apparently conflicting claims that, on the one hand, there are approaches to outdoor experiential learning that speak globally to the human condition transcending nations and cultures and, on the other hand, that each community should develop its own authentic approach to experience, learning and the outdoors. In the context of these questions the bias of my perspective is, potentially, a significant factor in my interpretation of which the reader should be critically aware.

The Algorithmic Paradigm

What are the characteristics of this algorithmic paradigm of outdoor learning? What are thought to be the problems with it? What other approaches are there, either hidden by the dominant discourse or lacking a voice in the English language? What good would these other approaches be and for what?

Martin Ringer[4] first used the term "algorithmic" to describe approaches to outdoor learning. It can be characterized in a number of ways, for example by the language that is used to describe it. Typical words include programming, processing, framing, funnelling, front loading, sequencing, cycles, outcomes, task, leader and team.

It can also be recognized by the beliefs that are taken as axiomatic. Those mentioned by the critics of this paradigm as potentially problematic are:

- Programs have predetermined outcomes, which are measured.
- Programs are sequenced according to a conceptual framework such as the learning or training cycle.

- Action and conversation are the central ingredients. You are not learning unless you are doing.
- The world of the learning experience is understood as metaphor and so **is** not entirely real.
- Raised self-esteem is typically the dominant outcome.
- The principles of challenge by choice, informed consent and other ethical concerns are seldom questioned.
- A belief in personal development and human progress and the centrality of the ego.
- There is an uncritical stance to the social context in which the learning occurs.
- Groups are understood as teams in the context of a shared goal and not as communities with a multiplicity of needs and dreams.
- Self reliance and leadership are widely practised taught and celebrated at the expense of human interdependence.
- Nature is understood as an assault course, gymnasium or puzzle to be resolved and controlled. It is a resource to be commodified instead of a home to which to relate.

The presence of some of these can indicate a program influenced, perhaps overly influenced, by the algorithmic paradigm.

A Modernist Tradition

I think there are three distinctive features of the paradigm that attract critical comment. They are all features of the currently dominant, western capitalist, post-renaissance paradigm called modernism. They are the scientific rationale, the production line metaphor that lends itself to mass production and the notion of learning as a product and so a marketable commodity.

1) A Scientific Rationale
Programmable, formulaic approaches are influenced by the positivist scientific paradigm. This positivist approach has set out to discover the theory behind all observable phenomena and seeks to express these theories

as algorithms. The benefit to society is that these general algorithms can then be "plugged in" to a particular problem and deliver a solution. Computer language works like this. Input the data, select the algorithm for the task you want undertaken and the result is a consistent solution.

Applying this method to the study of human behaviour has been under severe attack by other methodologies that do not treat people as predictable phenomena. Nevertheless the positivist paradigm has had a major influence as a metaphor for a course design understood as an algorithm with the capacity to deliver a consistent solution, hence Ringer's use of the term "algorithmic paradigm" to describe this approach. When this metaphor is attached to the metaphor of the production line a powerful combination of ideas capable of widespread influence is forged.

2) A Production Line Metaphor

Loading and processing are lifted straight from the world of production lines; programming, loading and sequencing form the world of computers. Both describe rational, mechanistic, technological, deterministic and linear approaches to a task. The raw materials or data are loaded at one end; they are then assembled and manipulated in a predetermined sequence to deliver a uniform outcome of a predictable standard as efficiently as possible. Applying the metaphor to a learning experience provides a rational proposal with measurable outcomes predetermined during the negotiations with the client. The linear rationality of models used widely in the outdoor learning literature such as Kolb's learning cycle or Tuckman's team development[5] only help to emphasize a progression through a defined sequence of steps or stages to a desirable outcome, learning in Kolb's case and performance in Tuckman's

The production line approach tempts the provider and the client to consider participants as objects, resource or labour, manufactured to fulfil their potential as a cog in a machine rather than as a human being. The positivist approach reinforces the idea that this object can be manipulated to a formula. Likewise it tempts the facilitator to focus on certain learning objectives to the exclusion of others. The result, pushed to an extreme, is a participant who is oppressed rather than empowered by their managed experience.

Of course there is often perceived to be all sorts of mutual benefits to the client and the participant and everyone is happy. Evaluation forms designed for this approach are widely referred to as "happy sheets." However, if a participant dares to suggest that they learned nothing, were unhappy about what they learned or simply learned something else unintended, heads roll, usually that of the facilitator who "failed" to deliver the "right" script.

3) A Marketable Commodity

Providers have developed technological solutions that attempt to enhance, accelerate and guarantee the product in order to achieve the predictable outcomes increasingly demanded by the client. This is partly cost driven, as the naturalistic qualitative approaches are both staff and time intensive. Technological solutions include both hard and soft elements. The high ropes course is a hard response to the need for a guaranteed adrenaline buzz with guaranteed safety delivered quickly anywhere. The reviewing (processing in North America) techniques are often seen as a soft solution to establishing conscious and rational learning outcomes from the experiences. These are then readily available for collection by the evaluation tools after the program.

Considered from the business perspective, treating the experience as product and packaging it for marketing has at least one drawback. One provider confided that they could sell any programme provided it was a two day ropes course experience, Fordism alive and well in the learning market place. This approach does wonders for the program marketing. The off the shelf product lends itself to branding, costs are driven down and the mass market can be accessed. Peter Drucker[6] claimed that "the only benefits in business are marketing and innovation; everything else is cost." This provider has solved the marketing question. However, their ability to innovate has been seriously hampered by the "off the shelf" approach. Even in business terms this will give their product a limited life cycle. They will then have to come up with another product.

Considered from an educator's approach, transforming the participant into a consumer can only lead closer to the oppressive end of the spectrum of outdoor learning. The product is predetermined and the benefits to the consumers decided for them. Even the facilitation is influenced towards convincing the consumers that they have got what they asked for and that they liked it. In this sense I believe that an "off the shelf" approach to outdoor learning cannot be properly described as experiential. This accolade can only be attached to bespoke services, those that have been tailor made or, even better, are emergent.

If you want to learn to navigate throw away the map!

Although the algorithmic approach is often tagged as "American," the origins can be traced back to British military traditions. Of the several candidates for these early influences I have chosen map reading. Map reading and navigation are often regarded as one and the same thing. Here, I will treat map reading as one of many practical techniques by which navigation is conducted. I think understanding these concepts as different ideas is important because the way in which navigators find their way makes a difference to how they encounter the places they are exploring and there are other ways to explore a place than with a map. Actually, what I really want to do is put the map away rather than throw it away. It does still have some uses!

Part of the culture of outdoor life in the U.K. involves linear routes, time plans, journeys, expeditions, destinations and self-reliance. This latter quality is particularly British. It means to be independent of others when finding your way probably in a landscape that is considered to be wild, remote and hostile. This approach involves a high degree of control over what is essentially a dynamic situation engaged in by, hopefully, a dynamic and lively imagination.

Map reading entered outdoor youth work via the Scout Association and Baden-Powell.[7] Baden-Powell was an army officer in the Boer War. He was impressed by how young men, too young to use weapons and so sent out to scout the terrain ahead of the army, rapidly became very competent at their tasks. In addition, he noted how they "grew up" equally quickly through the demands of their role. On return to the U.K., he founded the Scout Movement in order to raise the moral standing of young men at home through a "moral equivalent to war."[8] Navigation with maps and compasses became a core activity and the landscape became "hostile" terrain.

This approach to navigation is not common to approaches to journeying in other European countries but has, I believe through cultural links to U.K. outdoor education, crossed the oceans to North America, Australia and New Zealand.

The values of independence, control and hostility have consequences. In order to exercise this control groups spend a great deal of time learning to use maps. The key skills are those of planning a journey from a map and the using the map to keep to a linear route and a time plan once embarked on a journey. Landscapes are understood as potentially unsafe, challenging and risky. I am not suggesting that the values of militarism are embedded in this way of navigating, though they may be embedded in other aspects of the Scout Movement. However, I am suggesting that the underlying values of independence, control and hostility are, and that they do transfer to new contexts down the ages. The scouts on the battlefields of South Africa needed these values to survive and succeed. This all sounds sensible and worthwhile. However, my premise is that they may not always be desirable in other situations. At the very least we may benefit from not taking this approach for granted so that it becomes the only way navigators navigate especially in contexts where the educational benefits sought after may be different from those aspired to by Baden-Powell. Under the values of self-reliance and control, groups are unable to respond creatively to the landscape of the day except to control for their safety. An unexpected, moonlit nights and alluring extra summits are off limits because they are not in the plan. The knowledge of local people and even other walkers is excluded because the group are independent without a guide and discouraged from encounters with others.

However, other traditions without a historical link to militarism provide an alternative approach. There was a time when climbing courses taught primarily rope work and belaying. Little was offered to help the aspirant climber move on rock. Nowadays it is the other way round. Movement is at the centre of the classes. The rope is seen as an important safety devise and taught in secondary workshops that allow the climber to climb safely. Rope work is not climbing. It is simply a safety devise. If the map and compass were treated as safety devises how would this affect the art of navigation? Navigation would become the skill of reading a landscape and responding to it with the idea of a line to take or point to reach or a place to spend time. The navigator would also respond to the weather and the imaginations of the others in the group. A plan would emerge and yet remain open to adaptation as conditions, aspirations or information about what lies ahead changes. If conditions do not allow the navigator to navigate then, unless some imperative dictates otherwise, the group can simply stay put until circumstances change. If the group still need to keep moving then out come the safety devises, the map, compass and, these days, the global positioning system and mobile phone.

Adopting such an approach might mean a change to the activities that navigating a landscape offers. It would almost certainly mean change to risk management strategies. However, it is not far fetched. There are many landscapes navigated by educational groups without maps because they operate in countries where they do not exist or are of such a small scale to be of little use. Additionally, there are educators in the U.K. working with young children who want to introduce them to the aesthetics and sensuality of landscapes but find maps an impediment. Other educators have found great value in getting groups to create maps or other devises for each other to use to reproduce their respective journeys. Trekkers in many exotic places rely more on trails and guides

than maps for conducting their walks. So, by freeing up the approach to understanding the art of navigation a wider range of experiential options for engaging with place are created.

The Wider Problem of Control as a Value

I have argued that following maps, that is following an abstract and partial representation of a landscape, is a different experience to that of navigating a landscape. Map work gets in the way of an engagement with a place, the people and the moment. It is, as Ringer put it, algorithmic. It is hard to deviate from the plan. The person is challenged to keep in control and stay on course. This has educational benefits but can impede some of the educational outcomes possible from exploring a landscape in other ways.

I want to extend the critique of the value of control in navigation to a wider critique of U.K. outdoor education. Edmund O'Sullivan,[9] in one of the prominent books from the environmental movement that addresses education, argues that we do need a global vision of one world and one species. However, he points out that to make this vision active in the lives of everyday people it needs many and diverse interpretations at local level. Andrew Brookes[10] has made a similar point. He reminds us that a landscape is a living landscape brought to life by the interaction of a particular nature and culture. Yet often we import practices from other cultures and environments or take our students to those other landscapes because our local setting is thought to be lacking in the necessary resources for these standard activities.

Robbie Nicol[11] discussed the claims made by outdoor adventure education for environmental learning. The rhetoric, often convincing to policy makers, clients and even staff does not, in his view stand up to scrutiny. Education "in" the environment does not lead to education concerned with the environment unless it gets some additional curriculum or pedagogic support. A recent review of research on outdoor learning[12] concluded that education about the environment, often called field studies in the U.K., also does not lead to education concerned with the environment. That reminds me of Patrick Geddes, the nineteenth century

Scottish educational philosopher, who coined the educational values of "head, heart and hands." "In," that is the hands, "about," that is the head, leaves out the "with" that is the heart. At best, feeling is left to its own devises. Colin Mortlock,[13] an influential British adventure educator, sensed the importance of this emotional world when he wrote of love and respect for the environment as one of his driving educational values.

The problem is that even the serendipitous encounters of the heart with the landscape can be squeezed out by the map work approach to the outdoors. It might be tempting to assume that the rigour of the scientific method adopted by field studies is the antipathy of anarchic outdoor adventure. The truth is both are prone to following a predetermined, outcome driven path that leaves those who follow it unable to turn to the side or take a pace measured in their own time. Both the activities that engage us with a place and the theories, practices and curricula we have mapped out to help us work effectively in that place in fact close the practitioner and the student down to the possibility of a creative engagement with a living landscape.

Why do we allow this to happen? My opening remarks claim that one factor is simply an uncritical eye on the roots of our practice and their implications. I think there are also several influences that have encouraged us down this path. For example feminist eco-psychologists argue that the masculine controlling and dominating values of the enlightenment are manifesting themselves in this domain. This could be understood in outdoor education in several ways. In part it could be activity in the environment, the doing, gets in the way of being in or with the environment, the being. It is also possible that simple activities to enable people to make journeys in the landscape, cycling or canoeing for example, have been replaced by more technological ones that focus more on the ego of the participant than the aesthetics of the place, mountain biking or play boating for example. It is the case that educational goals have shifted their focus towards the personal and the social rather than the environmental and attention has moved from process to outcome. It may be that outdoor practitioners want to look like their school-based cousins adopting strategies better suited to classrooms (but perhaps not to pupils in those classrooms!). It is clear that an outcome-based school curriculum has rubbed off on those practitioners determined to make the value of outdoor education apparent to school teachers and policy makers. Certainly the spectre of risk has caused many to be overly concerned with risk management to the extent of avoiding or controlling activity to a degree that even those responsible for ensuring our safe practice consider unnecessary.   Another aspect is that policy makers from the institutions representing order in society have seen how effective outdoor experiences can be at instilling certain values in people. This may have led to the preponderance of courses concerning teamwork and leadership. It may also have led to their willingness to fund outdoor approaches to many of the social ills I identified earlier in my opening remarks. The algorithmic, closed approach works if what you want to achieve is citizens claiming to be modelled to your own vision.

Sometimes, of course, we do. We need a certain order in society. One generation needs to hand on what has been learned to another for it to make its own. Perhaps part of what I am arguing for is some kind of balance and that the outdoors is a place where the more generative, transforming and creative aspects of education could and should be practised. However, this politicking is only partly relevant here.

The part that is relevant is that part that has been arguing for aliveness in our relations with our culture and our landscape. I have stated earlier that we have lost our links with our surroundings and that restoring these links in some way is vital for our own health, the health of our societies and the health of the planet. Yet, by treating the landscape as a backdrop for other social enterprises, we lose the potential to engage with it actively.

Problems with the Algorithmic Paradigm

I have argued that the hierarchical, scientific, technological and mass production elements of this paradigm are unsuited to an experiential education practice. When Ringer coined the term "algorithmic," he commented:

> It is my view that in the field of adventure education and outdoor leadership there has long been an implicit and hence invisible discounting of aspects of group leadership that do not fit into algorithmic schemes.

In explaining the term, he adds:

> My concern is that the current political and economic
> climate in most of the western world supports the trivi-
> alisation and fragmentation of complex fields of endeav-
> our such as group facilitation and leadership. In this
> vein, the title of this paper was a deliberate play on the
> word facile. If the meaning of the word – as derived from
> the French facile (easy) – signifies the state of being easy,
> then facilitation translates into the term 'making easy.'
> However, the meaning of facile in English has migrated
> to something akin to 'trivial.' Bending a few grammatical
> rules enables us to see 'Facile-itation' as trivialisation.
> Isn't the activity of 'making easy' a group so simple as to
> warrant trivialisation? Should we not simply chunk
> facilitation into a number of algorithms, and derive
> from each algorithm the requisite competencies?

Ringer sees the reductionist approach popular with modernist science
applied to facilitation in order to create simple, and therefore trainable,
portable and assessable, competencies. He claims that, while this may
help beginners to start their professional development, this is no reason
to apply such a straight jacket to sophisticated practice. In discussing the
militarist legacy, Steve Bowles[14] comments:

> The correspondence with both military and masculine
> aspects remains both in-force and in-vogue. This is per-
> haps as it should be and this is necessary in the light of
> outdoor, adventure-based work having a history within
> war. War has been so hard on folk and we might say that
> it is only human to seek out alternatives. War hurts. War
> hurts men as it hurts women. War is ugly for all. Perhaps
> it is not so much the military and the masculine aspects
> that need to be addressed, as it is the reasonable alterna-
> tives that are possible that need attention. This was one

of the questions of the day that was a day of the last hundred years. Hahn, following William James and others,
sought a moral equivalent to war. Lord Hunt carried on
that search even through to the 1990s in the UK. Perhaps
we might, today, seek out alternative adventures that are
an alternative to war-like atmospheres. Perhaps we
might en-vision today adventures that are not just any
mere equivalent to war. There is both hope and there is
potential here. Such maybe. Such maybe for all. The
questions will thereby be put thus: Is an adventure programming atmosphere the alternative to war-like
atmospheres or does it both express and reflect, at times,
the condition of war and the conditions that do create
war? Perhaps to ask such questions is the only reasonable way in our work with OAE that wonderfully wob-
bles towards maturity.

These commentators raise the question that the dominance of the
algorithmic paradigm in practice and in the literature is not only a matter of diversity corrected by a fuller description and dissemination of
other paradigms. It is a deeper issue of a paradigm attached to a modern
worldview, a view that is also critiqued by these commentators. The
implication is that an ethical educational practice attached to the development of people in the context of community and environment would
find this algorithmic paradigm wrong in our current world context.

Before I take up this question I want to consider the paradigm that is
the focus of this book. I will also attempt an early description of what I
believe to be a new, emerging paradigm to see if this will inform the critique of these commentators.

An Ecological Paradigm

Recent attention in Europe has been given to friluftsliv, a Scandinavian
pedagogy rooted in culture and history as much as nature. Literally translated as nature free life, it acknowledges the importance of a particular

style of relationship with nature as defining of the culture's identity. If there are equivalent approaches in America they might be rooted in the idea of the pioneer, the cowboy, the settler or the Native People.

Scandinavia is a western region that has not yet lost the idea of a connection with community and place as important. In Norway, friluftsliv was championed by the explorer Nansen in an attempt to embed these values in the education system of a nation. Critically, it was seen as important for this to be an experiential education, felt and practised as well as understood. This sensual intimacy with the land and the people has strong links with ideas about indigenous traditions and the notion of authentic experience.[15] Yet here a non-modern feeling has been brought forward into a modern nation state.

Friluftsliv has more to offer than another reform of the old ways valuable as this may be. Building on the tradition, Naess[16] developed his ideas of deep ecology, an idea that is rapidly establishing political and educational expressions. Deep ecology offers something different because it sees the planet as a whole and the person as a member of a species, not just a community, living on that planet, not just in a neighbourhood. Further, it offers a visionary framework and advocates that people engage critically and consciously with these ideas.

Edmund O'Sullivan,[17] who explores the contribution of thinkers like Naess to a new education, claims that the adoption of such a vision in education would be more than a reform, it would be a transformation that would have far reaching consequences to an emerging post modern society. This, O'Sullivan sees as important because, in a world in which the consequences of our actions have worldwide significance to ecosystems and communities, he claims it is essential to have a vision that offers the individual a way to engage with the planet as an idea. He believes that, in our world context, we need the experiential intimacy of the local but combined with the visionary cosmology of the global.

Some Ways Forward

We are faced with a problem, a complex and extended period of values development for an increasingly independent young person in an increasingly plural and urban consumerist culture. We have sought to address this problem with an uncriticized outdoor education with its roots now two centuries old. I have tackled the value of control and its possible implications. Other pilot and radical outdoor learning projects are exploring ways to work with less control and ego in the wider sense of this critique and in the context of the development of new values in relation to social justice, economics and the environment. They highlight some interesting criteria for success that may provide solutions to this problem.

The Emerging Generative Paradigm

Outdoor learning could be a journey of discovery of a personal ontology and epistemology for the participant. It incorporates actions based on the experiences inspired by learners choosing for themselves how to make a difference. The individual moves through the role of participant and narrator, and becomes an agent in their world.

So far this particular radicalism could be criticized, as it seems to applaud the individualism that is attached to the ideas of modernism that define the algorithmic paradigm I am critiquing. However, there are qualities within individualism that this alternative worldview might consider worth retaining. For example, the liberation experienced by a shift of power to the individual and the creativity as each individual struggles to reinvent a personal world view with which they can live are both values this radical perspective seeks to hold on to. Nevertheless, these qualities can only be transforming when the experiences supporting them do not occur in the context of the market. In this world the individual is constructed as no more than a consumer or as labour.

The emerging paradigm is thus critiquing the context of outdoor learning as much as the approach. The activity of participants and practitioners radicalised in the context of a wider social and environmental field takes them into the political realm. Here is the potential for a synergy with the emerging vision, described by O'Sullivan, of sustainable communities in congruence with the planetary ecosystem. In the politics of sustainability action finds a local and personal expression linked to the community and the land. Such a new and radical approach seems to be in congruence with the critical stances of some eco-feminist views[18] already benefiting the practice of outdoor learning, and the transformative learning concept espoused by O'Sullivan, a critique from which the field might benefit.

The emerging paradigm sits firmly in the domain of political action and indeed informs it. By incorporating this paradigm in outdoor experiential learning it is possible to confront the technological, market place and image politics that have been allowed in by the algorithmic approach. Without such a position the dynamics of living with self, community and planet will be a lost battle rather than a hope filled struggle.

The Characteristics of the Emerging Paradigm

I have called the emerging approach the generative paradigm after Robin Hodgkin who first coined the term in the context of education's role in supporting young people in the creative interpretation of their experience and a transforming influence on their culture. From this point of view its characteristics are:

- Instead of a rational approach it could best be described as valuing intuition.
- Rather than being production oriented and valuing standards and predictability it is creative and founded on hope and possibility.
- It takes its metaphors from spirituality and the journey rather than positivist science and productive business, being subject rather than object oriented.
- It is not outcome focused or process oriented; it is emergent as described by the educational thinkers Robin Hodgkin[19] and John Heron[20] valuing the twilight and the firelight where intuition and conceptualisation meet through storytelling. Meaning and value emerge within the experience rather than being represented or defined by the program structure or the facilitator. Empowerment, rather than being represented as the gift of a tool, is understood as establishing congruence with an inner sense of self.
- The facilitator accompanies rather than leads the participants as

in David Boud's[21] advocacy of animation rather than facilitation. Its principles are egalitarian and not hierarchical as in O'Sullivan's transformative learning.

- Learning is goal free, the experience offered a step on the road rather than a solution; the metaphor of the journey emerges as an alternative to the production line or computer programme.
- Relational mutuality and trust replace transactional consent and choice.
- It is influenced by feminine as much as masculine ideologies.
- It restores place as a central and critical dimension of equal value for learning and meaning as the self and the group.
- It subscribes to a sustainable vision in relation to, and congruent with, ideas of community and the environment.
- It replaces egocentric evolutionary biology with ecocentric Gaian ecology.
- It is politically engaged. Justice and congruence rather than progress and consumption are its highest values.

A Critical Stance

Just as the algorithmic paradigm can be criticized for treating people as labour and perpetuating a culture of violence,[22] so the generative model is open to a critical appraisal. Some commentators recognize that it contains the potential for indoctrination. Critics of Dieter May,[23] for example, would draw parallels between the traditions of rites of passage that he advocates and approaches that support fascist tendencies. The potential for this paradigm to degenerate is as real as they were for German liberal education. It requires a liberal and critical approach to this radical form in order to keep clear of such possibilities.

The potency of the generative paradigm lies in the dance between the emerging participant and the, potentially, mutable, even transformable social order. As is the algorithmic paradigm, this paradigm is politicized, but its worldview is a possibility for the future and not one of the established but increasingly unsupportable past. Its worldview of sustainability and justice is also explicit, rather than the hidden and uncriticized agendas of the older paradigm. O'Sullivan believes that, in this context, change can best be achieved by helping people to act within their own communities, developing their critical faculties and valuing the diverse results of the solutions that emerge, values close to the roots of experiential education philosophy.

What the new paradigm offers is the possibility of a dance floor and not a production line or an arena; and an experience judged, if at all, on impression and not technical performance!

Just a Nice Idea?

I have suggested that the generative paradigm might be an emerging, collective dream of a possible future for outdoor experiential learning, one that the commentators I have spoken with are intuitively moving towards as they sense its emerging form around them. If there were some truth in this notion it would be surprising if only the watchers were attuned to the possibilities. Just as they are articulating these ideas in their critiques I would expect others to be creating the ideas in practice. Without such an expression the generative paradigm will remain the product of imagination rather than intuition, and stay in the realm of narrative and not practice.

In fact I could give you many accounts to support this approach. Here is one.

We were visiting an unfamiliar and medium sized island with a group of students. They were invited to explore the island to see what it might have to offer us. One small group set off to follow the beautiful seashore. They met a local fisherman collecting seashells and asked him about the coastline ahead. They got talking to him about his work. He invited them to his home where his wife cooked the group local food and gave them tea. As the conversation unfolded they learned about the way of life and the place from these friendly people. Meanwhile the word went around that there were visitors and neighbours dropped in for a chat. Someone got out a fiddle and started up a tune. Someone else began a long saga about the dramatic history of the island. Before they knew it the chat had turned in to a dance, the whisky had come out, the sun went down and then, before they'd even thought of sleep or returning to our camp, the sun had come up again. Bleary eyed they eventually made it back. Their stories about the island and its people provided the basis for many walks, a football match, several more "ceilidhs" (visits) and another dance. Educationally I think that was arguably more valuable than following the values of independence and control. Indeed the opposite values of interdependence and serendipity led to the benefits we experienced. Whether you agree with me or not I think this approach certainly offered more of value to a curriculum of sustainability. The students learned a great deal about a landscape they discovered was rich in history and culture and not wild. More importantly they learned a great deal about people who were in touch with that history and landscape and living with it still.

A critical eye on this brief example might suggest that this is simply another rhetoric from a different but equally entrained worldview. This is of course possible. Even if such programmes contain strong elements of creativity, spontaneity and vitality and are relational and generative in approach they could be the beginning of something that becomes institutionalized. I suspect that generative programmes have always emerged around the edges of the so-called outdoor education world and others are always drifting into bounded convention. Perhaps it is a characteristic of experiential approaches that they transform convention from time to time even if we resist it. Perhaps acknowledging these deeper processes in our field's best work will help us develop structures that sustain more rather than less generative outdoor learning experiences.

One way of seeing the generative paradigm at work is to understand it as work in progress drawing on the traditions of older paradigms, adding new ideas and gaining a particular, community and planetary political focus. If this is so, seeds of these ideas will be emerging in writing such as this and in the practice of experiential education organizations old and new.

NOTES

Preface: Is a Tree Transplanted to Another Continent the Same Tree? Some Reflections on Friluftsliv in an International Context (Brookes and Dahle)

1. Andrew Brookes, "Gilbert White Never Came This Far South: Naturalist Knowledge and the Limits of Universalist Environmental Education," in *Canadian Journal of Environmental Education,* 7 (Spring) 2002a.
2. Andrew Brookes, "Lost in the Australian Bush: Outdoor Education As Curriculum," in *Journal of Curriculum Studies,* 34:4 (2002) 405–425.
3. B. Riffenburgh, *The Myth of the Explorer* (Oxford: Oxford University Press, 1994).
4. Børge Dahle, *"Naturfovaltning og friluftsli" I local samfrunn, localbefolkningens medvirkning: Sosialisering til friluftsliv* (Notator og rapporter fra Norges idrettshøgskole 93) Norwegian University of Sport and Physical Education (NIH), 1989.

INTRODUCTION

A Canadian Meets Friluftsliv (Henderson)

1. The Conference was titled DEEP – Conference 2000. Deep Environmental Education Practice: Friluftsliv sponsored by Norge Idrettshøgkole, at Hæverstølen Renneba on January 14–18, and at Oslo on January 19–20, Norway. The conference description read as follows: "Places for outdoor education in the 21st century: Local, national and global perspectives on outdoor education theory and practice."
2. Arne Naess, *Ecology, Community and Lifestyle: Outline of an Ecosophy.* (Cambridge: Cambridge University Press, 1989). Dave Rothenberg Translation.
3. R.M. Pyle, "The Rise and Fall of Natural History: How a Science Grew that Eclipsed Direct Experience," in *Orion.* 20:4 (2001) 17–23; Andrew Brookes, "Astride a Long-Dead Horse: Mainstream Outdoor Education Theory and the Central Curriculum Problem," in *Journal of Australian Outdoor Education.* 8:2 (2004) 22–33.
4. Sharon Butala, *The Perfection of the Morning: An Apprenticeship In Nature* (Toronto: HarperCollins, 1994) 89.

5. Henry David Thoreau, *Walden and Civil Disobedience* (New York: New American Library, 1960); Sigurd Olson, *Reflections from the North Country* (Minneapolis: University of Minnesota Press, 1978); Aldo Leopold, *The Sand County Almanac: And Sketches Here and There* (New York: Oxford University Press, 1987.

6. N. Adelson, *Being Alive Well: Health and the Politics of Cree Well-Being* (Toronto: University of Toronto Press, 2000); Bob Henderson, "Healthy Words/Meanings from an Outdoor Educator," taken from *Healing Matrix,* www.healingmatrix.ca, released on July 10, 2005.

Feet on Two Continents: Spanning the Atlantic with Friluftsliv? (Vikander)

1. "Adrienne's Junket," in *The National Post*, September 12, 2003.

2. W.L. Morton, *The Canadian Identity* (Toronto: University of Toronto Press, 1961).

3. E.O. Wilson, *Biophilia: The Human Bond with Other Species* (Cambridge: Harvard University Press, 1984).

4. Ipso-Reid, "Give Us a Break," in *The National Post*, January 2004, (54).

5. P. Reed and D. Rothenberg (eds.), *Wisdom in the Open Air: The Norwegian Roots of Deep Ecology* (Minneapolis: University of Minnesota Press, 1993).

6. *Leirskolekatalogen,* (Norway: Norsk Leirskoleforening, 1998).

7. T. Tilton, *What is the Future of Swedish National Parks?* (Stockholm: The Swedish Institute, No. 419, 1998).

PART I: SCANDINAVIAN

Chapter 1: Norwegian Friluftsliv: A Lifelong Communal Process (Dahle)

1. Børge Dahle, Naturforvaltning og friluftsliv I lokale samfunn. Sosialisering til friluftsliv. Nora nr. 93. (Oslo: Norges idrettshægskole, 1989).

2. Nils Faarlund, "Defining Friluftsliv," in *Pathways: The Ontario Journal of Outdoor Education*, 14:3 (Summer 2002) 18–19.

3. Børge Dahle, "Støy og stillhet i friluftsliv," in *SFT Rapport*, 1992, 39.

Chapter 2: Friluftsliv as Slow Experiences in a Post-modern "Experience" Society (Gelter)

1. H. Gelter, "Friluftsliv: The Scandinavian Philosophy of Outdoor Life," in *Canadian Journal of Environmental Education* (5) 2000, 77–92.

2. H. Gelter, "Genuine Friluftsliv as a Way to Great Natural Experiences and Professional Experience Production," in *Articles on Experiences* 2, M.

Kylänen (ed.), Lapland Centre of Expertise for the Experience Industry, Rovaniemi, 2005, 8–26.

3. John Muir, *Nature Writings: The Story of My Boyhood and Youth, My First Summer in the Sierra, the Mountains of California, Stickeen, Selected Essays* (New York: Library of America 1997); J. Muir, H.B. Kane and E.W. Teale, *The Wilderness World of John Muir* (Mariner Books E.A. Mills, 1920), republished 2001; Aldo Leopold, *A Sand County Almanac* (Oxford University Press, 1949).

4. J. Dybwad, *Nansens röst* (Oslo: Jacon Dybwads Forlag, 1942).

5. Free nature is a very common phrase in Scandinavia. It means a nature free from human constructs – like wilderness, but better. People belong there and can be present.

6. G. Sessions, *Deep Ecology for the 21st Century* (Boston: Shamnhala. 1995).

7. Snofed 2005, Snofed Nytt 11, www.snofed.se, accessed on Sept. 11, 2005.

8. B.J. Pine II and J.H. Gilmore, *The Experience Economy* (Boston: Harvard Business School Press, 1999).

9. V.A. Shetty, "Take Your Time," in *The Times of India*, May 12, 2005. See also SlowDesign at www.slowdesign.org, accessed on June 15, 2007, Slow-Food at www.slowfood.com, accessed on Nov. 12, 2003.

10. Mihály Csikszentmihályi, *The Psychology of Optimal Experiences* (New York: Harper Perennial, 1991).

11. Pine and Gilmore, *The Experience Economy*, 1999.

12. S. Priest, "The Semantics of Adventure Education," in J.C. Miles & S. Priest (eds.), *Adventure Education*. (State College, PA: Venture Publ., 1990), 113–117.

Chapter 3: Deserving the Peak: When Norwegian Friluftsliv Meets the World (Ese)

1. Heidi Richardson, Kraftanstrengelse og ensomhet – En analyse av det norske friluftslivets kulturelle konstruksjoner (Bergen: Universitetet i Bergen, 1994).

2. Anette Bischoff, and Alf Odden "Nye trender i norsk friluftsliv. Utvanning eller forsterkning av gamle mønstre og idealer." *Rapport fra konferansen forskning i friluft*. Comp. Lerkelund, Hans Erik (Oslo: Frifo 2003). 231–247: Alf Odden, and Øystein Aas (2003) "Motiver for friluftsliv-sutøvelse" *Rapport fra konferansen forskningi friluft*. Comp. Lerkelund, Hans Erik (Oslo: Frifo 2003) 120–139.

3. Ketil Skogen, "Ungdom og nature – Postmoderne identitetskonstruksjon eller repsoduksjon av klassekultur?" *Tidsskrift for samfunnsforsking*, 1995.

4.   Odd Inge Vistad and Marie Skaar "Regionale skilnader i synet på endring av regelverket om bruk av snøskuter i utmark," *Utmark 1*, 2005.
5.   Vorkinn Marit, Joar Vittersø and Hanne Riese. *Norsk friluftsliv på randen av modernisering* (Lillehammer: Østlandsforskning, 2000).

Chapter 4: Defining Friluftsliv (Faarlund)

1.   From an encounter at Hæverstølen/Norway April 2002 to study modernity and the Norwegian tradition of friluftsliv. "Defining Friluftsliv," in *Pathways: The Ontario Journal of Ontario Education,* Summer 14 (3) 2002, 18–19
2.   C.W. Rubensen, "On the Peaks: Friluftsliv in V or Sport," in *Norsk Fjellsport Journal*, 1914.

Chapter 5: What is Friluftsliv Good For? Norwegian Friluftsliv in a Historical Perspective (Tordsson)

1.   Jon Teigland, *Nordmenns friluftsliv og naturopplevelser. Et faktagrunnlag fra en panelstudie av langtidsendringer* (Vestlandsforskning Sogndal: VF-rapport 7/00. 1986–1999).
2.   Mari-Lise Sjong, *Friluftsliv I behandlingen av belastede grupper, en oversikt over forskning og utredning* (Trondheim: Direktoratet for naturforvaltning. 1993).
3.   Ottar Hellevik and Henning Høie, "Vi bekymrer oss mindre for miljøet" in *Samfunnsspeilet* 4, 1999, 53–61.
4.   Worldwatch Institute, *State of the World* (Oslo: J.W. Cappelens Forlag A.S., 2002) Norwegian Edition.
5.   Marit Vorkinn, Joar Vittersø, Hanne Riese, *Friluftsliv – påranden av modernisering?* ØF-rapport 02/2000 (Lillehammer: Østlandsforskning, 2000).

Chapter 6: Norwegians and Friluftsliv: Are We Unique? (Gåsdal)

1.   Odd Frank Vaage, *Til alle døgnets tider: Tidsbruk 1971–2000* (Oslo: Statistics Norway, 2002).
2.   J.E. Dølvik, Ø. Danielsen, and G. Hærnes. *Kluss i vekslinga: fritid, idrett og organisering.* FAFO rapport 080 (Oslo: FAFO, 1988).
3.   Marit Vorkinn, and Anne Mari Aamelfot Hjelle. *Friluftsliv: Delrapport 2 fra forskningsprogrammet Bruk og forvaltning av utmark* (Oslo: The Research Council of Norway, 2001).

4. Nils Faarlund, "Norsk friluftslivs verdigrunnlag og forskningsmessige forsøk på bestemmelse og bidrag til levendegjøring." *Konferansen Forskning i friluft. Stjørdal 18–19 November 1998*: Friluftslivets fellesorganisasjon, 1999.

5. Tove Nedrelid, *Ut på tur – på nordmanns vis* (Oslo: Cappelen, 1993).

6. Ola Vaagbø, *Den norske turkulturen: Friluftslivetsår 1993* (Oslo: FRIFO, 1993).

7. B.L. Driver, H.E.A. Tinsley and M.J. Manfredo, "The Paragraphs about Leisure and Recreation Experience Preference Scales: Results from Two Inventories Designed to Assess the Breadth of the Perceived Benefits of Leisure" in B.L. Driver, P.J. Brown and G.P. Peterson (eds.), *The Benefits of Leisure* (State College, PA: Venture Publishing, 1991) 263–86.

8. Odd Gåsdal, "Deltakelse i friluftsliv: Sosiale mål og fysiske hindringer." Dissertation, University of Trondheim, 1995.

9. Nils Faarlund, "Norsk friluftslivs verdigrunnlag og forskningsmessige forsøk på bestemmelse og bidrag til levendegjøring." Konferansen Forskning i friluft. Stjørdal 18–19 November 1998: Friluftslivets fellesorganisasjon, 1999.

10. H.K. Cordell et al, "United States of America: Outdoor Recreation," in *Free Time and Leisure Participation: International Perspectives*, Grant Cushmann, A.J. Veal and Jiri Zuzanek (eds.) (Wallingford, UK: CABI Publishing, 2005) 245–64.

11. Odd Frank Vaage, *Trening, mosjon og friluftsliv: Resultater fra Levekårsundersøkelsen 2001 og Tidsbruksundersøkelsen 2000*. Statistics Norway Reports 13 (Oslo: Statistics Norway, 2004).

12. Statistics Sweden. 5 May 2006. http://www.scb.se/statistik/LE/LE0101/_dokument/Tabell3PRM.xls

13. C.L. Craig et al, *Increasing Physical Activity: Building a Supportive Recreation and Sport System* (Ottawa: The Canadian Lifestyle and Fitness Research Institute, 2001).

14. Alberta Community Development, "Alberta Recreation Survey Report: Summery of Results," 2000. Alberta Community Development, http://www.cd.gov.ab.ca/building_communities/sport_recreation/recr eation_survey/surveypdf/2000_ARS_Alberta_results.PDF, accessed on May 25, 2006.

15. Statistics Finland, http://www.stat.fi/til/vpa/2002/vpa_2002_2006-04-13_tau_025_en.xls, accessed on May 25, 2006.

16. Anne D. Wallace, *Walking, Literature, and English Culture: The Origins and Uses of Peripatetic in the Nineteenth Century* (Oxford: Oxford University Press, 1993).

17. Inger-Marie Bjønness, "Outdoor recreation and its impact upon a boreal forest area Bymarka, Trondheim" in *Norsk Geografisk Tidsskrift* 35:2 (1981) 57–77.
18. Rebecca Solnit, *Wanderlust: A History of Walking* (New York: Penguin, 2000).
19. Björn Tordsson, "Å svare på naturens åpne tiltale: En undersøkelse av meningsdimensjonene i norsk friluftsliv på 1900 – tallet og en drøftelse av friluftsliv som sosiokulturelt fenomen." Dissertation. Norwegian School of Sport Sciences, 2003.
20. Simon Schama, *Landscape and Memory* (London: Fontana, 1996).
21. Gudrun M. König, *Eine Kulturgeschichte des Spatzierganges: Spuren einer Bürgelichen Praktik 1790–1859* (Vienna: Böhlau, 1996).
22. Roderick Nash, *Wilderness and the American Mind* (New Haven, CT: Yale University Press, 1980).
23. David E. Shi, *The Simple Life: Plain Living and High Thinking in American Culture* (New York: Oxford University Press, 1985).
24. Tom Selwyn, "Landscapes of Liberation and Imprisonment: Towards an Anthropology of Israeli Landscape," in Eric Hirsch and Michael O'Hanlon (eds.), *The Anthropology of Landscape: Perspectives on Place and Space* (Oxford: Clarendon, 1995) 114–34.
25. Nicholas Green, *The Spectacle of NATURE: Landscape and Bourgeois Culture in Nineteenth-Century France* (Manchester: Manchester University Press, 1990).
26. Anthony Giddens, *Modernity and Self-Identity: Self and Society in the Late Modern Age* (Cambridge: Polity, 1991).
27. Ibid, Björn Tordsson, 2003.

Chapter 7: The Ash-Lad: Classical Figure of Norwegian Ecophilosophy (Kvaløy-Sætereng)

1. Herbert Hendin, *Suicide and Scandinavia* (New York: Green and Stratton, 1967).

Chapter 8: The Right of Public Access: The Landscape Perspective of Friluftsliv (Sandell)

1. K. Sandell, & S. Sörlin, *Friluftshistoria – från 'härdande friluftslif' till ekoturism och miljöpedagogik: Teman i det svenska friluftslivets historia* (Stockholm: Carlssons Bokförlag, 2000). B. Tordsson, *Å svare på naturens åpne tiltale: En undersøkelse av meningsdimensjoner i norsk friluftsliv på*

1900 – tallet og en drøftelse av friluftsliv som sosiokulturellt fenomen (Oslo: Norges Idrettshøgskole, 2003).

2. C. Watkins (ed.) "Rights of Way: Policy," in *Culture and Management* (London: Pinter, 1996). H. Millward, "Public Access in the West European Countryside: A Comparative Survey," in *Journal of Rural Studies*, Vol. 9, No. 1 (1993) 39–51.

3. B. Tordsson, "Rötter i 'barbari' och 'romantik'," in K. Sandell and S. Sörlin, *Friluftshistoria – från 'härdande friluftslif' till ekoturism och miljöpedagogik: Teman i det svenska friluftslivets historia* (Stockholm: Carlssons bokförlag, 2000) 47–61. Also see T. Wiklund, *Det tillgjorda landskapet: En undersökning av förutsättningarna för urban kultur i Norden* (Göteborg: Korpen, 1995).

4. K. Sandell, "Access Under Stress: The Right of Public Access Tradition in Sweden," in N. McIntyre, D. Williams and K. McHugh (eds.), *Multiple Dwelling and Tourism: Negotiating Place, Home and Identity* (Wallingford and New York: CABI Publishing, 2006) 278–294.

5. O. Brox, *Ver felles eiendom: Tar vi vare på allemannsretten?* (Oslo: Pax Forlag, 2001); K.T. Colby, "Public Access to Private Land: Allemansrätt in Sweden," in *Landscape and Urban Planning*, Vol. 15 (1988) 253–264. H.K. Cordell and C.J. Betz, "Trends in Outdoor Recreation Supply on Public and Private Lands in the USA," in C.W. Gartner and D.W. Lime (eds.), *Trends in Outdoor Recreation, Leisure and Tourism* (Wallingford and New York, CABI Publishing, 2000) 75–89. K. Højring, "The Right to Roam the Countryside: Law and Reality Concerning Public Access to the Landscape in Denmark," in *Landscape and Urban Planning*, Vol. 59 (2002) 29–41; B. Kaltenborn, H. Haaland and K. Sandell, "The Public Right of Access: Some Challenges to Sustainable Tourism Development in Scandinavia," in *Journal of Sustainable Tourism*, Vol. 9, No. 5 (2001) 417–433.

6. E. Daléus and K. Sandell, "From A Sense of Place to A Sense of Marketplace: Outdoor Recreation and Public Right of Access to Nature in Sweden and Canada," paper presented at the international workshop "Outdoor Recreation – Practice and Ideology from an International Comparative Perspective" Umeå, Sweden, September 2–6, 1998. Also see H. Millward, "Public Access in the Canadian Countryside: A Comparative Survey," in *The Canadian Geographer*, Vol. 36, No. 1 (1992) 30–44.

7. Y.F. Tuan, *Topophilia: A Study of Environmental Perception, Attitudes, and Values* (New York: Columbia University Press, 1990). Also see D.R. Williams and N. McIntyre, "Where Heart and Home Reside: Changing Constructions of Place and Identity," in D. Stynes (ed.), *Trends 2000:*

Shaping the Future (Lansing, MI: Department of Park Recreation and Tourism Resources, 2001) 392–403.

8. "Whose Common Future? A Special Issue," in *The Ecologist*, Vol. 22, No. 4 (1992). Also see G. Snyder, "Ecology, Place, and the Awakening of Compassion," in A. Drengson and Y. Inoue (eds.), *The Deep Ecology Movement* (Berkeley, CA.: North Atlantic Books, 1995) 237–242.

Chapter 9: The Value and Necessity of Tumbling and Fumbling (Jensen)

1. Conwaying leadership: Sharing the experiences of free nature in accord with the patterns of thought and values of the Norwegian tradition of friluftsliv in smaller groups for the joy of identification, as well as for finding in modernity routes towards lifestyles where nature is the home of culture. See Nils Faarlund, "Defining Friluftsliv," in *Pathways the Ontario Journal of Outdoor Education*, 14:3 (Summer 2002) 18–19.

2. *Kjennskap* (definite form is *Kjennskapen*) is very difficult to translate into English. It is made up of two words: *ä kjenne*, which means to feel, to know, to experience, etc., and *skap*, which is a wholeness or a gestalt. Possible words to use are perhaps "acquaintedness, embodied knowing" or the French *connaissance*.

Chapter 10: How Modern Friluftsliv Started: Fridtjof Nansen, Instigator and Model (Repp)

1. L.N. Høyer, *Eva og Fridtjof Nansen* (Oslo: Cappelen, 1955).

2. E. Shackleton, *Nansen the Explorer* (London: Witherby Ltd., 1959). The first edition of *Eskimoliv* (Kristiania: Aschehoug, 1891), Nansen's book about the life and culture of the Inuit people in Greenland, was published in Norwegian (1891), Swedish (1891) and German (1893). It was also published in Budapest (1922). Regrettably, it has never been published in English.

3. E. Shackleton, 1959, 73. Readers will be able to find very concise information in many dictionaries and reference books, e.g. *Chambers' Biographical Dictionary* (2002) or *Chambers' Dictionary of World History* (2000). Besides many articles about Nansen in various languages, the books of R. Huntford in English – *Nansen* (1997) and *Scott and Amundsen* (1993) – can be recommended. As far as shorter works in English are concerned, however, articles by Rygg (1931), Breivik (1989), Lippe (2002) and Repp (2004) should be mentioned. A summary in English about the artistic approach of Nansen is written by the Norwegian historian

of fine arts, L. Oestbye, *Fridtjof Nansen as an Artist* (Oslo: Unuversitets-
forlaget, 1980) 41, 42.

4. R. Huntford, *Nansen* (London: Duckworth, 1997) 56.
5. This account about Nansen and his "long wooden pieces" is translated from
    the German historian Karl Ziak (1965). Cf. "Da eilte 1888 die Sensation-
    snachricht durch die Welt, da – Fridtjof Nansen auf Skiern in 40 Tagen
    Grönland durchquert habe, und plötzlich war alle Welt an den langen
    Hölzern interessiert." See p. 171.
6. F. Nansen, "Friluftsliv: Professor Fridtjof Nansen's tale paa Den norske
    tuirstforenings møte for skoleungdommen I juni 1921," in Den norske
    turistforening (ed.), *Den norske turistforenings aarbok 1922* (Kristiania:
    Grøndahl, & Søn, 1922).
7. M.N. Greve, *Fridtjof Nansen* (Oslo: Aschehoug, 1994) M.E. Daivies, transla-
    tion. For English translations of Peter Wessell Zapffe's writings, see
    Peter Reed and David Rotherberg (eds.), *Wisdom in the Open Air* (Min-
    neapolis: University of Minnesota Press, 1993).
8. L. Øestby, *Fridtjof Nansen as an Artist*, 1980, 41.
9. F. Nansen, *Sporting Days in Wild Norway: Pages from My Diary* (London:
    Thornton Butterworth, 1925); F. Nansen, *Adventure* (London: Leonard
    & Virginia Woolf at the Hogarth Press, 1927); G. Breivik, "F. Nansen and
    the Norwegian Outdoor Life Tradition," in *Scandinavian Journal of
    Sports Sciences*, 11:1 (1989) 9–14; G. Lippe, "Fridtjof Nansen: The Mak-
    ing of His World of Men," in *The Sports Historian*, 22:2 (2002) 98–118.
10. Most of this theoretical approach is a summarized discussion from central
    parts and themes belonging to my dissertation, "Values and ideals of our
    generation's outdoor life 'friluftsliv': Nansen as a model? Thinking and
    formulations about 'friluftsliv' today reflecting the values and ideals of
    Nansen? A comparative study." Also used is material from my other stud-
    ies of Nansen. Two written arenas of formulation were compared, the first
    one concerning the "friluftsliv" of Nansen and the second one that of our
    generation. More than a century ago Nansen urged that an alternative
    rearing of youth should emphasize traditional knowledge and firsthand
    meetings with nature, developing a sense of joy in being in nature. For the
    last four decades debates and confrontations have arisen about correct use
    and understanding of the concept "friluftsliv," about attitudes to nature,
    about ecological thinking, environmental responsibility and social com-
    mitment. See G. Repp, *Verdiar og ideal for dagens friluftslive. Nansen som
    føredøme* (Oslo: Norges idrettshøgskole, 2001); "Friluftsliv and Adventure:
    Models, Heroes and Idols in a Nansen Perspective," in *Journal of Adven-
    ture Education and Outdoor Learning*, 19:5 (2004) 265–285.

11.   A.N. Rygg, "Fridtjof Nansen," in *The American-Scandinavian Review*, 19:5 (1931) 265–285.

Chapter 11: Nature Guidance and Guidance in Friluftsliv (Ulstrupp)

No notes

Chapter 12: Friluftsliv with Preschool Children (Brügge)

1.   B. Brügge, M. Glantz, och K. Sandell, *Friluftslivets pedagogic: För kunskap, känsla och livskvalitet* (Stockholm: Liber, 2004).
2.   A. Lenninger and T. Olsson, *Lek äger rum* (Forskningsrådet Formas, 2005).
3.   Utbildningsdepartementet Läroplaner för det obligatoriska skolväsendet och de frivilliga skolformerna, 1994, Lpo 94 .
4.   Lenninger and Olsson, 2005.
5.   T. Olsson, *Skolgärden som klassrum, Året runt på Coombes school* (Runa förlag, Bokserien Stad & Land 168, Movium, SLU, Alnarp, 2002).
6.   B. Brügge, Glantz and Sandell, 2004.
7.   R. Kaplan and S. Kaplan, *The Experience of Nature: A Psychological Perspective* (Boston: Cambridge University Press, 1994).
8.   A. Dahlgren, L.O. och Szczepanski, *Utomhuspedagogik – Boklig bildning och sinnlig erfarenhet. Ett försök till bestämning av utomhuspedagogikens identitet.* (Linköpings universitet, Skapande Vetande No. 31, 1997); A. Dahlgren, L.O. och Szczepanski, *Outdoor Education: Literary education and sensory experience.* (Kinda Education Centre, 1998).
9.   The Comenius Program is one specific project among many under the European Union "Comenius" umbrella. The Comenius Progam facilitates cooperative ventures among students and teachers in European schools.

Chapter 13: The "Oslomarka" Greenbelt: Protection and Use in Friluftsliv (Lund)

1.   Bob Henderson, Simon Beames and David Taylor, "You Came to Norway, Just to Ski" in *Snø & Ski,* May 2004, 37–39.

PART II: CANADIAN

Chapter 14: An Effort to Capture an Elusive Friluftsliv (Henderson)

1.   The Conference was titled DEEP – CONFERENCE 2000. Deep Environmental Education practice – Friluftsliv sponsored by Norge Idrettshøgskole,

at Hæverstølen Renneba January 14–18, and Oslo 19–20, Norway. The conference description read as follows: "Places for outdoor education in the 21st century. Local, national and global perspectives on outdoor education theory and practice."

The papers at this conference explored ways in which "outdoor life" may maintain links with nature weakened by developments in the last century, and maintain traditions of knowledge and respect, which have been placed at risk by globalization and modernization. The role of globalization and modernization within current forms of outdoor life will be critically examined. International perspectives and comparisons will highlight the tension between the local, the national, and the global in outdoor experience. In different ways, each of the papers will explore the imperatives for developing deeper analysis of the environmental and cultural dimensions of outdoor life, with a particular emphasis on pedagogical implications.

2. I kept detailed notes at the two January 2000 gatherings. Many of the quotes in this paper are directly connected to formal and informal presentations and conversations shared at these gatherings. Indeed, this conference over a five-year period has remained the leading impetus toward collecting this set of papers for an English friluftsliv anthology. When a passage is not referenced, it has come from conversations held at the January 2000 gatherings.

3. Petr Kubala, "Friluftsliv: The Mysterious, the Ordinary, the Noticeable, and the Extraordinary," proceedings from the International Symposium, *Outdoor Sports Education* November 18–21, 2004, Hrubá Skála, Czech Republic. Edited by Jan Newman and Ivana Turčová.

4. Mizamoto Musashi, *A Book of Five Rings: The Classic Samerai Guide to Strategy* (London: Allison Busby, 1982).

5. Eugene Herigel, *Zen and the Art of Archery* (Toronto: McGraw-Hill, 1964).

6. Fred Bodsworth, "Our Threatened Heritage," in Borden Spears (ed.), *Wilderness Canada* (Toronto: Clarke Irwin, 1970).

7. John Livingston, in David Cayley, *The Age of Ecology* (Toronto: James Lorimer, 1991) 11. Sigurd Olson, *Reflections from the North Country* (New York: Alfred A. Knopf, 1976) 27.

8. For a full version of this story, see "Thoughts on the Idea of Adventure," in *The Soul Unearthed: Celebrating Wilderness and Spiritual Renewal Through Nature*, edited by Cass Adams (Boulder, CO: Sentient Publications, 2002).

9. Thomas Berry, *The Great Work: Our Way into the Future* (New York: Bell Tower 1999) 20.

10. Thomas Berry, *The Great Work*, 15.

11. Arnes Naess, *Ecology, Community and Lifestyle: Outline of an Ecosophy*, translated by Dave Rothenberg (Cambridge: Cambridge University Press, 1989) 179.

12. Nils Faarlund, Peter Reed and David Rothenberg (eds.), *Wisdom in the Open Air* (Minneapolis: University of Minnesota Press, 1993) 164.

Chapter 15: Dwelling Where I Teach: Connections with Friluftsliv (Elrick)

1. Wendell Berry, "History" from *Collected Poems of Wendell Berry, 1957–1982* (San Francisco: North Point Press, 1987).

2. Bert Horwood, "Integration and Experience in the Secondary Curriculum," in *McGill Journal of Education*, 29:1 (1994) 89–101; Sona Mehta and Bob Henderson, "Exploring Notions of Schooling" in *Pathways: The Ontario Journal of Outdoor Education.* July/August Vol. 8, No. 4 (1996) 11–17.

3. Editor's Note: Michael Elrick was a member of Canadian National White Water Kayak Slalom team from 1983 to 1988.

4. *The Long Range Deep Ecology Movement and Arne Naess*, Alan Drengson (ed.), *The Trumpeter: Journal of Ecosophy* (theme issue), Vol. 9, No. 2 Spring 1992. See specifically Melissa Nelson, "An Exploration of Intuition: Its Relationship to the Deep Ecology Movement and Ecosophy."

5. Bob Henderson, *Every Trail Has a Story: Heritage Travel in Canada* (Toronto: Natural Heritage, 2005).

6. Steve Van Matre, *Earth Education: A New Beginning* (Warrenville, IL: The Institute for Earth Education, 1990)

7. Murray Bookchin, *Remaking Society: Pathways to a Green Future* (Boston: South End Press, 1990).

8. Steve VanMatre, *Earth Keepers* (Cedar Grove, Greensville, WA: The Institute for Earth Education, 1987).

9. Chief Gary Potts of the Bear Island Indian Reserve, Temagami, Ontario. Quoted in "Temagami: The Last Stand," in *The Nature of Things*, Canadian Broadcasting Corporation, 1989.

10. Bill Reese, excerpt from keynote speech at EECOM (Canadian Network for Environmental Education and Communication) conference "Creating Ripples," Oct 1, 2005, at Camp Tawingo, Huntsville Ontario.

11. Sharon Butala, *The Perfection of the Morning: An Apprenticeship In Nature* (Toronto: HarperCollins, 1994) 65.

12. Aldo Leopold, *A Sand County Almanac* (New York: Ballantine Books, 1970) 243.

Chapter 16: Duct Tape and Rabbit Wire: Getting by in the Big Land (Innes)

1. For more information on Innu culture, history and contemporary political struggles, see Georg Henriksen, *Hunters of the Barrens* (St. John's: ISER, 1973), *Life and Death Among the Mushuau Innu of Northern Labrador* (St. John's: ISER, 1993); Camille Fouillard, (ed.), *Gathering Voices: Finding Strength to Help Our Children* (Vancouver: Douglas and McIntyre, 1995); *Innu Nation Task Force on Mining Activities, Ntesinan Nteshininman Nteniunan* (Sheshatshiu: Innu Nation, 1996); Stephen Loring, "The Innu Hunting Way of Life," in *Journal of American Indian Higher Education*, 7, 4, 1996, 20–27; José Mailhot, *The People of Sheshatshit: In the Land of the Innu* (St. John's: ISER, 1997); and Marie Wadden, *Nitassinan: The Innu Struggle to Regain Their Homeland* (Vancouver/Toronto: Douglas and McIntyre, Ltd., 1996). Innu Nation, the political organization representing the Labrador Innu, maintains a Web site at www.innu.ca. See also the award winning site www.tipatshimuna.ca

2. Survival International, *Canada's Tibet: The Killing of the Innu* (London: Survival for Tribal Peoples, 1999).

3. Nils Faarlund, "Defining Friluftsliv!" in *Pathways: The Ontario Journal of Outdoor Education*, 14 (3), Summer 2002, 18–19.

4. Examples include the Next Generation Project in Natuashish, focused on women in that troubled community and the Innu Guardians and Innu Youth Experiential Learning projects offered by Innu Nation to develop environmental skills among Innu youth in preparation for the responsibilities of resource management under a future self-government agreement. The work of the Tshikapish Foundation is also notable. Tshikapish is a not-for-profit organization with a mission to provide leadership and healing opportunities for Innu youth by reconnecting them with their heritage. It operates from a remote lodge at Kamestastin, in the Labrador interior.

Chapter 17: Embracing Friluftsliv's Joys: Teaching the Canadian North Through the Canadian Wilderness Travel Experience (Hvenegaard and Asfeldt)

1. B.S. Guy, W.W. Curtis and J.C. Crotts, "Environmental Learning of First-Time Travelers," in *Annals of Tourism Research*, 17 (1990) 419–431.

2. A. Ewert, "Experiential Education and Natural Resource Management," in *Journal of Experiential Education* 19:1 (1996) 29–33.

3. S. Priest and M. Gass, *Effective Leadership in Adventure Education* (Champaign, IL: Human Kinetics, 1997).

4. J. Raffan, and M.J. Barrett, "Sharing the Path: Reflections on Journals from an Expedition," in *The Journal of Experiential Education* (Summer 1989) 29–36.

5. A. Jensen, "The Value and Necessity of Tumbling and Fumbling," in *Pathways: The Ontario Journal of Outdoor Education*, 14:3 (2002) 20–21.

6. N. Faarlund, "Defining Friluftsliv," in *Pathways: The Ontario Journal of Outdoor Education*, 14:3 (2002) 18–19.

7. D. Pepi, "The Mechanics of Nature Appreciation," in *Journal of Environmental Education*, 25:3 (1994) 5–13.

8. M. Weilbacher, "The Renaissance of the Naturalist," in *Journal of Environmental Education*, 25:1 (1993) 4–7.

9. D.W. Jardine, "Birding Lessons and the Teachings of Cicadas" in *Canadian Journal of Environmental Education* 3 (1998) 92–99.

10. A. Bell, "Natural History from a Learner's Perspective," in *Canadian Journal of Environmental Education* 2 (1997) 132–144.

11. M.S. Quinn, "Knowing Your Friends," in *Pathways: The Ontario Journal of Outdoor Education* 7:6 (1995) 5–8.

12. B. Henderson, "Lessons from Norway: Language and Outdoor Life," in *Pathways: The Ontario Journal of Outdoor Education* 13:3 (2001) 31–32.

13. B. Hampton and D. Cole, *Soft Paths: How to Enjoy the Wilderness Without Harming It* (Mechanicsburg, PA: Stackpole Books, 2003).

14. E.J. Stewart, B.M. Hayward and P.J. Devlin, "The 'Place' of Interpretation: A New Approach to the Evaluation of Interpretation," in *Tourism Management*, 19:3 (1998) 257–266.

15. B. Dahle, "Outdoor Life: Based on Whose Values?" in *Pathways: The Ontario Journal of Outdoor Education*, 13:3 (2001) 26–27.

16. J.S. Rowe, *Home Place: Lessons in Ecology* (Edmonton, AB: NewWest Books, 1990).

17. A. Leopold, *A Sand County Almanac* (New York: Oxford University Press, 1949).

18. M. Asfeldt, "Finding a Place for Technology in Outdoor Education," in *Pathways: The Ontario Journal of Outdoor Education*, 16:3 (2004) 18–20. Also see M. Asfeldt and G. Hvenegaard, "The Purposeful Use of Technology" in *Pathways: The Ontario Journal of Outdoor Education*, 15:2 (2003) 4–7. *Pathways* has maintained a focus on technology and outdoor education from 2002 to 2006.

Chapter 18: The Role of Craft-Making in Friluftsliv (MacEachren)

1. See Zabe MacEachren, "Craftmaking: A Pedagogy for Environmental

Awareness." Unpublished PhD Dissertation, York University, Toronto, Canada, 2001.

2.   Many people associate Baden-Powell with founding the Scout Movement. Prior to Powell being considered the head of the organization, many prominent youth leaders with their own established organizations were corresponding in order to discuss amalgamating efforts and to decide who had the most appropriate role models for youth. Dan Beard promoted the "Pioneer" or "Frontier" person. Seton promoted the "Indian Brave" and his woodcraft lore. Unfortunately, Seton's original unpublished manuscript, which he shared with Powell, was adapted and used to promote Powell's interest in the "Military Scout" as the role model within the organization he would eventually lead. See John Wadland, "Ernest Thompson Seton: Man in Nature and the Progressive Era 1888–1915." Unpublished PhD Dissertation, York University, Toronto, Canada, 1977. Also note that The Woodcraft Folk Movement, which still exists in the United Kingdom and arose as a partial objection to the military tone the Scout Movement, is based on many of Seton's ideas that emphasized learning indigenous crafts from one's local area.

3.   See Ernest Thompson Seton, *Two Little Savages* (New York: Dover Publications, 1962) and *The Book of Woodcraft* (New York: Garden City Publishing, 1912, 1921).

4.   M.K. Gandhi, *My Views on Education* (New Delhi: Gandhi Peace Foundation, 1970).

5.   Anthony Richards, "Kurt Hahn: The Midwife of Educational Ideas." Unpublished Ph.D Dissertation, University of Colorado, USA, 1981.

6.   Patricia Livingston, "The Importance of Handwork in the Waldorf School," in *Renewal Magazine*, Spring/Summer 9 (2000).

7.   For more information on William Morris, see Edward Lucie-Smith, *The Story of Craft* (Oxford: Phaidon Press, 1981).

8.   Charlene Spretnek, *The Resurgence of the Real* (New York: Routledge, 1999).

9.   Blair Stevenson, "Culture Behind the Craft: Teaching Traditional Sámi Handicraft in Norway," in *Pathways, The Ontario Journal of Outdoor Education*, 16:1 (2004).

Chapter 19: Friluftsliv Transplanted: The Norwegian Immigrant Experience in Alberta (Urberg)

1.   I have interviewed over 30 Norwegian immigrants in conjunction with "The Norwegian Immigrant Experience in Alberta." The participants currently reside in Alberta, and they immigrated to Canada before 1965. The

purpose of this project is two-fold: 1) to record the experiences, recollections and voices of Norwegian immigrants to Alberta before they disappear; and, 2) to examine issues of identity and place in these immigrant experiences. I have received ethics approval for this project from my home institution. I am using the full names of my participants here with their permission. This article and project would not be possible without their generosity and willingness to share their experiences.

Interviews Cited

Ardiel, Solveig. Personal interview, June 21, 2002. Phone interview, July 21, 2004.

Berg, Reidun & Thorleif. Personal interview, August 8, 2001.

Brittner, Kari. Personal interview, May 20, 2002. Phone interview, July 20, 2004.

Fimrite, Karen. Personal interview, August 15, 2001.

Haga, Knut. Personal interview, August 16, 2001. Phone interview, July 20, 2004.

Hazanoff, Anne Marie. Personal interview, August 2, 2002. Phone interview, July 23, 2004.

Hellum, Kaare. Personal interview, January 22, 2001.

Nyhus, Kirstian. Personal interview, January 17, 2001.

Schneider, Inga. Personal interview, May 14, 2003. Phone interview, July 23, 2004.

Steinbru, Verner. Personal interview, June 22, 2002. Phone interview, July 23, 2004.

Terning, Olga. Personal interview, August 15, 2001. Phone interview, July 22, 2004.

2.   www.edmontonnordic.ca, accessed June 7, 2007.

3.   According to Dr. Gary Gibson, Professor Emeritus of Physical Education of the Augustana Faculty, University of Alberta, some 3,000 to 4,000 people came to watch the early ski jumping competitions in Camrose. Camrose Ski Club was originally called the Fram Ski Club, and it is among the oldest ski clubs in Canada. Additional information about Camrose Ski Club can be found at www.camrose.com/ski.

4.   Nils Faarlund, "Defining Friluftsliv," in *Pathways: The Ontario Journal of Outdoor Education* 14:3 (2002) 18–19.

Part iii: International

Chapter 20: *The Czech Outdoor Experience: Turistika and Connections to Friluftsliv (Martin, Turčová and Neuman)*

1. G. Repp, Norwegian relationships to nature through outdoor life," in J. Neuman, I. Mytting and J. Brtník (eds.), *Outdoor Activities: Proceedings of International Seminar Prague '94 Charles University* (Lüneburg: Verlag Edition Erlebnispädagogik, 1994) 32–42.

2. J.E. Comenius, (M.W. Keatinge, ed.), *The Great Didactic of John Amos Comenius* (London: Black, 1907). Original work published 1632.

3. Czechoslovakia was only founded in 1918 and separate Czech and Slovak republics were later formed in 1993.

4. M. Waic and J. Kössl, "The Origin and Development of Organized Outdoor Activities in the Czech countries," in J. Neuman, I. Mytting and & J. Brink (eds.), *Outdoor Activities: Proceedings of International Seminar Prague '94 Charles University* (Lunenburg: Vela Edition Erlebnispädagogik, 1994) 18–22.

5. J. Guth-Jarkovský, *Turistika: Turistický katechismus* (Praha: Baset, 2003). Original work published 1917.

6. J. Neuman, "Outdoor activities: various opportunities of application and development," in J. Neuman, I. Mytting and J. Brtník (eds.), *Outdoor Activities: Proceedings of International Seminar Prague '94 Charles University* (Lüneburg: Verlag Edition Erlebnispädagogik, 1994) 23–71.

7. I. Turčová, J. Neuman and A.J. Martin, "Diversity in Language: Outdoor Terminology in the Czech Republic," in *Journal of Adventure Education and Outdoor Leadership*, 5:1 (2005) 99–116.

8. E.T. Seton, *Woodcraft Manual for Boys: The Sixteenth Birch Bark Roll (Woodcraft League of America)* (Garden City, NY: Doubleday, Page & Co. 1917).

9. A.B. Svojsík, *Základy Junáctví* (Praha: Merkur, 1991). Original work published 1912.

10. J. Foglar, *Hoši od Bobří řeky* (Praha: Kobes, 1937).

11. F. Nansen, *The First Crossing of Greenland* (London: Longmans, Green, 1890). Translated by H.M Gepp.

12. J. Neuman, "Introduction to Outdoor Education in the Czech Republic," in A. Nilsson, (ed.), *Outdoor Education: Authentic Learning in the Context of Landscapes* (Kisa, Sweden: Kinda Education, 2001) 31–41.

13. J. Kratochvíl, "The Actual Comparison of Physical and Outdoor Education in Czech Educational System," in J. Neuman, I. Mytting and J. Brtník (eds.), *Outdoor Activities: Proceedings of International Seminar Prague '94 Charles University* (Lüneburg: Verlag Edition Erlebnispädagogik, 1994) 102–105.

14. J. Neuman, "The Czech Way of Outdoor Experiential Education," in F.H. Paffrath and A. Ferstl (eds.), *Hemingsles erleben* (Augsberg: Ziel, 2001) 329–338.

15. J. Neuman, I. Mytting and J. Brtník (eds.), *Outdoor Activities: Proceedings of International Seminar Prague '94 Charles University* (Lüneburg: Verlag Edition Erlebnispädagogik, 1994).

16. S. Polišenská, *Norský friluftsliv: teorie a praxe.* Diplomová práce. (Praha: UK FTVS, 1995). Z. Svatošová, *Friluftsliv v Norsku. Hnutí návratu člověka k přírodě.* Diplomová práce (Praha:UK FTVS, 1991).

17. A.J. Martin, D. Franc and D. Zounková, *Outdoor and Experiential Learning* (Aldershot, UK: Gower, 2004).

Chapter 21: Friluftsliv and America (Gilligan)

1. Kevin Crossley-Holland, *The Norse Myths* (New York: Pantheon Books, 1980) 3–6. There is an extensive literature on Norse mythology, ranging from the Icelandic sagas to fully illustrated children's books. Crossley-Holland's *The Norse Myths* (1980) is a good middle ground account – accurate, accessible, and in English. His notes are particularly valuable.

2. Børge Dahle (ed.), *Nature: The True Home of Culture* (Oslo: Norges Idrett-thogskole, 1994). Børge Dahle edited this important booklet around the time of the 1994 winter Olympic games (held in Norway). The booklet was translated into English and circulated during the Olympics. It included important contributions from Norwegians such as Fridtjof Nansen, Børge Dahle, Thor Hyerdahl, among others. This is one of the few references (in English) documenting the philosophical evolution of friluftsliv.

3. F. Nansen, "Friluftsliv," in B. Dahle (ed.), *Nature: The True Home of Culture,* (Oslo: Norges Idretthogskole, 1994). Roland Huntford's excellent biography, *Nansen* (London: Duckworth and Co., 1997), is another valuable source.

4. Peter Reed and David Rothenberg (eds.), *Wisdom in the Open Air* (Minneapolis: University of Minnesota Press, 1993) is another important collection that chronicles the evolution of Norwegian nature philosophy.

5. Bob Henderson as journal editor has also made recent contributions to the literature on friluftsliv in articles in *Pathways: The Ontario Journal of Outdoor Education,* Summer 2000 and Summer 2002.

6. Neil Rolde, *The Interrupted Forest: A History of Maine's Wildlands* (Gardiner, ME: Tilbury House Publishers, 2001). Speck (1997), Maine Indian Program of the Friends of America Service Committee (1989), and Leland (1992) are also excellent sources on indigenous cultures in

Maine and the Maritimes. (See additional references at the end of this section.)

7. Jared Diamond, *Guns, Germs, and Steel: The Fates of Human Societies* (New York: W.W. Norton & Co., 1999) 35–52. There is a vast (and often controversial) literature on this topic. Other accessible and interesting sources include Brian M. Fagan and Paul Shepard, among others. (See additional references at the end of this section.)

8. Gary Snyder, *Practice of the Wild* (San Francisco: North Point Press, 1992).

9. Henry David Thoreau, *Walden* (Boston: Shambhala Publications, 1992) 73.

10. Henry David Thoreau, *Walking* (Bedford, MA: Applewood Books, 1862) 5.

11. Ibid, 33.

12. Ibid, 30.

13. John Muir, "Yellowstone National Park," in *Atlantic Monthly*, April 1898, 515–516.

14. Roderick Nash, *Wilderness and The American Mind* (New Haven: Yale University Press, 1967). Max Oelschlaeger, *The Idea of Wilderness* (New Haven: Yale University Press, 1991). Both Nash and Oelschlaeger are mandatory reads for understanding Thoreau, Muir and Leopold in the context of wildness and wilderness.

15. Aldo Leopold, *A Sand County Almanac with Essays on Conservation from Round River* (New York: Oxford University Press, 1966) 240.

16. Ibid, 251.

17. Ibid, 264.

18. Ibid, 261–262.

19. P.R. Erlich and A.H. Erlich, *The Population Explosion* (New York: Simon & Schuster, 1990).

20. Rand McNally & Co., *Deluxe Illustrated Atlas of the World* (Chicago: Rand McNally & Co., 1999).

Additional References

Brian M. Fagan, *The Journey From Eden: The Peopling of our World* (London: Thames and Hudson, 1990).

Bob Henderson, "Lessons from Norway: Language and Outdoor Life," in *Pathways: The Ontario Journal of Outdoor Education*, Summer 2000.

Bob Henderson, "Lessons from Norway: Language and Outdoor Life II," in *Pathways: The Ontario Journal of Outdoor Education*, Summer 2002.

Charles Leland, *Algonquin Legends* (New York: Dover Publications, 1992).

Maine Indian Program of the American Friends Service Committee, *The Wabenakis of Maine and the Maritimes* (Bath, ME: Maine Indian Program of the American Friends Service Committee, 1989).

Paul Shepard, *Coming Home to the Pleistocene* (Washington D.C.: Island/Shear-
water, 1998).

Frank Speck, *Penobscot Man* (Orono, ME: University of Maine Press, 1997).

*Chapter 22: From Tomte Wisdom to Friluftsliv: Scandinavian Perspectives of
Nature (Hulmes)*

1. Claire, Boss (ed.), *Scandinavian Folk & Fairy Tales* (New York: Avenel
    Books, 1984) 285. This collection of folk and fairy tales provides an
    excellent spectrum of stories and beliefs from the Scandinavian coun-
    tries.
2. C.A. Bowers, *The Culture of Denial: Why the Environmental Movement
    Needs a Strategy for Reforming Universities and Public Schools* (Albany:
    State University of New York Press, 1997) 4, 209. C.A. Bowers has writ-
    ten several books that challenge the cultural assumptions of the Amer-
    ican economic and educational system with respect to our
    anthropocentric views of nature He also argues for the importance of
    retaining the intergenerational wisdom handed down through stories
    and traditions that he refers to as our "mythopoetic narratives."
3. P. Reed and D. Rothenberg (eds.), *Wisdom in the Open Air* (Minneapolis:
    University of Minnesota Press, 1993) 12. Henrik Ibsen's poem "Paa Vid-
    derne" is quoted in part by Peter Reed and David Rothenberg, in their
    introduction to *Wisdom in the Open Air*, and provides a historical
    explanation of the term friluftsliv.
4. Max Oelschlaeger, *The Idea of Wilderness* (New Haven: Yale University
    Press, 1991) 96.
5. Henry David Thoreau, *Walden* (New York: New American Library, 1960)
    66.
6. Roderick Nash, *Wilderness and the American Mind* (New Haven: Yale Uni-
    versity Press, 1967) 128.
7. Aldo Leopold, *A Sand County Almanac with Essays on Conservation from
    Round River* (New York: Ballantine Books, 1978) 238.
8. Ibid.
9. Barry Lopez, *Arctic Dreams* (New York: Bantam Books, 1987).
10. P. Reed and D. Rothenberg (eds.), *Wisdom in the Open Air* (Minneapolis:
    University of Minnesota Press, 1993) 9.
11. Selma Lagerlof, *The Wonderful Adventures of Nils* (New York: Doubleday,
    Page & Company, 1913). Selma Lagerloff was the first women to receive
    the Nobel Prize for literature. *The Wonderful Adventures of Nils* shares
    the nature and geography of Sweden through a story that has captured

the hearts of children and from the tompte, taught them the importance of kindness to humans and animals.

12. Elsa Beskow, *Children of the Forest* (Edinburgh: Floris Books, 1982). Translated from Swedish, this book tells the story of a year in the life of a
tompte family that lives deep in the forest.

13. Harold Jacobsen and Jørn R Sollum, *Kulturminner I Skog* (Skogbrukets:
Kursinstitutt, 1997) 84–85. *Kulturminner I Skog* can be translated as cultural memories in the forest. This forest management text that
describes the Norwegian tradition of planting a tree in the middle of
the farmyard was shared with me by two Norwegian friends, Hilde
Nystuen and Halgrim Breie, who, upon completion of their masters
degrees, plan to return to Hilde's family farm near Tynset, where they
hope to continue traditions handed down from several generations.

Additional References

Peter Christen Asbjørnsen and Jøorgen Moe, *Norwegian Folk Tales* (Oslo: Drey-
ers Forlag, 1982).

Rachel Carson, *Silent Spring* (New York: Houghton Mifflin Company, 1962).

Edwin Teale, Way, *The Wilderness World of John Muir* (Boston: Houghton Mifflin Company, 1954).

*Chapter 23: Experience of Place: Lessons on Teaching Cultural Attachment to Place
(Wattchow)*

1. John Miles, "Wilderness As a Learning Place," in *Journal of Environmental
Education*, 18:2 (1986/87) 33–40.

2. John Miles, "Wilderness Keeping by Wilderness Educators," in *Journal of
Experiential Education*, 13:3 (1990) 42–46.

3. Andrew Brookes, "Lost in the Australian Bush: Outdoor Education As Curriculum," in *Journal of Curriculum Studies*, 34:4 (2002) 405–425.

4. Aldo Leopold, *A Sand County Almanac and Sketches Here and There* (New
York: Oxford University Press, 1949) 166.

5. Ibid, 223.

6. E. Relph, "Modernity and the Reclamation of Place," in D. Seamon (ed.),
Dwelling, Seeing, and Designing: Toward a Phenomenological Ecology
(New York: State University of New York Press, 1992) 37.

7. Arne Naess, "The Norwegian Roots of Deep Ecology," in B. Dahle (ed.),
Nature, The True Home of Culture (Oslo: Norges Idrettshogskole, 1994) 15.

8. Nils Faarlund, "Friluftsliv: A Way Home," in B. Dahle (ed.), *Nature, The True
Home of Culture* (Oslo: Norges Idrettshogskole, 1994) 21–26.

9. B. Dahle, "Socialisation to Life: In Harmony with Nature," in *International*

Seminar in Environmental Education Research, Christchurch College of
Education, New Zealand, December 8–11, 1997.

10. Ibid, 2.

11. B. Dahle, *Smajutulan: I Barnas Naturverden* (Rennebu: Jutullauget) 1995.

12. See, for example, J. Cameron, "Responding to Place in a Post-Colonial Era:
An Australian Perspective," in W.M. Adams and M. Mulligan (eds.),
Decolonizing Nature (London: Earthscan, 2003), 172–196. Also see D.
Orr, *Ecological Literacy: Education and the Transition to a Post-Modern
World* (Albany: State University of New York Press, 1992) and D. Orr,
Earth in Mind: On Education, Environment and the Human Prospect
(Washington, DC: Island Press, 1994).

13. Wendell Berry, *Home Economics* (San Francisco: North Point Press, 1987) 146.

14. Lucy Lippard, *The Lure of the Local: Senses of Place in a Multicentered Society* (New York: The New Press, 1997).

Chapter 24: Landfullness in Adventure-Based Programming: Promoting Reconnection to the Land (Baker)

1. R.M. Pyle, "The Rise and Fall of Natural History: How a Science Grew That
Eclipsed Direct Experience," in *Orion*, 20 (4) (2001) 17–23.

2. A. Leopold, *A Sand County Almanac with Essays on Conservation from
Round River* (New York: Oxford University Press, 1966) 210.

3. B. Lopez, *The Rediscovery of North America* (Lexington, KY: University Press
of Kentucky, 1990) 31.

4. J. Hilten and R.F. Hilten, "A Sense of Place for Environmental Education
and Interpretation," in *The Interpretive Sourcebook: The Proceedings of
the 1996 National Interpreter's Workshop* (Fort Collins, CO: The
National Association for Interpretation, 1996) 59–61.

5. P. Hawken, "A Declaration of Sustainability," in *Utne Reader*, 59 (1993)
54–61.

6. M.A. Baker, "Sense of Place: Connecting People to Places," in *Interpscan*,
26:3 (1999) 20–21; R. Haluza-Delay, "Navigating the Terrain: Helping
Care for the Earth," in J.C. Miles and S. Priest (eds.), *Adventure Pro-
gramming* (State College, PA: Venture, 1999) 445–454; T. Miner, "The
Role of the Environment in Adventure and Outdoor Education," in
Taproot, 13:4 (2003) 6–8; Andrew Brookes, "Astride a Long-Dead Horse:
Mainstream Outdoor Education Theory and the Central Curriculm
Problem," in *Journal of Australian Outdoor Education*, (2) 2004, 22–33.
The critique of outdoor adventure education has grown steadily in the
last decade particularly concerning a lack of attention to "Place."

7. S.J. Meyers, *Lime Creek Odyssey* (Golden, CO: Fulcrum, 1989).

8. Y. Tuan, *Topophilia: A Study of Environmental Perception, Attitudes, and Values* (Englewood Cliff, NJ: Prentice-Hall, 1974).
9. R. Carson, *The Sense of Wonder* (New York: HarperCollins, 1956).
10. D.A. Kolb, *Experiential Learning* (Englewood Cliffs, NJ: Prentice-Hall, 1984).

Additional References

D. Kriesberg, "Creating a Sense of Place with Children's Literature," in *The Interpretive Sourcebook: The Proceedings of the 1999 National Interpreter's Workshop* (Fort Collins, CO: The National Association for Interpretation, 1999) 81–83.

A. Leopold, *Round River* (New York: Oxford University Press, 1953).

Chapter 25: Why Outdoor Learning Should Get Real (Loynes)

1. Chris Loynes, "Adventure in a Bun," in *Journal of Experiential Education* 21:1 (1998) 35–39.
2. George Ritzer, *The McDonaldization of Society* (New York: Sage, 2004).
3. Charlene Spretnak, *The Resurgence of the Real* (Harlow, England: Addison-Wesley, 1997).
4. Martin Ringer, "The Facile-Itation of Facilitation? Searching for Competencies in Group Work Leadership," in *Scisco Conscientia* 2 (1999) 1–19.
5. For example, see Simon Priest and Michael A. Gass, *Effective Leadership in Adventure Programming* (Champaign, IL: Human Kinetics, 1997).
6. Peter F. Drucker, *Management Challenges for the 21st Century* (Oxford: Butterworth-Heinemann, 1999).
7. M. Smith, "Robert Baden-Powell as an Educational Innovator," available at www.infed.org/thinkers/et-bp.htm, accessed August 8, 2002.
8. Robbie Nicol, "Outdoor Education: Research Topic or Universal Value. Part One," in *Journal of Adventure Education and Outdoor Leadership*, 2:1 (2002) 29–41.
9. Edmund O'Sullivan, *Transformative Learning* (London: Zed Books, 1999).
10. Andrew Brookes, "Gilbert White Never Came This Far South: Naturalist Knowledge and the Limits of Universalist Environmental Education," in *Canadian Journal of Environmental Education* 7:2 (2002) 73–87.
11. Robbie Nicol, "Outdoor Education for Sustainable Living: An Investigation into the Potential of Scottish Local Authority Residential Outdoor Education Centres to Deliver Programmes Relating to Sustainable Living." Unpublished PhD thesis, University of Edinburgh, 2000.
12. M. Rickinson et al, *A Review of Research on Outdoor Learning* (Preston Montford, UK: Field Studies Council, 2004).

13. Colin Mortlock, *The Adventure Alternative* (Milnthorpe, England: Cicerone Press, 1984).

14. S. Bowles, Personal communication, 2000.

15. Graham Ellis-Smith, "Rediscovering Our Indigenous Heart: An Adventure with Nature," in *The Human Face of Outdoor Education*, Camping and Outdoor Education Association of Western Australia (Perth, Australia: Australian Outdoor Education Council, 1999) 54–58.

16. Arne Naess, *Ecology, Community and Lifestyle* (Cambridge: Cambridge University Press, 1989).

17. Edmund O'Sullivan, *Transformative Learning* (London: Zed Books, 1999).

18. For example see Karen Warren, "Women's Outdoor Adventures: Myth and Reality," in Karen Warren (ed.), *Women's Voices in Experiential Education* (Dubuque, ID.: Kendall Hunt, 1996).

19. Robin Hodgkin, *Born Curious: New Perspectives in Educational Theory* (London: Wiley, 1976).

20. John Heron, *Feeling and Personhood: Psychology in Another Key* (London: Sage, 1992).

21. David Boud, *Developing Student Autonomy in Learning* (London: Kogan Page, 1988).

22. J. Suoranta, "The Possibilities of Education in the Culture of Violence," in *Journal of Adventure Education and Outdoor Leadership*, 13:2 (1996) 40–46.

23. Dieter May, "Aspects of Tradition and Possible Relationships to Present Day Western Society," in *Journal of Adventure Education and Outdoor Leadership* 13:2 (1996) 30–33.

An English-Language Friluftsliv Bibliography

This bibliography comprises direct friluftsliv-based writing. For this reason, such things as the Scandinavian rights to wander – *allemansrätt* literature and deep ecology literature – have not been a focus. And, the many classic articles that bespeak the friluftsliv tradition in spirit without knowledge of the connection have also not been included. Also omitted are texts that have proven quite difficult to locate, including some conference proceedings. The articles that have been selected, then, are readily retrievable in Canadian libraries and are primarily friluftsliv-based.

For anyone wishing to further their own research in this area, I would encourage them to include content from Norwegian roots of ecophilosophy, *allemansrätt* (rights to wander), and Norwegian identity, history and recreation.

Bowles, S., "Crossing the Borders as a Critical and Experiential Pedagogy" in *Pathways: The Ontario Journal of Outdoor Education*, Winter 2001.

Breivik, G.F., "Nansen and the Norwegian Outdoor Life Tradition" in *Scandinavian Journal of Sports Science II*, (1) 1989.

Dahle, B., (ed), *Nature: the True Home of Culture*. Oslo: Norges Idrettshogskole (1994).

Gelter, H., "The Scandinavian Philosophy of Outdoor Life" in *Canadian Journal of Environmental Education*, Summer (5), 2000.

Gelter, H., "Genuine Frilufsliv as a Way to Great Natural Experiences and Professional Experience Production" in *Articles on Experiences* 2, M. Kylänen (ed.), Lapland Centre of Expertise for the Experience Industry, Rovaniemi, 2005.

Gundersen, Dag E., and Ølstrem, Ketil., "Outdoor Guidance: A Norwegian Perspective" in *Friluftsliv: Entwicklung, Bedeutung und Perspektive*," (Gunnar Liedtke and Dieter Lagersrøm eds.). Aachen, Germany: Meyer & Meyer Verlag, 2007.

Henderson, B., "Friluftsliv" in *Trumpeter: Journal of Ecosophy* 14, (2), 1997.

Henderson, B., "A Canadian Friluftsliv from a Guide and Student Perspective." In *Friluftsliv – Entwicklung, Bedeutung und Perspektive*," (Gunnar Liedtke and Dieter Lagersrøm eds.), Aachen, Germany:Meyer & Meyer Verlag, 2007.

Højring, K., "The Right to Roam the Countryside: Law and Reality Concerning Public Access to the Landscape in Denmark" in *Landscape and Urban Planning*, Vol. 59, 2002.

Kaltenborn, B., Haaland, H., and Sandell, K., "The Public Right of Access: Some Challenges to Sustainable Tourism Development in Scandinavia." in *Journal of Sustainable Tourism*, Vol. 9, No. 5, 2001.

Kubala, Petr., "Friluftsliv: The Mysterious, the Ordinary, the Noticeable, and the Extraordinary" in Proceedings from the International Symposium, *Outdoor Sports Education* November 18–21, Jan Newman and Ivana Turčová (eds), Hrubá Skála, Czech Republic, 2004.

Kvaloy, S., "Ecophilosophy and Ecopolitics: Thinking and Acting in Response to the Treats of Ecocatastrophe." in *North American Review*, 264 (3) 1977.

Kvaloy, S., "Complexity and Time: Breaking the Pyramid's Reign" in *Resurgence*, Autumn, 1984.

Liedtke, Gunnar, and Lagersrøm, D. (eds.), "*Friluftsliv – Entwicklung, Bedeutung und Perspektive*." Aachen, Germany: Meyer & Meyer Verlag, 2007.

Naess, A., *Ecology, Community and Lifestyles*. Cambridge, MA: Cambridge University Press, 1989.

Pendleton, S., "The Norwegian Nature Life Approach" in *Journal of Experiential Education*, Spring, 1983.

Priest, S., "Outdoor Education in Norway: Folkehogskolen, Friluftsliv and Deep Ecology" in *Australian Journal of Outdoor Education*, 2 (3), 1998.

Reed, R. & Rothenberg, D., (eds), *Wisdom in the Open Air*. Minneapolis: University of Minnesota Press, 1993.

Repp, G., "Outdoor Adventure Education and 'Friluftsliv' Seen from Sociology of Knowledge Perspective" in *The Journal of Adventure Education and Outdoor Leadership*, 13 (2), 1996.

Repp, G., "Friluftsliv and Adventure: Models, Heroes and Idols in a

Nansen Perspective" in *Journal of Adventure Education and Outdoor Learning*, 19 (5), 2004.

Rygg, A.N., "Fridtjof Nansen" in *The American-Scandinavian Review*, 19 (5), 1931.

Sandell, K., "Outdoor Recreation and the Nodic Tradition of "Friluftsliv": A Source of Inspiration for a Sustainable Society" in *Trumpeter: Journal of Ecosophy*, 10 (1), 1993.

Sandell, K., "Access Under Stress: The Right of Public Access Tradition in Sweden" in N. McIntrye, D. Williams and K. McHugh (eds.), *Multiple Dwelling and Tourism, Negotiating Place, Home and Identity*. Wallingord and New York: CABI Publishing, 2006.

Stevenson, B., "Culture Behind the Craft: Teaching Traditional Sámi Handicraft in Norway" in *Pathways: the Ontario Journal of Outdoor Education*, 16 (1), 2004.

Toft, M., "Finding High Level Wellness Through Outdoor Pursuits" in *Explore*, Fall, 1985.

Vikander, N., "Trekking in the Landscape of the Mind: Ruminations on 'Friluftsliv' from Afar" in *Pathways: The Ontario Journal of Outdoor Education*, 16 (2), 2004.

Vikander, N., "Personality Dispositions in the Outdoors: Leadership as 'Compelling Demonstration'?" in *The Norwegian Journal of 'Friluftsliv'*, 2007. www.hint.no/~aaj/articles07.html

Vikander, N., "The Function of the Outdoors in Education: The Contribution Potential of Physical Education" in N.F. Rønbeck, (ed), *Artikkelsamling I Friluftsfilosofi, Historie – og Utadanning*. Alta: Finnmark University College, 1990.

Westersjø, J. H., "Friluftsliv in Norway" in *Friluftsliv – Entwicklung, Bedeutung und Perspektive*. Gunnar Liedtke and Dieter Lagersrøm (eds.), Aachen, Germany: Meyer & Meyer Verlag, 2007.

Also see two theme issues of *Pathways: The Ontario Journal of Outdoor Education*, Summer, 13 (3), 2007 and Summer 14 (3), 2002. Contact Bob Henderson, Chair of Editorial Board for *Pathways*, 1990–2006 and *The Norwegian Journal of 'Friluftsliv'* and e-journal published in Norway, www.hint.no/~aaj/articles.html, contact Aage Jensen aage.Jensen@hint.no

Index

About the Contributors

Morten Asfeldt is an Associate Professor of Physical Education at the University of Alberta, Augustana Campus. He was born in Denmark but grew up in northern Newfoundland and the Yukon. Being in wilderness for expended periods is a way of life for Morten and his love for the Canadian north is enduring. He has guided wilderness canoe and raft trips in the Yukon, Northwest Territories and Nunavut for over 20 years and, as a part of his teaching, has been engaging students in 3-to-4-week expeditions for 15 years. The student expeditions saturate the students in wilderness, and the wilderness travel experience helps them to develop lifelong relationships with nature and wild places. (See Chapter 17.)

Molly Ames Baker was the co-director of the Colgate University Outdoor Education program for twelve years where she worked closely with students to develop and implement the "landfull" framework. She is now a full-time mother of three, working with her kids to nurture a sense of belonging in the northern Michigan landscape near Lake Michigan. (See Chapter 24.)

Andrew Brookes (Ph.D.) has taught and researched outdoor education at La Trobe University in Bendigo, Australia, since 1988. He has made several visits to Scandinavia, and has a particular interest in the relationships between outdoor education and particular places, people and histories. He lives in the Lyell forest with his wife and two children. He is never heard to sing around a campfire. (See Preface.)

Britte Brügge is a teacher of outdoor environmental education. She has taught friluftsliv for 18 years at folk high school. After that she has worked as teacher trainer at Linköpings University, which also includes the Master program in Outdoor Environmental Education and Outdoor Life for teachers. This work has involved teaching a wide variety of students, who range from primary school pupils to adults. She reminds us that with friluftsliv the viewing of small flowers near her home is a splendid experience. (See Chapter 12.)

Børge Dahle teaches friluftsliv at Norges Idrettshogskole, Oslo, Norway. Together with Andrew Brookes, he was the prime organizer of Deep Conference January 2000 (Deep Environmental Educational Practice) in Rennebu, Norway. This conference was the catalyst in the creation of this book. He has written children's books concerning friluftsliv and was the editor of *Nature: The True Home of Culture*, 1994. Børge has travelled widely promoting friluftsliv in Scandinavia and the rest of the world. (See Chapter 1.)

Michael Elrick has been teaching high school Environmental Integrated Programs for over 13 years. He teaches in the same community in which he was born and raised, and lives on the street where he delivered papers as a child. His ancestry on his mother's side is fully Norwegian, linked through the great emigrations of the late 1800s. Michael and his family recently attended a reunion in Norway, which was held on a farm that has been in his family for over a thousand years. (See Chapter 15.)

Jo Ese has done research on development and conflict in the Norwegian friluftsliv culture. He now holds an administrative position at Østfold University College, Southern Norway. (See Chapter 3.)

Nils Faarlund has been described as a foundational figure to the evolution and meaning of Norwegian friluftsliv. He has served as the Managing Editor of the *Norwegian Outdoor Journal, Mestra Fjelle*, since the early 1970s and has run an outdoor mountain guiding school for over 30 years. Translations of his writings can be found in Peter Reed and David Rothenberg (eds.), *Wisdom in the Open Air* (Minneapolis: University of Minnesota Press, 1993). (See Chapter 4.)

Odd Gåsdal (Ph.D. in Sociology) is Associate Professor in the Department of Sociology at the University of Bergen. He teaches Research Methods, Economic Sociology and Social Aspects of Nature Resource

Management. He has formerly worked as a researcher in the Norwegian Institute for Nature Research's Friluftsliv Department where he specialized in studies of Urban Area Friluftsliv. In more recent years he has conducted some research on recreational hunting and fishing with a particular emphasis on the economic and resource management aspects of these activities. (See Chapter 6.)

Hans Gelter (Ph.D. in Biology) holds a faculty position as Associate Professor in Biology and as education program co-ordinator for the Master program in Professional Experience Production at the Department of Music and Media, Luleå University of Technology, Sweden. He teaches various subjects within the Experience Production Study Program, such as Hospitality, Interpretation and Guiding, Environmental and Outdoor Education, Experience Production, Creativity Management, etc. Gelter has participated in scientific expeditions on Greenland and along the Northern Russian Arctic coast, as well as private nature tours in northern Canada, U.S.A., Europe, Central Russia, Australia and New Zealand. He is also a keen mountaineer with climbing expeditions in the Alps, Alai and Himalayas. (See Chapter 2.)

David S. Gilligan has taught natural history and outdoor education at Prescott College, Arizona, and Sterling College/The Center For Northern Studies, Vermont from 1999–2007. He has travelled by foot, ski, snowshoe, canoe and sea kayak in remote areas throughout North America, as well as Scotland, Scandinavia, Switzerland, Nepal and New Zealand. He is the author of *The Secret Sierra* and *In the Years of the Mountains*. His upcoming book focuses on North American canoe country. (See Chapter 21.)

Bob Henderson has taught Outdoor Education at McMaster University, Hamilton, Ontario, Canada, for over 25 years. He has served as editor of *Pathways: The Ontario Journal of Outdoor Education* and is author of the 2005 book *Every Trail has a Story*, which promotes heritage travel and place-based education in Canada. Bob travels widely in Canada and is known to share many a song and story around the campfire, including the occasional Ash-Lad story. (See Introduction and Chapter 14.)

Douglas Hulmes is a Professor of Environmental Studies and Education at Prescott College in Prescott, Arizona. He has received numerous awards for his teaching, environmental advocacy and performances of Scottish/American naturalist John Muir. Doug has spent considerable time teaching and travelling in Norway and Sweden, where he taught with a Friluftsliv program at Olavskolen Folkehøgskole, and was a guest professor at Høgskule i Telemark in one of Norway's first interdisciplinary environmental studies programs. (See Chapter 22.)

Glen Hvenegaard has taught Environmental Science and Geography at the Augustana Campus of the University of Alberta since 1994. He co-teaches a geography and canoe expedition course in the Canadian North. He works at several levels (international organizations, local community groups, students and canoeing with his own family) to enhance human interactions with nature, by way of wildlife tourism, protected areas and environmental education. He has published widely on these topics. (See Chapter 17.)

Larry Innes is the executive director of the Canadian Boreal Initiative, an independent organization working with conservationists, First Nations, industry and others to link science, policy and conservation solutions in Canada's Boreal region. He is also an environmental and Aboriginal rights lawyer, and works with the Innu of Labrador and other First Nations across the North on lands and resource issues. He lives in Goose Bay, Labrador, with his wife and young daughters, and plays outside with them every chance he gets. (See Chapter 16.)

Aage Jensen is teaching pedagogy for friluftsliv students at Nord Trøndelag University. He gives another course in nature philosophy for the same category of students. He has written about conwaying in Friluftsliv in different books meant for students at high schools and colleges. He loves hiking up in the mountains, both in summertime and especially in wintertime when he can be seen on his old wooden skis with his homemade rucksack. (See Chapter 9.)

Sigmund Kvaløy-Sætereng (Sigmund Kvaløy) has been, and continues to be, a philosopher, deep ecologist, mountain climber and activist. From the late 1960s to the present he has been a spokesperson against global unidimensionality in favour of regional multidimensionality. A leader in promoting ecophilosopy, he has been a leader in important environment protests and currently teaches at the University of Trondheim, Norway. (See Chapter 7.)

Chris Loynes lectures in Outdoor Education at St. Martin's College. He also consults in the UK and internationally for universities and outdoor education organizations. His first post at a comprehensive school involved the development of an outdoor education program as an alternative curriculum. He was the founder and editor of the *Journal of Adventure Education and Outdoor Leadership*. Chris is a keen naturalist, mountaineer, offshore sailor and sea kayaker. (See Chapter 25.)

Oddvin Lund is responsible for the conservation measures and land use policy for Nordmarka, Oslo. He is a regular contributor to *Sno & Ski* magazine. He works for the large ski federation Skiforeningen. (See Chapter 13.)

Zabe MacEachren (Ph.D.) is the Outdoor and Experiential Education coordinator for the Faculty of Education at Queen's University, Kingston Ontario, Canada. She has made a wood and canvas canoe she named *Instinct* and, when the lakes are open, she can usually be found paddling her way across Canada. In the winter when the lakes are frozen, she hauls the nine-foot-long birch toboggan she made and named *Intuition*. Although her students often seek her out in an academic office, she prefers to chat with people on a trail or around a campfire. (See Chapter 18.)

Andrew Martin (Ph.D.) is a Senior Lecturer in the Department of Management, Massey University, Palmerston North, New Zealand. His intrigue into the Czech way of outdoor education led to the book *Outdoor and Experiential Learning*, which focuses on the outcomes and educational process of courses involving the Czech dramaturgy method and turistika activities. (See Chapter 20.)

Jan Neuman (Ph.D.) is an Associate Professor and head of the Department of Turistika, Outdoor Sport and Outdoor Education, Faculty of Physical Education and Sport, Charles University, Prague, Czech Republic. He is one of the leading Czech experts in the field of Experiential Education. (See Chapter 20.)

Gunnar Repp (Ph.D.) is an Associate Professor in the Department of Physical Education, Sports and Outdoor Life: Friluftsliv, at Volda University College, Norway. He was lecturer/tutor in friluftsliv at The Norwegian University of Sports and Physical Education for five years dre, speaking generally, and with a view to the matter of friluftsliv in particular. (See Chapter 10.)

Klas Sandell (Ph.D.) is professor in human geography at Karlstad University, Sweden, and has worked in a number of scientific projects on human ecology, environmental history and outdoor recreation. Also, he has been a teacher in friluftsliv in practice for about a ten-year period at a folk-high school and he is the co-editor of several popular science books in the field. Building his own kayaks in wood and canvas and paddling in the archipelago of his ancestors is one of the best qualities in life he thinks. (See Chapter 8.)

Björn Tordsson (Ph.D.) was born in Sweden and has, since 1979, been teaching friluftsliv in Sweden, Norway, Denmark and Finland. From 1988 he has been at the Friluftsliv Studies Program at Telemark University College, Norway, where he is Associate Professor. Besides writing practical handbooks on friluftsliv, he has worked with epistemological and educational topics and published studies on the relations between friluftsliv and culture/society, different ideologies in the friluftsliv tradition, and the political and institutional framework around friluftsliv. He loves sailing in traditional working boats along the Scandinavian coasts. (See Chapter 5.)

Ivana Turčová (Ph.D.) is a Lecturer in the Department of Outdoor Sports and Outdoor Education, Faculty of Physical Education and Sport, Charles University, Prague, Czech Republic. Her doctoral thesis examined the diversity in outdoor language in relation to Czech and British English. (See Chapter 20.)

Svend Ulstrup is a renowned Greenlandic kayak builder. He runs a folk school in Denmark with craft and ecologically sustainable lifestyle as central themes. Svend is also a friluftsliv guide in Denmark. Currently he is completing a project to build a bronze-age replica seafaring vessel. (See Chapter 11.)

Ingrid K. Urberg has taught Scandinavian Studies on the Augustana Campus of the University of Alberta since 1994. In addition to teaching Norwegian language and Scandinavian literature and culture courses, Ingrid co-teaches an interdisciplinary course called "Explorations of the Canadian North." Her research focuses on personal narratives and polar literature, which has brought her to northern Norway, Greenland and Svalbard. She enjoys cross-country skiing, running and hiking in Canada and in Norway. (See Chapter 19.)

Nils Vikander has taught friluftsliv since 1991 at North Troendelag University College in Levanger, Norway. Starting his all-weather explorations of the outdoors as a child in Sweden, he followed his family to Canada where he became an academic roamer from east to west, interspersed with years of work/play in cross-country skiing. The latter took him yet further afield-to the US Midwest and Montana, and to the farthest reaches of the Canadian Arctic. In the late 1980s his curiosity took him back to Scandinavia, this time to Norway, where his teaching and outdoor immersion brought him many deep nature experiences, taking advantage from time to time of the nearness to Sweden and Finland. From 2003 to 2005 he returned to Canada as a visiting scholar at Brock University and found deeply intriguing comparative teaching experiences in the outdoors. Nils delves deeply into the philosophy of the nature experience. His greatest passion is to search familiar or unknown vistas with paddle or ski, simply, intimately and tracelessly. (See Introduction.)

Brian Wattchow (Ph.D.) is a Senior Lecturer with Monash University's Faculty of Education, Australia. He has been teaching, leading and lecturing in outdoor education both in Australia and overseas for the last 20 years. He has a long-standing interest in researching and writing about sense of place. In 2000 he spent six weeks living and travelling in Norway, much of that time spent in the outdoors with friluftsliv staff and students from the Norwegian University of Sports and Physical Education. (See Chapter 23.)

Visuals

Margot Peck

Bob Henderson

Bob Henderson began his passion for outdoor life as a camper at an Algonquin Park children's camp. Later, as a camp canoe-tripping guide, with family and friends he began exploring Canadian trails – winter and summer, coast to coast. He also teaches outdoor education at McMaster University, Hamilton, Ontario.

After first exploring friluftsliv through literature, he began, following the DEEP conference in Rennebu and Oslo in January 2000, to make regular trips to Norway to explore cultural themes through stories, workshops and outdoor travel. Bob has remained convinced through these years that friluftsliv ideas and methods offer a wisdom that should cast a wide net for Nordic countries, in particular.

Bob can be reached at bhender@mcmaster.ca

Nils Vikander

Nils Vikander has taught widely in Scandinavia and North America promoting outdoor education and cross-country skiing. He believes that, for the voice of nature to be truly heard, most urban dwellers need to be out at least a few nights – again, preferably more. Only then does the engine of the city recede.

Once the dependence on mechanical existence begins to wither away, then friluftsliv becomes not an optional decoration for a life, or even a natural part of life. Rather, it begins to be seamlessly integrated in life, much as we eat and sleep without feeling we have to decide whether or not to. When the student is ready, the master appears; the master who has been there all along – nature – and no other teacher can compare.

Nils can be reached at Nils.Vikander@hint.no

MEMBER OF SCABRINI GROUP

Québec, Canada
2007